GOVERNMENT BEYOND THE CENTRE

SERIES EDITORS: GERRY STOKER AND DAVID WILSON

The world of sub-central governance and administration – including local authorities, quasi-governmental bodies and the agencies of public-private partnerships – has seen massive changes in the United Kingdom and other western democracies. The original aim of the **Government Beyond the Centre** series was to bring the study of this often-neglected world into the mainstream of social science research, applying the spotlight of critical analysis to what had traditionally been the preserve of institutional public administration approaches.

The replacement of traditional models of government by new models of governance has affected central government, too, with the contracting out of many traditional functions, the increasing importance of relationships with devolved and supranational authorities, and the emergence of new holistic models based on partnership and collaboration.

This series focuses on the agenda of change in governance both at sub-central level and in the new patterns of relationships surrounding the core executive. Its objective is to provide up-to-date and informative accounts of the new forms of management and administration and the structures of power and influence that are emerging, and of the economic, political and ideological forces that underlie them.

The series will be of interest to students and practitioners in central and local government, public management and social policy, and all those interested in the reshaping of the governmental institutions which have a daily and major impact on our lives.

Government Beyond the Centre
Series Standing Order
ISBN 0–333–71696–5 hardcover
ISBN 0–333–69337–X paperback
(outside North America only)

You can receive future titles in this series as they are published by placing a standing order. Please contact your bookseller or, in the case of difficulty, write to us at the address below with your name and address, the title of the series and the ISBN quoted above.

Customer Services Department, Macmillan Distribution Ltd
Houndmills, Basingstoke, Hampshire RG21 6XS, England

GBC

GOVERNMENT BEYOND THE CENTRE

SERIES EDITORS: GERRY STOKER AND DAVID WILSON

Working Across Boundaries

Collaboration in Public Services

Helen Sullivan
and
Chris Skelcher

palgrave
macmillan

First published 2002 by
PALGRAVE MACMILLAN
Houndmills, Basingstoke, Hampshire RG21 6XS and
175 Fifth Avenue, New York, N.Y. 10010
Companies and representatives throughout the world

PALGRAVE MACMILLAN is the global academic imprint of the Palgrave
Macmillan division of St. Martin's Press, LLC and of Palgrave Macmillan Ltd.
Macmillan® is a registered trademark in the United States, United Kingdom
and other countries. Palgrave is a registered trademark in the European
Union and other countries.

ISBN-10: 0–333–96150–1 hardback
ISBN-10: 0–333–96151–x paperback
ISBN-13: 978-0-333-96150-6 hardback
ISBN-13: 978-0-333-96151-3 paperback

This book is printed on paper suitable for recycling and made from
fully managed and sustained forest sources. Logging, pulping and
manufacturing processes are expected to conform to the environmental
regulations of the country of origin.

A catalogue record for this book is available
from the British Library.

Library of Congress Cataloging-in-Publication Data
Sullivan, Helen (Helen C.)
Working across boundaries : collaboration in public services / Helen
Sullivan and Chris Skelcher.
     p. cm.—(Government beyond the centre)
Includes bibliographical references and index.
ISBN 0–333–96150–1
1. Privatization—Great Britain. 2. Public–private sector cooperation—
Great Britain. 3. Privatization. 4. Public–private sector cooperation.
I. Skelcher, Chris, 1951–II. Title. III. Series.
HD3850 .S8732 2002
338.9'25—dc21
                                                             2002022907

Printed and bound in Great Britain by the MPG Books Group, Bodmin and King's Lynn

Contents

List of Tables, Figures and Boxes

Tables

vii

List of Abbreviations

ABI	Area-Based Initiative
ACPO	Association of Chief Police Officers
AGM	Annual General Meeting
ASBO	Anti Social Behaviour Order
CAT	City Action Team
CCT	Compulsory Competitive Tendering
CCTV	Closed Circuit Television
CDP	Community Development Project
CIPFA	Chartered Institute of Public Finance and Accountancy
CSR	Comprehensive Spending Review
CURL	Centre for Urban Research and Learning
CVS	Council of Voluntary Services
DBFO	Design, Build, Finance, Operate
DEFRA	Department for Environment, Food and Rural Affairs
DETR	Department of the Environment, Transport and the Regions
DTLR	Department for Transport, Local Government and the Regions
DfEE	Department for Education and Employment
DfES	Department for Education and Skills
DoH	Department of Health
DHSS	Department of Health and Social Security
DSS	Department of Social Security
EA	Estate Action
EAZ	Education Action Zone
EPA	Education Priority Area
EU	European Union
EYDCP	Early Years Development and Childcare Partnerships
EZ	Employment Zone
FEMA	Federal Emergency Management Agency
GATS	General Agreement on Trade and Services
GEAR	Glasgow Eastern Area Renewal
GOR	Government Offices for the Regions
HAT	Housing Action Trust
HAZ	Health Action Zone
HEAT	Health Equality Action Team
HIMP	Health Improvement and Modernisation Programmes

HO	Home Office
ICPP	Inner City Partnership Programme
IPS	Industrial and Provident Society
JASP	Joint Approach to Social Policy
JCC	Joint Consultative Committee
LEA	Local Education Authority
LEC	Local Enterprise Companies
LGMB	Local Government Management Board
LSC	Learning and Skills Council
LSP	Local Strategic Partnership
NAO	National Audit Office
NCR	New Commitment to Regeneration
NCVO	National Council for Voluntary Organisations
NDC	New Deal for Communities
NGO	Non-Governmental Organisation
NHS	National Health Service
NPM	New Public Management
NRF	Neighbourhood Renewal Fund
NSNR	National Strategy for Neighbourhood Renewal
PAC	Public Accounts Committee
PALS	Patient Advice and Liaison Services
PCG	Primary Care Group
PCT	Primary Care Trust
PFI	Private Finance Initiative
PIC	Public Interest Company
PIU	Performance and Innovation Unit
PPP	Public Private Partnership
PSA	Public Service Agreement
QUANGO	Quasi Autonomous Non-Governmental Organisation
RCS	Regional Co-ordination Unit
RDA	Regional Development Agency
SAZ	Sports Action Zone
SCVO	Scottish Council of Voluntary Organisations
SDA	Service Delivery Agreement
SRB	Single Regeneration Budget
TEC	Training and Enterprise Council
UDC	Unitary Development Corporation
VAP	Value-Added Partnership
VfM	Value for Money
WHO	World Health Organization

Preface

A radical transformation is taking place in the way communities are governed. Funding and authority for the development and delivery of public policy are increasingly located in collaborative ventures involving a range of governmental, business, voluntary and community agencies. These are most typically termed 'partnerships' and are found in all fields of public policy. Although an international phenomenon, the UK has undergone a major expansion of partnerships, many stimulated by central government and operating at the sub-national level. This change poses major challenges for the ways in which power and governmental activity are understood, and for the practice of public service managers and others involved in collaborations.

This book sets out to map the nature of collaborative activity and to provide a theoretically informed analysis of its emergence, operation and impact. We draw in part on our own research in the field, which is described briefly in Appendix 1. We are grateful to several journals for permission to utilise parts of four articles. These are: *Local Governance* (Sullivan, H. and Potter, T. [2001] vol. 27, no. 1, 19–31), *Journal of Health Services Research and Policy* (Judge, K. [2000] vol. 5, no. 1, 1–3), *Public Administration* (Lowndes, V. and Skelcher, C. [1998] vol. 76, no. 2, 313–34 and *Public Policy and Administration* (Skelcher, C. [2000] vol. 15, no. 3, 3–19). We are also grateful to the Policy Press for permission to use an extract from Skelcher, C. *et al.* [1996] *Community Networks in Urban Regeneration* (Bristol). Every effect has been made to contact all copyright-holders, but if any have been inadvertently omitted the publishers will be pleased to make the necessary arrangement at the earliest opportunity.

Much of our research on collaboration has been undertaken with colleagues, and we owe them particular thanks for the insights developed over the years and the critical yet helpful comments that we received on draft chapters. Ideas have also been stimulated in teaching and discussion with our postgraduate students, most of whom themselves are practising public service managers caught up in the collaborative agenda. Amongst the many we would wish to mention, special thanks go to: Marian Barnes,

Michael Hughes, Vivien Lowndes, Janet Newman, Sue Richards, Mike Smith and John Stewart, and the Palgrave series editorial and publishing team of Steven Kennedy, Gerry Stoker and David Wilson. Finally, we give particular appreciations to Deborah and Barbara for supporting us in our single-minded approach to authorship.

HELEN SULLIVAN
CHRIS SKELCHER

1 The Collaborative Agenda

Collaboration is now central to the way in which public policy is made, managed and delivered throughout the world. It is a way of working with others on a joint project where there is a shared interest in positive outcomes. The pre-existing and rigid boundaries between public and private sectors, different tiers of government and voluntary and community agencies are becoming more permeable as actors reach across these organisational divides and explore new ways of developing and delivering public purposes. The most familiar form of collaborative arrangement is the multi-organisational partnership, a formal expression of shared commitment to act in the common interest. Globally, partnership is the new language of public governance – whether through the use of private capital to fund infrastructure projects, the engagement of community organisations in economic development or the integration of state health and social care services.

Partnership is about sharing responsibility and overcoming the inflexibility created by organisational, sectoral and even national boundaries. For example, the 1992 Rio Summit firmly established environmental sustainability as an international priority and highlighted the need for collaborative effort to reduce the rate of global warming. Subsequent action has involved inter-governmental negotiation and transnational activity by non-profit environmental groups together with domestic collaborations under the Local Agenda 21 banner as public, private, voluntary and community sectors have cleaned and greened their local environments (S. Young, 1999). The notion of working together for the common good that underpins collaborative action is also found in changing approaches to northern hemisphere international development policies, where aid is intended to be allocated in discussion with users rather than as a reflection of the donor's priorities (James, 2001). A web of interpersonal relationships which arise through networking, however, often supports the formality of a partnership. These constitute a type of social capital (Putnam, 1993). They provide a context within which can be mediated those questions of power, trust and motive that are central to any form of collaboration. Collaborations for public purpose, therefore, are both about the formal structures that emerge and the micro-politics of individual actors as their roles intersect across organisational, sectoral and geographical boundaries. This book investigates the place of collaborative action in the achievement of public purpose. Its prime focus is on collaboration that occurs beyond the centre – that takes effect at regional, local and neighbourhood levels. However, in an era of multi-level governance such an assessment necessarily involves an examination of the impact of national and, in the case of EU member states, European institutions. Partnerships have become the preferred delivery mechanisms for many aspects of European and national policy, including those related to economic restructuring, social inclusion, environmental sustainability and the knowledge society. These policy initiatives stimulate activity at sub-national levels and in some cases, as we discuss later, become the means through which very specific policy intentions are expected to be realised. Collaboration, therefore, involves both horizontal and vertical forms of inter-organisational engagement.

Motivations for collaboration

The first question this book addresses is why collaboration happens and what the key imperatives are that result in this approach to achieving public purpose. An important explanatory variable is the changing role of the state in the late twentieth and early twenty-first centuries. The nature of the state's transformation has been the subject of much debate by those concerned with the rise of collaboration (such as Montanheiro *et al.*, 1999; Rhodes, 1997; Taillieu, 2001) as well as those interested in changing patterns of governance world wide (including Giddens, 2000; Hirst and Thompson, 1999; Pierre and Peters, 2000). At its heart is a discussion of whether in the prevailing context the state itself has the necessary capacity and resources to deliver public policy goals and, if not, how those gaps can be filled. One response to this capacity problem is to involve other sectors in providing services. In the 1980s the belief that improved services could be provided at lower costs by external providers led to a world-wide fascination with public–private partnerships which began in the UK and throughout the following decade spread to North and South America, Asia and the former Soviet Union and eastern European countries (G. Clarke, 2000; Savas, 2000). For others the motivation was not about effecting improvements but establishing coverage of basic services in the face of state failure. Slater's (2001) account of the development of voluntaristic partnerships among local private and not-for-profit agencies in South Asia gives evidence of this latter impulse.

There are other important motivations to collaboration beyond the changing configurations and expectations of the state. Collaborating in an attempt to resolve conflict is powerfully illustrated by the difficult endeavours under way in the peace processes in Northern Ireland (Hughes *et al.*, 1998) and other regions experiencing inter-communal violence. Collaboration is also driven by a desire to achieve a shared vision of the future. This is evident in the World Health Organization's (WHO) mission to improve health and reduce health inequalities. Action to achieve this vision occurs internationally through the work of annual global conferences which lead to joint statements of intent such as the Mexico Ministerial Statement on Health Promotion signed by 87 ministers of health or their representatives in 2000. However, work also takes place at other levels, including the international 'Healthy Cities' movement which promotes cross-sector collaborative action on health improvement in cities, towns, villages and islands. Collaboration to achieve a shared vision is also evident in relation to economic regeneration programmes promoted by national governments and transnational institutions, for example the European Union's (EU) 'cohesion policy' which seeks to revitalise declining rural areas through the medium of local public–private–community partnerships. Finally, collaboration is stimulated by common problems. For example, the WHO Mega Country Health Promotion Network is a partnership of the most populous countries in the world, a grouping that also has the potential to make the greatest impact in improving world health.

Implicit in these experiences is a recognition that the challenges facing communities and countries in the twenty-first century are sufficiently complex in scope and scale as to require the involvement of a range of actors with complementary perspectives, expertise and resources. However, the extent to which actors from the private, voluntary and community sectors are engaged in collaborative action will be influenced by the nature of the state and its historical relationships with them. So the experience of the US with its tradition of 'small government' will be very different to that of Western Europe where the state has played a much more prominent role in service provision. Similarly, both will differ from the experience of post-communist nations where the state was the monopoly provider in most parts of the social and economic realm (Devas and Horváth, 1997). Collaboration is catalysed by changes in state relationships with these sectors but in turn this motivates further change in the prevailing patterns of governance. So the emergence of multi-level governance, defined by Peters and Pierre as 'negotiated, non-hierarchical exchanges between institutions at the transnational, national, regional and local levels' (2001, p. 131) is both a consequence of and contributor to increasing collaboration within and between states. This point is important. It emphasises the dynamic nature of the public policy environment and highlights the need to explain collaborative activity in terms of these more fundamental dynamics.

Forms of collaboration

The myriad imperatives to collaboration are matched by the multiplicity of collaborative arrangements that are entered into. In one recent text the following collaborative arrangements were among those cited in the index: community-led initiatives, contracts, inter-organisational co-operation, joint ventures, partnerships, policy networks, principal–agent relationships, public–private partnerships, relational contracting, social networks, strategic alliances and voluntary sector compacts (Osborne, 2000). Further illustration of this variety is presented by Parsons (1995) who identifies more than 30 alternatives to direct service delivery by government employees in the United States. Given this world of possibilities the second question that this book will address is: what are the prevailing forms of collaboration and how widely do they manifest themselves across levels of government and sectors of society?

Notwithstanding the range of potential operational arrangements, all collaborative relationships derive from one of three governance forms: contracts, partnerships or networks (Thompson *et al.*, 1991). Contractual relationships are most closely associated with the delivery of public services by non-state bodies such as companies or voluntary organisations, or by state agencies operating on a trading basis at arm's-length from the purchaser. In its simplest form a contract is a principal–agent relationship where decision-making about what to provide and the act of production are undertaken by separate bodies. The contract spells out what will be provided, at what level of quality and for what cost. It is a legal document and failure to deliver on the contract specification may result in the application of sanctions. Savas (2000) reports that between 1982 and 1992 there was a 121 per cent increase in privatisation in a sample of 596 US cities, the majority of which was the subject of contracts between government and external providers. He further reports that at least 200 different services are provided to government by contractors (private, voluntary or public). Research in the UK, cited in the next chapter, reveals a similar picture.

Contracts for the most part are formal, specific and legally binding agreements between organisations. Networks, however, are constituted on the basis of informal relationships regulated by obligations of trust and reciprocity. Networks are frequently grounded in individual relationships that transcend organisational boundaries and even organisational agendas. They have a boundary-spanning, reticular and entrepreneurial flavour (Friend *et al.*, 1974; Ayres and Davis, 2000), and consequently are fluid relationships that may grow up in response to a particular policy or service issue and will continue to operate for as long as the need exists and the network members are willing to sustain the relationship.

The most common manifestation of collaboration – partnership – is far harder to define (Lawless, 1991; Mackintosh, 1992; Roberts, 1995). It is a word that is sprinkled liberally through academic texts and policy documents and has acquired a strong normative and virtuous association in the contemporary governance environment. Part of the difficulty associated with trying to define partnership pertains to the dynamic and fragmented nature of the policy environment. Very often differing policy fields begin with a bespoke interpretation of partnership that is not shared beyond that policy area. For example, voluntary sector definitions of partnership with the state are typically imbued with notions of dialogic and consensual decision-making and inclusive structures and processes. State agencies' views of partnership with the voluntary sector typically operate on design principles of committee decision-making shaped by powerful actors through pre-meeting caucusing. Conceptually, however, partnerships are distinctively different to contract or network. They can best be described as collaboration through 'joint decision making and production' (Klijn and Teisman, 2000, pp. 85–6). In other words partners share responsibility for assessing the need for action, determining the type of action to be taken and agreeing the means of implementation. So in regeneration:

> a working definition of partnership ... might be the mobilisation of a coalition of interests drawn from more than one sector in order to prepare and oversee an agreed strategy for the regeneration of a defined area. (Bailey *et al.*, 1995, p. 27)

The literature suggests that there are three other key constituents of partnership. The first is that it involves negotiation between people from diverse agencies committed to working together over more than the short term. As such:

> partnership entails a long-term commitment and reflects a condition of mutual dependency .... Partnership is a set of normative rules determining

what behaviour is permissible and what constitutes a violation of trust. The rules are designed to facilitate exchange in a situation otherwise open to exploitation. (Lorenz, 1991, pp. 189–90)

Secondly, partnership aims to secure the delivery of benefits or added value which could not have been provided by any single agency acting alone or through the employment of others (Mackintosh, 1992). This notion is expressed by Huxham (1996) in the phrase 'collaborative advantage'. The basic requirement is that autonomous organisations agree to work together to achieve shared goals, that in doing so they cede some power and influence over decisions in order that their chances of achieving their joint objectives are enhanced. In addition there has to be some way in which the achievements of a public policy partnership are subject to the assessment of intended beneficiaries. Governments at all levels are promoting partnerships as a means of improving the performance of service delivery, and user and citizen perspectives are therefore vital in the collaborative process. Consequently, in the local government context, 'partnership is a process in which a local authority works together with partners to achieve better outcomes for the local community as measured by the needs of local stakeholders' (Newchurch, 1999a, p. 1).

Partnership is thus differentiated from contracts because of the requirement for joint decision-making over more than the short term. Partnership also differs from a network because the delivery of joint decision-making and service delivery will require the formal articulation of a purpose and plan to bind the partners together. Further, the significance of the joint activities – especially where they require the expenditure of public money and accountability to the wider community – will mandate the creation of a formal partnership board. However, such hard and fast conceptual distinctions between contract, network and partnership do not always easily translate into practice. This is illustrated by developments in thinking about contractual forms. There is considerable interest in moving beyond fixed-term principal–agent contracts to those that encompass a broader, longer-term commitment between the parties (Coulson, 1998). These 'relational contracts' are based upon partners' intention to invest in stable and enduring collaboration that transcend the letter of any formal agreement. Johnston and Lawrence describe the incidence of relational contracts in the private sector as 'value added partnerships'. They argue that 'for a VAP to exist, its partners must adopt and adhere to a set of ground rules that generates trustworthy transactions. The sense of partnership must become an enforceable reality, despite the many uncertainties and opportunities for playing games' (Johnston and Lawrence, 1991, p. 201). As we discuss further in the book, such developments blur the apparently neat boundary between contracts, networks and partnerships.

Factors influencing collaborative performance

Collaborative activity is now commonplace, but so too are the expressions of frustration by those involved. There can be considerable political, operational and financial obstacles to making collaboration work. Complaints relate to the level of resources that need to be invested to support collaborative endeavours, slow progress towards goals, lack of inclusiveness and domination by some partners (Davoudi and Healey, 1995; Barnes, Sullivan and Matka, 2001; Williamson, 2001). Conversely, there are also collaborations that are notable successes. In the US, for example, the Federal Emergency Management Agency (FEMA) transformed its role from disaster response to disaster prevention by refocusing its activities upon the development of local public, private and community partnerships to build preventive capacity within neighbourhoods. The charismatic leadership of the Agency's new director was identified as a key factor in overcoming obstacles and delivering a new collaborative arrangement (Kerestes and Lenniham, 2001). Elsewhere, a study of collaborative programmes by non-governmental organisations (NGOs) to support the development of grass-roots activity found that the quality of relationships rather than management or technical capacity was more significant in explaining success. Those NGOs that could establish mutual trust and respect with their partners were far better equipped to develop sustainable programmes (James, 2001).

How, therefore, can collaborative performance be explained? This is the third question addressed in the book. It is considered in two separate but related ways. The first is an examination of the essential skills and resources necessary to enable organisations, professionals, politicians, users and communities to work together in building effective collaborations. Once established, however, collaborations continue to present challenges. For example, Geddes' (2000) work on social exclusion partnerships within the EU identifies the power imbalances between partners and the danger that they operate as exclusive rather than inclusive arrangements, thereby perpetuating the issues they were designed to tackle. Questions of power and its distribution are a matter of considerable concern for those studying the involvement of citizens and communities in collaborative endeavours with the state (Himmelman, 1996; Razzaque, 2001; Smith and Beazley, 2000).

This issue is important because of the changes that need to be made in collaborations if citizens are to participate as equal partners. It is also significant because it draws attention to the accountability of collaborative arrangements and the need to secure good governance.

Evaluating collaboration

The trend towards partnership can be expected to continue over future years as a consequence of economic globalisation. The negotiation of GATS – the General Agreement on Trade and Services – through the World Trade Organization in the early years of the twenty-first century is likely to open up new areas of public service to private competition and hence to further radically transform the nature of the state and its relationship with other sectors of society domestically and globally. Yet theoretically informed and empirically supported analysis of the value, type and role of collaboration in delivering public purpose is severely constrained. The ideological environment is uncritically pro-collaboration. The policy agenda promotes collaboration as the primary delivery mechanism. There are strong pressures from grass-roots, NGOs and business organisations for partnerships with government. Practitioner-oriented guides containing prescriptive advice based on case studies which purport to illustrate success dominate the management literature. The academic literature is only now moving beyond a preoccupation with partnership creation and rather static analyses of power relations between actors. There has, however, recently been a growing interest in evaluating collaboration – and especially partnerships. These evaluations are often commissioned by partnerships themselves or their sponsoring bodies, but nevertheless provide a basis from which generalisation, hypothesis building and theory development can take place.

Consequently the fourth question that this book explores is how collaborative activity can be evaluated. A number of evaluative frameworks have been produced in recent years. For example, the WHO introduced its 'Verona' evaluation methodology which can be employed to assess the fitness for purpose and performance of partnerships (WHO, 2000). Academic institutions and government agencies have developed other frameworks. The Nuffield Institute introduced a '10 step framework' to partnership building and evaluation based upon academic research into collaboration between health and social care agencies (Hardy *et al.*, 2000), and the Audit Commission (1998) published a similar tool. At the same time there has been growing interest in assessing the capacity of joint action to achieve desired outcomes. Attention has been paid to the development of evaluative frameworks that explain the ways in which collaborative interventions contribute to shared goals, for example 'Theories of Change' (Connell and Kubisch *et al.*, 1995), while other studies have focused on examining the consequences of collaborative action for specific stakeholders such as users and communities (Barnes *et al.*, 1999; Carley *et al.*, 2000).

The focus of the book

The book addresses questions which are of international relevance and draws on an academic literature that reflects this. However, much of the empirical material and examples come from the UK. The rate of change in the UK public sector since the early 1980s has resulted in partnership practice that in general has a high level of variety and innovation relative to international comparisons. These domestic developments have been driven by governments that, from the early 1980s, have been committed to reforming the public sector and reshaping its relationship with other sections of society. This is found in the new right philosophies of the Conservative governments which promoted new public management and latterly the modernisation agenda of the Labour governments post-1997. The pace of the collaborative agenda, as one element of this major reform programme, shows no sign of reducing. Indeed the emphasis on the achievement of outcomes in key policy areas such as community safety, health, regeneration and education is predicated upon the operation of local partnerships established to deliver targets set out in national strategies.

One consequence is the substantial institutional growth generated by the collaborative agenda in the spaces between and around the established structures of democratic government. At the same time there has been devolution to Scotland, Wales and London and the strengthening of the English regional tier of government. These developments provide an environment of multi-level governance with new opportunities for collaboration and different points of accountability for partnerships. Added to this is the desire of Labour administrations to re-connect citizens with the policy process, and to do so in a way that involves them as partners in achieving desired outcomes. So, for example, local regeneration programmes emphasise the need for communities to take ownership of the process by becoming members of local partnership boards, and in some cases managing regeneration resources and taking responsibility for the provision of services. The emphasis upon

'taking responsibility' is an essential component of the New Labour programme. This move to recreate citizens as joint producers of welfare with a
collective commitment to common ends (Barnes and Prior, 2000; Newman,
2001) highlights in an acute form issues pertaining to citizen participation in
collaborative contexts – issues about skills and capacities for partnership, the
inclusion/exclusion of particular groups, the power relationships that pertain
within partnerships and the limits of collaborative endeavour with citizens.
The recent experience of the UK, therefore, provides fertile ground for an
examination of collaboration for public purpose.

Devolution to Scotland and Wales, combined with the separate constitutional arrangements in Northern Ireland, has resulted in increased policy
differentiation. The UK government is now principally concerned with
external relations and the government of England. We have tried to reflect
collaborative developments throughout the UK, but the English context
tends to predominate because of its scale and the focus of academic
research to date.

The argument and structure of the book

The central argument of the book is that the collaborative agenda for public
purpose has been both under-theorised and overlooked. It is under-theorised
because the UK tradition of empirical social science finds fertile ground in
the demands of practitioners and government research sponsors for 'good
practice' advice. It is noticeable that much of the theoretical work relevant
to inter-organisational partnerships and collaboration arises from academics working in the US (for example Benson, 1975; Fukuyama, 1995;
Williamson 1985) and continental European traditions (for example
Kooiman and van Vliet, 1993; Kickert *et al.*, 1997). The collaborative agenda
is overlooked because the assumptions of the unitary English state are
deeply embedded. As we have argued elsewhere, the growth of collaborative institutions is

> an important and dynamic field [which] typically features as a minor part
> of British Government text-books, and it would probably not be an exag-
> geration to conclude that it has made little impact on university syllabi.
> While undergraduates are studying the finer points of prime ministerial
> rule of the reform of the House of Lords, there is a whole world of part-
> nership boards determining the future shape of our communities and
> regions. If there is joining-up to do, it is of the radical transformation of

government with the knowledge and understanding imparted to citizens in the educational process. (Skelcher, 2000, pp. 16–17)

Chapters 2 and 3 provide the foundation upon which the central argument of the book is built. Chapter 2 provides an analysis of the changes to the form and relationships of the British state. It examines the process of hollowing-out which fragmented the organisational structure of government and shows how collaborative institutions reintegrated the state in new ways, and especially by tying business, voluntary and community organisation into partnership bodies. We argue that the emergent pattern can best be presented through the metaphor of the congested state, although in the concluding chapter we return to this proposition and – on the basis of our subsequent analysis – suggest a somewhat different formulation. The chapter then discusses the collaborative agenda as it is reflected in the Labour governments' modernisation programmes. It highlights the distinctive features of the emergent partnerships. Finally, the chapter maps the scale of formal partnership activity stimulated by national government. Data is presented on the number and expenditure of public policy partnerships and the composition of their boards. Specific attention is given to their impact on individual localities.

Chapter 3 examines a number of theoretical perspectives that contribute to an understanding of the field. Theoretical perspectives on collaboration tend to be located in a variety of disciplines and in general do not seek to provide a comprehensive explanation (Faulkner and de Rond, 2000). The chapter examines and discusses those theories that have particular value in relation to the four questions identified above and with which the book is concerned. These theories include: exchange, resource dependency and political economy theories from the organisational sociology literature; policy network, regime and community empowerment theories from the political science literature; and new institutional theory. The chapter employs these perspectives to develop a framework for understanding collaboration, which is elaborated further in Chapters 4–10.

Chapter 4 examines the imperatives for collaboration in the UK context. It examines three policy fields where the achievement of positive outcomes is necessarily reliant upon the collaboration of a number of organisations. These three cross-cutting issues are urban regeneration, community safety and health and social care. The chapter demonstrates the way in which the collaborative agenda has developed over time in each policy field and highlights the dominant imperatives for collaboration. The extent to which these imperatives are able to influence the genesis of collaborations, however, is dependent upon the incidence of key contextual factors. The interplay between imperatives and context is examined and the similarities and differences between policy areas explained.

The comparison of collaborative activity is continued in Chapter 5 where the focus is on collaboration across major spheres of activity. The chapter examines the way in which the UK government's drive for partnership has impacted on relationships with business and voluntary sectors. It charts the increasing complexity and scale of public–private collaboration, from relatively simple contracting-out, through public–private partnerships to strategic partnering. Change is also apparent from a chronological analysis of government–voluntary sector relations. We show how the structure of collaboration has been transformed from grant-aid, through the contract culture to the contemporary idea of compacts. Beside these essentially horizontal collaborations, the chapter discusses the incidence of vertical partnerships between levels of government in a European context. This opens up an examination of the range of collaborative relationships that pertain between localities, regions, national governments and the European institutions and highlights their significance to the debate about multi-level governance.

Although collaborative activity in the UK has increased substantially, the capacity of the different partners to effect joint action remains questionable (Benyon and Edwards, 1999; Hall *et al.*, 1996; Hudson *et al.*, 1999). Chapters 6 and 7 examine those factors that support and hinder the implementation of collaboration in practice. In Chapter 6 the emphasis is on identifying and examining the components that contribute to the necessary 'collaborative capacity' between partners and within a partnership. The chapter explores the skills and resources required by individuals to participate in collaborations, the facets of organisational culture that contribute to collaborative capacity among partner bodies and the structural features that support sustainable relationships. Chapter 7 develops this analysis by investigating the dynamics of collaboration and in particular by discussion of an empirically-derived partnership life-cycle. This enables an understanding of the way in which different kinds of capacity are necessary at different points in the relationship. It also shows how hierarchical, network and market forms of governance may all be utilised within a partnership arrangement.

Chapter 8 opens up the question of partnership governance, a topic of considerable significance given the public policy agendas with which these institutions are concerned. A discussion of the nature and significance of 'good governance' in the contemporary public sector sets the context for an examination of the constitutional forms which partnerships take and the implications of these for accountability. The chapter argues that partnerships exhibit a democratic deficit in the same way as quangos and illustrates this through an analysis of their political, financial and performance accountability arrangements.

The concern with accountability draws attention to the role of citizens in partnerships. Chapter 9 examines the consequences of the Labour government's agenda to re-connect with citizens as it impacts on their involvement in collaborative activity. It explores the extent to which partnerships are open to citizen participation, and the nature of the involvement offered, for example through consultative mechanisms or board membership. The chapter examines the factors that facilitate and obstruct effective citizen participation in partnership working. A significant issue addressed in this chapter is that understandings of the 'success' of a partnership are plural and relative.

This issue is developed in Chapter 10 as part of a wider consideration of the evaluation of collaboration. Evaluation is currently fashionable in the UK and forms an important part of the drive to establish evidence-based management and practice. However, establishing 'what works', let alone explaining how it can be replicated from one setting to another, is a highly contentious issue epistemologically, methodologically and politically. The chapter explores the debates about the evaluation of public policy and presents a number of challenges arising specifically from the field of collaboration. It then reviews and critiques the prevailing frameworks that have been used to evaluative recent collaborative ventures and identifies alternative approaches that offer a more helpful way forward.

The final chapter of the book reviews the challenges and problems presented by collaborative activity. It returns to the four key questions posed in Chapter 1 and discusses these in terms of the evidence and theories considered in the book. In doing this, a number of dilemmas are identified. These set an agenda for research and practice. The book closes by considering the implications for the governance of societies where collaborative forms evolve into the primary means of delivering core public policy intentions.

2 Collaboration and the State

The UK case provides a powerful example of the way in which the collaborative agenda has become a central instrument of public policy, particularly in the context of the government's modernisation project from the late 1990s. Collaboration across the public sector, and between it and business, community and voluntary organisations, reflects a desire by government to overcome the organisational and professional boundaries that separate services and to build an integrated approach to the development of policy, exercise of management and delivery of real improvements in outcomes. Yet collaborative activity has its roots in earlier periods. Inter-agency working between health and social care has a long legacy, with various mechanisms being developed in the 1960s and 1970s to undertake joint planning and ease users' transition between the National Health Service (NHS) and social service provision. During this period partnership arrangements between the public and voluntary sectors were also developed in response to problems of urban deprivation (Chapter 3). The consequences of new public management, however, gave a stimulus to the collaborative agenda. The deconstruction of large welfare bureaucracies and consequent fragmentation of organisational responsibilities and authority generated a need to create integrative mechanisms.

In this chapter we explore these processes in more detail. We show how the collaborative agenda has developed in the context of the changing institutional structure of the public sector and the emergence of new philosophies of public management and governance. Particular attention is given to the idea that the state has been hollowing-out and to the new collaborative configurations that have arisen in response. We argue that this new configuration can best be understood through the metaphor of the congested state – a complex web of interconnections whose negotiation and steering requires considerable energy on the part of organisations and individuals – and that the modernisation agenda has had a particular impact on the nature of these collaborative structures. We then map the public policy partnerships found in the UK and discuss their purpose, number, expenditure and membership. This analysis reveals the complexity of inter-agency relationships in the modern state and the way in which collaborative arrangements have become the focal point for the delivery of new policy initiatives arising from government, relegating mainstream public sector organisations to something of a supporting role.

The changing pattern of the state

The legacy of departmentalism

The explanation of the current popularity for collaboration and partnership has its origins in the major processes of public sector restructuring that took place in the 1980s and early 1990s. Then, there was a strong view that the UK public sector was in crisis – that the institutions of government had over-reached themselves and were unable to deliver their policy objectives. Big government was, in King's (1975) terminology, 'overloaded' with responsibilities and required refashioning in order to establish effective implementation and regain popular legitimacy. One aspect of the critique was that the capacity of government to address issues that required co-ordinated action was limited because of the functional principle which underlay organisational design (Richards and Jervis, 1997). This resulted in authority being divided between separate governmental empires, with health, social services, housing, planning and the various other activities of the public sector each being the responsibility of an individual minister, council committee or quango board. The annual budgetary process was often the arena where these tensions became exposed, especially since in this era the ability of politicians to maintain and increase spending on their service was perceived as a sign of political virility (Heclo and Wildavsky, 1981). The political structures oversaw a department or organisation that often had a strong professional orientation. Each professional group brought a particular approach to the way in which both problems were defined and solutions were prescribed, adding to the barriers that existed between services (Hudson, 1987). The policy and operational conflicts between the various branches and levels of government were accentuated by their overlapping jurisdictional responsibilities. For example, NHS bodies and social services authorities both had responsibilities for client groups such as young children and older people, but attempts at co-ordination were hindered by their contrasting political accountabilities:

> The National Health Service ... has always been a national bureaucracy subject to direct political control only at the very highest level in central

government. By way of contrast, the personal social services have always been delivered by local authorities which are 'autonomous' of central government and closely controlled by elected local politicians. (Webb, 1991, p. 230)

These factors combined to create an environment of jurisdictional tension rather than collaboration, despite an apparent common interest between agencies.

Hollowing-out

The policy prescriptions that were introduced during the 1980s and into the 1990s challenged a number of the underlying design principles of this overloaded welfare state, including its large welfare bureaucracies, professional rather than managerial control, reliance on representative forms of democracy and the notion of a passive community. This process of hollowing-out had four broad features: the loss of legitimacy by government, the implementation of public management reform programmes, the changing relationship between public employees on the one hand and politicians and citizens on the other, and the impact of transnational and regional institutions on the nation state (Peters, 1993, 1997; Rhodes, 1994, 1996, 1997). It is the second of these – the reform of public management – that is of particular salience in terms of the emergence of partnerships (Table 2.1).

At the core of what came to be called new public management (Hood, 1991; Pollitt, 1993) was a set of beliefs that government should be smaller, more concerned with identifying what services needed to be provided and less with delivering them itself, and that market forces had a key role to play in this respect. These prescriptions were heavily influenced by the analyses of public choice theorists. In broad terms, they argued that the utility maximising motivations of politicians and officials caused public sector resources to be used less productively than they might otherwise be (Lane, 1987; Niskanen, 1994). Exposing the public sector to competitive processes would improve the economy and efficiency of activities and, if markets could be created in which users had choices, increase the responsiveness and consumer-orientation of services. Whatever the academic virtues of this argument, its political impact was striking. Here was a powerful analysis which chimed with the emerging political dominance of the New Right. The policy prescriptions arising from this understanding were developed and implemented with increasing confidence and scope by the populist governments of Prime Minister Thatcher during the 1980s, and by other governments throughout the world.

Table 2.1 *Key features of overloaded, hollowed-out and congested states*

	Overloaded state	Hollowing-out	Congested state
Political Agenda	Desire to deliver on mainstream welfare programmes	Desire to deliver on state reduction	Desire to deliver in relation to cross-cutting issues
Mode of Organisation	Large welfare bureaucracies linked to elected political authority (primary bodies)	Fragmentation of government bodies and use of appointed arm's-length agencies (secondary bodies)	Complexity of organisational domains and responsibilities leads to emergence of partnerships (tertiary bodies)
Pattern of Accountability	Reliance on representative democracy	Development of accountability through patronage and market-based systems	Plurality of forms of governance and mechanisms of accountability
Extent of Transparency	Visibility of key decision-centres	Partial visibility of key decision-centres	Invisibility of key decision-centres
Role of Senior Public Employees	Policy advice and administration	Tempered, managerial	Active, networking
Role of the Public	Passive community of recipients and voters	Active customers informing service delivery	Active citizens and stakeholders informing policy and delivery

Source: Adapted from Skelcher (2000, p. 6).

Hollowing-out had two main consequences on public service bureaucracies – fragmentation arising from the separation of the service commissioning and purchasing role from that of the provider and decentralisation of
authority within state bureaucracies in order to manage these new and more
complex relationships. An increasing scale of provision was contracted-out
to private companies or the voluntary sector, or to public sector units operating at arm's length. The latter include the direct service organisations created by many local authorities to deliver contracted-out activities such as
refuse collection and street cleaning, and the executive agencies responsible
for welfare benefits, driving licences and other central government responsibilities. Fragmentation also arose from the transfer of responsibility for
the management and delivery of public programmes from multi-purpose bodies controlled by directly elected politicians to quangos (quasi-autonomous
non-governmental bodies) – single-purpose agencies overseen by a board of
appointees. Quangos have been a long-standing feature of the British governmental system, but what was significant about this period was the major
increase in their number and the scope of their activities across the public
domain (Stewart and Davis, 1994). Quangos proved attractive to governments of the period because they offered a means of depoliticising and
managerialising areas of public sector activity, and especially those that
were the responsibility of local authorities – who were perceived to be trou-
blesome. Quangos are characterised by their appointed boards of national
and local *notables* chosen because of their individual expertise or, in some
cases, support for the policy agenda pursued by the government of the day
(Skelcher, 1998). The expansion of quangos and their governance characteristics accentuates the organisational, policy and cultural divisions in the
structure of the British state.

The impact of hollowing-out

Being 'hollowed-out' provides a useful metaphor for the state, especially
when contrasted with the earlier notion of 'overload'. It suggests a process
of extraction which leaves government with a core of activity, including
the policy-making functions of the core executive, regulation of natural
monopolies and privatised and contracted-out services and the oversight and monitoring of residual direct provision functions. Consequently
hollowing-out produces an environment of organisational and political fragmentation in which the old certainties about the location of responsibility,
accountability and authority for public action are lost. Transparency, one of

the key conditions for good governance, is obscured by the complexity of purchaser and provider roles linked through a variety of contractual arrangements and overseen by boards that may be elected but are more likely to be appointed. Yet at the same time the political focus turned towards those intractable problems that cut across the boundaries of this fragmented organisational landscape. Social exclusion, community safety, the environment and regeneration became politically salient issues by the late 1990s, as did the problem of how to enable action on these 'wicked issues' when they do not 'belong' to any one organisation (Richards *et al.*, 1999).

The conjunction of hollowing-out and a new political imperative towards cross-cutting issues has stimulated the creation of numerous partnerships. Such partnerships can be viewed as a tertiary level of governmental organisation since they sit at one remove from both elected (that is, primary) and appointed (that is, secondary) bodies. This is illustrated in Figure 2.1, where we show how the traditional core relationship between citizen and elected authorities, mediated through the electoral process, is supplemented by a number of other linkages with quangos and partnerships. In terms of democratic theory these relationships are weaker than those with bodies controlled by elected politicians. This is because citizens are not directly involved in selecting the members of quango and partnership boards (although there are a few specific exceptions) compared with the voting mechanism and constituency role which applies to MPs and

Figure 2.1 *Basic patterns of democratic control in the congested state*

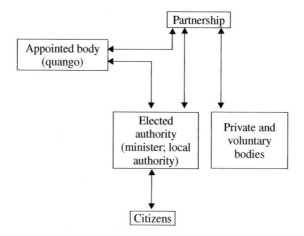

Source: Adapted from Skelcher (2000, p. 14).

councillors and which gives a degree of democratic purchase on their activities.

Collaborative arrangements have always been a feature of governmental activity, but they are now more significant than in earlier periods. As Clarence and Painter (1998) have demonstrated, the discourse of collaboration emerged from the Labour governments post-1997, although in policy terms it had its roots both in the urban policy initiatives of the preceding Major government (especially SRB [Single Regeneration Budget]) and the community planning experiments of local authorities in the mid-1990s (Rogers, 1998; Newman *et al.*, 2000). Yet the notion of the state being hollowed-out does not seem adequately to reflect this plethora of activity going on between its fragmented agencies and a variety of other bodies. Peters observes this when he comments that 'hollow vessels sometimes contain a great deal, and what is needed is ... a better conception of just how governance can be exercised by hollow states' (1997, p. 52). Hollowing-out, therefore, may be better conceived as a *process* rather than an *end-state*. From this perspective, to refer to the UK state of the late 1990s as hollowing-out is accurate. But in turn there has been the major development of integrating mechanisms at the tertiary level associated with the realignment of policy networks and formation of partnership structures. This suggests that a new conceptualisation of the state is required.

The congested state

This new pattern can be understood through the metaphor of the congested state. The congested state reflects

> an environment in which high levels of organisational fragmentation combined with plural modes of governance require the application of significant resources to negotiate the development and delivery of public programmes. (Skelcher, 2000, p. 12)

In terms of the institutional economics framework, fragmentation imposes significant transaction costs on organisations and collaborative structures provide one means of managing these. However, their creation requires the mobilisation of political, managerial and financial resources (Painter *et al.*, 1997; Prior, 1996). Putative partners must vest some of their authority in the collaborative venture and take the risk that working jointly with others will enhance the deliverability of their own objectives without damaging their status or resource flows. The tertiary partnership bodies that emerge may advise on ways in which the activities of primary (elected) and secondary (quango) bodies can be harmonised or better co-ordinated, while executive authority to act remains with the partners. Alternatively they may engage in the development of policy and delivery of programmes on behalf of partners, who cede them the necessary resources to act on their behalf. These relationships are mediated by means of hierarchy, market and network (Chapter 7), and hence constitute plural modes of governance. The growth of collaborative mechanisms can therefore be explained as a response to the transaction costs that arise from collaborative working in a hollowed-out environment.

Emerging forms of partnership

The partnerships that government has stimulated since 1997 are different in several respects from those in the preceding decade. In the first place they have a much stronger orientation to the delivery of those outcomes that will improve the well-being of particular groups or communities. In some cases this outcome focus is the local manifestation of the Public Service Agreement (PSA) system through which central government departments negotiate specific budgetary increases from the Treasury in return for their commitment to deliver on the government's key targets. Sure Start provides one example of this hierarchical linkage between local partnership and national intent (Chapter 8). Delivery of outcomes is also important in the local Connexions partnerships which are designed to integrate a range of services delivered by different agencies to support the participation of 13- to 19-year-olds in education and training. The imperative for achieving cross-cutting outcomes provides a longer-term agenda for partnerships and encourages the articulation of joint outcomes to which all partners subscribe but which are not necessarily organisationally specific.

The consequence of this process gives rise to the second feature of post-1997 partnerships – the longer time horizons towards which they are now focused. For example, the delivery of significant and sustained improvement in health and community well-being requires a commitment by agencies to work together and with stakeholders over a number of years. This means that the five years or so over which time-limited partnerships such as City Challenge and SRB operated is no longer sufficient. More recent initiatives such as New Deal for Communities, a local authority-led collaborative approach to regeneration, will normally operate for 10 years. This development does begin to question the value of time-limited partnerships. The original justification was that short-term interventions would enable particular clusters of issues to be tackled, and that this work could then be integrated into the mainstream budgets of relevant agencies. However, the new long-term partnerships institutionalise the collaborative arrangement to a much greater extent. There is now evidence of a process through which partnerships are transforming into more permanent organisations as a result of their longer-term time horizons. Some NHS/local authority partnerships created under the Health Act 1999 flexibilities are changing from essentially managerial arrangements which, for example, pooled budgets or undertook joint commissioning, into a more formalised arrangement by becoming a care trust – a statutory partnership body with formal accountability both through the NHS structure to the Secretary of State and locally to the local authority. We discuss these processes later in the book (Chapters 7 and 11).

Area-based initiatives (ABIs) are the third collaboration theme of Labour governments since 1997. Prior to this date there had been a number of centrally-initiated partnerships which were confined to specific designated localities. However, much greater weight then ever before has now been placed on this approach. Zonal initiatives – the Health Action Zones (HAZs), Education Action Zones (EAZs), Sport Action Zones (SAZs) and Employment Zones (EZs) – were an early manifestation. These have since been supplemented by a whole series of new partnerships, often focused on areas of disadvantage – for example Sure Start and projects related to the National Strategy for Neighbourhood Renewal (NSNR). However, the size of the targeted areas vary considerably. Some HAZs cover several local authorities, while Sure Start normally covers only a small group of wards within a council's jurisdiction.

The fourth development is the creation of overarching Local Strategic Partnerships (LSPs). These normally cover a single local authority's area, but some have a sub-regional scale or bring together county and districts where there is two-tier local government. They are intended to engage key actors in the development of a vision for the area and to align the programmes of individual agencies to support its delivery. This process can be understood through the insights of regime theory (Chapter 3). LSPs have an additional function. They provide a point at which the host of individual partnerships in the area can be integrated. Local Strategic Partnerships emerged autonomously in a number of localities, and the Local Government Association's New Commitment to Regeneration gave an added impetus to this process by sponsoring 'pathfinder' local authorities to actively build fora of public, business, community and voluntary sector leaders. However, in England and Wales LSPs are now being adopted by all local authorities as the mechanism by which the statutory duty to prepare a community strategy can be fulfilled. One example of a strategic partnership is provided by the arrangements in Northumberland (Figure 2.2). This brings

Figure 2.2 *The interconnections of agencies and partnerships – Northumberland's strategic and specific partnerships*

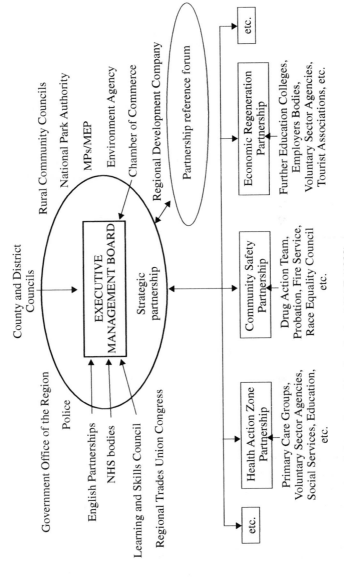

Source: Developed from information in Northumberland HAZ (1998).

Table 2.2 *A typology of partnerships*

Characteristics	Strategic	Sectoral	Neighbourhood
Purpose	Achievement of vision and cross-cutting goals over broad area	Design and/or delivery of service	Meeting needs of specific neighbourhood
Status	Locally agreed terms of reference; may arise from legislative requirement	Local policy and/or legislation; may be corporate body	Local policy and/or legislation; may be corporate body
Membership	Cross-sector, multi-agency	Representatives of commissioners, providers and users	Representatives of relevant organisations within area
Delivery Mechanism	Policies, programmes and budgets of partners	Some form of contract or agreement	Some form of contract or agreement
Time scale	10–20 year visions	Determined by nature of contract, between 3 and 30 years	Determined by nature of initiative, between 3 and 10 years
Governing mechanism	Partnership forum for deliberation and decision, but normally without executive authority	Board, which may have user representation and which may have executive authority	Board, which may have resident representation and may have executive authority
Accountability to members	Through forum, with accountability to wider stakeholders via regular reporting arrangements	Through board and/or accountable body to funding and/or initiating body	Through board and/or accountable body to funding and/or initiating body
Performance review	Prospectus; annual reports	Delivery plan; monitoring and evaluation	Delivery plan; monitoring and evaluation
Examples	Local Strategic Partnerships; New Commitment to Regeneration	Connexions; Community Safety Partnerships (Scotland); Local Health Alliances (Wales)	Sure Start; Education Action Zones; Partnership Action for Continuing Employment (Scotland)

together various public sector agencies, business, labour and community interests. It provides a forum for the development of policy and oversight of delivery in relation to cross-cutting issues that require inter-agency collaboration. The day-to-day business of the Strategic Partnership is handled through the Executive Management Board, comprising the chief executives of a sub-set of the agencies. There is also a Partnership Reference Forum whose members encompass a wider set of voluntary, community and business interests, and which is consulted intermittently. The Strategic Partnership manages its inter-agency programmes through a series of specific partnerships, including those on the Health Action Zone, community safety and economic regeneration.

The structure in Northumberland reflects the type of strategic partnership that is developing across the UK to supplement the more specific sectoral and neighbourhood collaborations (Table 2.2). This formulation adds an additional level of complexity to the earlier discussion of the congested state, since any locality will have a number of such collaborative bodies operating within it. Rather than reducing the transaction costs of inter-organisational working, this array of collaborative activity imposes its own demands on the time and resources of participants. The emergent complex of organisations with different legal forms, corporate governance arrangements and accountability structures poses a major problem both in theorising the new governmental realm and for its practical guidance and management.

The arithmetic of partnerships

The study of public policy partnerships in the UK raises some fundamental empirical questions: How many partnerships are there? What is their purpose? How much money do they spend? Who are their members? Data is partial and not always consistent. Nevertheless it is possible to gain an understanding of the scale and scope of partnership activity and an impressionistic view of the members of their boards.

The number of partnerships

There are no official statistics on partnerships nor is there an annual publication which lists their types, numbers and other relevant details. Despite their increasing significance to the British system of government, this is a somewhat surprising but not unexpected state of affairs. It means that any assessment of the numbers and types of public policy partnerships has to be constructed from those few studies that have tried to map the sector and from original research using official documents and web sites. The three main studies that have published data on partnerships are those by the Select Committee on Public Administration, the Regional Co-ordination Unit (RCU) and the Chartered Institute of Public Finance and Accountancy (CIPFA). All three studies map quangos that have arisen in response to government initiatives rather than local conditions, and this is an important limitation on the data to which we return later. The Select Committee on Public Administration requested government departments in England to provide details of the partnerships that they sponsored (House of Commons, 2001). The results provide an initial picture, but there are significant omissions. The Regional Co-ordination Unit (2000) created to oversee area based initiatives in England publishes its own list, based on an earlier study (Performance and Innovation Unit, 2000). This includes several ABIs that we would not classify as partnerships, and these have been excluded from our calculations. Nevertheless it presents an effective mapping of one class of partnership. A more wide-ranging review of partnerships was undertaken by CIPFA (2001). This report provides details of a considerable number of types of partnership in England, Scotland and Wales, although once again definitional questions and availability of data lead it to be not completely inclusive. We have employed these three sources and searches of government statements and documentation in order to produce the table in Appendix 2.

Our research gives a figure of some 5500 individual partnership bodies at local or regional level stimulated or directly created by government in England, Scotland, Wales and Northern Ireland. These cluster into almost 60 types of public policy partnership which cover a wide range of activities from health improvement and regeneration to child development and rural transport. However, this analysis inevitably remains incomplete. First, the list takes no account of those partnerships created autonomously by local councils, quangos or other local and regional bodies and therefore that are not part of a national initiative (see, for example, the case of Birmingham City Council in Chapter 8). Second, the scope of central government activity is so wide that we are not likely to have recorded all partnerships. Those we identified have an orientation towards the social agenda; there will be others in agricultural, defence or industrial policy. Third, forms of partnership are being announced or stimulated on a regular basis by government. The Rural White Paper, for example, promoted the development of strong and inclusive partnerships involving parish and town councils and other groups concerned with the rural economy, society and environment (Department for Environment, Food and Rural Affairs, 2001). In some areas these are likely to be included within the portfolio of LSPs, while in others separate collaborations may emerge. Finally, we have not included partnerships funded through European programmes (such as the district partnerships in Northern Ireland supported through the peace and reconciliation programme) or private finance initiative/public–private partnerships. Our list therefore has limitations, but at the time of writing it is, we believe, the most comprehensive available.

The expenditure of partnerships

Identifying the expenditure of partnerships is fraught with difficulties. Funding streams come from a variety of sources, and aggregate data are normally only available on central government spending allocated for specific types of partnership. We have been able to identify some £4.3 billion of expenditure by partnerships in 2001/02, of which three-quarters is provided by central government. This figure does not include matching funding and other support provided by partners nor spending from mainstream budgets that is influenced or controlled by partnerships (other than for Health Act partnerships) since data on these sources are not published in aggregate form. For example, Crime and Disorder Partnerships oversee and shape the crime-prevention spending of local councils, the police, voluntary organisations and other agencies. The impact of such partnerships will tend to be reflected in changes to the pattern of expenditure in mainstream budgets on, for example, street lighting, neighbourhood wardens and educational programmes and therefore not separately identifiable as crime-reduction spending. Consequently a conservative estimate of total annual direct and indirect expenditure by public policy partnerships at the sub-national level would be some £15–20 billion.

Although the proportion of total public expenditure directly allocated to partnerships is relatively small, it does have considerable significance. This is because it has the effect of redirecting the effort of mainstream public agencies towards government's key priorities. Three factors are important here. The first is that access to partnership funding provided by government often requires a competitive bid. This competition for resources engages public bodies in a process of thinking about how their policies and programmes can be modified to meet the criteria for a financial award. The second influence is that approval of government funds for a partnership sometimes requires the agencies involved to provide matching funding or in-kind support, once again reshaping their priorities. Finally, the funding is made available in a highly normative climate where winning or being nominated for special funds from a high prestige government initiative is seen as an indicator of status.

Members of partnership boards

One way of examining who has access to and influence over decision-making in partnerships is to consider the composition of their boards. Data on these are not available from a central source, but it is possible to make some estimates. Most of the partnerships listed in Appendix 2 have some form of board or management group. Assuming a conservative estimate of 10 members on each partnership board, this gives a figure of some 55 000 places. However, these ignore partnerships that emerge in response to the specific needs of the locality. If we also assume, very conservatively, that each local authority in England, Northern Ireland, Scotland and Wales is involved in five locally-initiated partnerships, each with a board of 10 members, this produces a figure of some 20 000 board places. Overall, therefore, we can estimate with reasonable confidence that there are some 75 000 board places on sub-national public policy partnerships in the UK. This compares with approximately 23 000 councillors and 60 000 members of local executive quangos (Wilson and Game, 1998; Skelcher, 1998).

We have gathered information on the membership of individual partnership boards from a number of regeneration, health, community safety and other forms of local partnership. This reveals that some boards are *agency-exclusive*, comprising nominees from the partner organisations but with little or no representation from the community or client group being served. Bradford HAZ provides an example. This has a top-level partnership board of senior managers from the key partner organisations, plus the Council leader and the social services portfolio holder as the two elected political representatives of the people of Bradford and two community health council representatives (Table 2.3). LSPs also typically have a small agency-inclusive executive group and a wider partnership forum which can have upwards of 60 members from the community and voluntary sectors (Local Government Association, 2001). SRB and Sure Start partnerships, in contrast, are examples of *community-inclusive* boards which typically have a significant level of representation from community and voluntary interests. In the case of an SRB studied by Smith (2001), community representation on the board

Table 2.3   *Original membership of Bradford HAZ partnership board*

Organisation	Status of representative
Bradford Health Authority	Chair; chief executive; deputy chief executive
Bradford Metropolitan District Council	Leader; social services chair; chief executive
Airedale NHS Trust	Chair; chief executive
Bradford Community NHS Trust	Chair; chief executive
Bradford Hospitals NHS Trust	Chair; chief executive
Airedale CHC	Chair
Bradford CHC	Chair
Bradford Primary Care Group	Chair
University of Bradford	Vice-chancellor
Bradford Race Equality Council	Director
Voluntary Sector	Representative
Bradford TEC	Chair
Bradford Chamber of Commerce	President
West Yorkshire Police	Superintendent
Regional TUC	Representative

Source: Adapted from Bradford HAZ (1998).

increased from four out of 21 places to five out of 17 over the life of the project. Community directors and chairs of local community fora were also part of the co-ordinating group who oversaw the implementation process. Our analysis of partnership board structures leads us to conclude that agency-inclusive boards are the norm and therefore that the great majority of their members are senior managers from relevant agencies. Community representation on partnership boards is more limited. This is not to say that community participation does not take place. Most partnership bodies with agency-exclusive board have some type of consultative forum (see Chapter 9). However, just as councillors have been typified as being male, middle-aged, middle-class and white, so we can say that the typical partnership board member is a senior-level public sector manager rather than an elected councillor or community or voluntary sector representative.

Regional partnerships

Most partnerships operate within localities or groups of neighbourhoods and local authorities play a leading role in facilitating their emergence and operation. However, there is a growing regional tier of partnerships. One example is the Regional Cultural Consortia in England. They were created by the Department of Culture, Media and Sport to support the development of a cultural strategy in each region (other than London, where a quango appointed by the Mayor undertakes this task). These partnerships consist of nominees of the regional quangos for arts, tourism, sports and heritage, the library and archive service, the Regional Development Agency (RDA) and local government. There is also representation from the creative industries, regional lottery boards, countryside and recreation bodies, educational interests and the voluntary sector. The chairs of the partnership are appointed by the Secretary of State (Skelcher *et al.*, 2000). Regional Transport Partnerships in Scotland similarly operate on a supra-locality basis. The four created to date are responsible for preparing co-ordinated transport strategies and resolving any problems arising from different approaches by conterminous organisations (CIPFA, 2001). Such regional partnerships are even more elusive and under-researched than those at locality level.

Partnerships and local government

It is local authorities, of any public body, who are involved in the greatest number and range of partnerships, as befits the scope of their functions and focal role in acting for a local community. A 1999 survey of local authorities identified a total of 5326 partnerships (Table 2.4). The survey adopted a wider definition of partnership than we employ in this book, and

Table 2.4   *Types of partnership in which local authorities are involved*

Type	Number	%
With one or more local authorities	866	17
With the private sector	1296	26
With the voluntary sector	1034	21
With one or more local authorities and one or more private, voluntary or public organisations	734	15
In a network with a combination of public, private and voluntary sector organisations	868	17
Other	232	4
TOTAL	5030	100

Source: Adapted from Newchurch (1999b).

therefore captured contracted-out service delivery to private companies and service level agreements with the voluntary sector (accounting for 30 per cent of all 'partnerships') as well as more strategic collaborations to do with regeneration. One county council, for example, had more than 500 'partnerships', of which 400 were individual contracts with nursing and

Table 2.5   *Partnerships in Nottingham*

Name of partnership	Period	Total public funding within initiative £m	Total leverage/ matched funding expected £m	Total investment £m
Time limited partnerships, including...				
SRB 2	1996–2002	13.2	45.5	58.7
SRB 3	1997–2003	4.5	4.8	9.3
SRB 4	1998–2004	5.3	3.0	8.3
SRB 5	1999–2005	12.0	13.1	25.1
SRB 6	2000–2006	8.8	14.9	23.7
Sure Start – Northwest Nottingham	2000–2007/10	1.7 revenue; 1.3 capital	0.7 in kind	3.7
Sure Start – St Ann's	2000–2003 with possible extension	1.0 revenue; 0.5 capital	0	1.5
EAZ	1999–2004	4.5	1.5 in cash and kind	6.0
HAZ	1999–2002	8.0	0	8.0
URBAN	1997–2001	5.4	At least 5.4	10.8
New Deal for Communities	2000–2010	55.0	0	55.0
Employment Zone	2000 Subject to possible extension	N/a	N/a	N/a
Phase Ten regeneration	2000–2005	12.0 capital plus other resources	0	12.0
Crime Reduction	1999–2002	Bid into national fund of £250 m over 3 years	50%	N/a
On-going partnerships, including...				
Local Strategic Partnership	Connexions	Community Legal Service Partnership		
Crime and Disorder Partnership	Local Agenda 21	Drug Action Team		

Source: Adapted from Nottingham CVS (2001).

private residential care providers. Although the data are heavily biased towards contractual arrangements, which fall outside our definition of public policy partnerships, they do reveal the level of inter-agency activity and hence the complexity involved at the local level.

The example of Nottingham illustrates the way in which partnerships have become integral to public service operations (Table 2.5). There are some 14 time-limited partnerships stimulated by government, to which must be added the various ongoing arrangements and locally developed collaborations. This has a major impact on the city, both in terms of the scale of public investment, the demands for community participation and the transaction costs involved. Many of the partnerships are concentrated on a small number of wards, and some wards receive several overlapping partnerships – as might be expected from initiatives designed to address problems of disadvantage and social exclusion and to stimulate regeneration. Nottingham is by no means an exception. Similar patterns are found in each local authority area across the UK. However, there will be a greater concentration of partnerships in localities that have a higher incidence of disadvantaged communities. The result is a complex mosaic of multi-agency collaboration spending considerable amounts of public money, topped up with in-kind contributions and leveraged funds.

Conclusion

The data presented here demonstrate the extensive use of partnerships and the variety of forms in which they are found. It also reveals how significant partnerships are to the delivery of public policy in a post-hollowing-out environment and one where there is a much stronger political imperative to deliver outcomes on cross-cutting issues. The complexity of the congested state poses a major challenge for the traditional norms of public administration which, despite the extensive public management reforms of the later twentieth century, still underlie the approach to government in the UK. Officials rather than politicians have a major role as decision-makers on partnership boards. There appears to be a low level of community-inclusiveness at board level, despite extensive consultation mechanisms. The processes of representative democracy are stretched to the extreme by the relationship between tertiary structures and primary and secondary bodies. And some services that are nominally the responsibility of local authorities are in reality shaped by partnerships.

Table 2.6 *Organising principles for public services*

Organising principle	Organisational response	Examples
Functionally-defined service	Public bureaucracy led by elected or appointed representatives	• Social housing – housing provision and management by local authority housing department or registered social landlord • Health care – primary care through PCT, involving GPs and community-based services; specialist care through hospitals
Outcome-defined issue	Multi-agency partnership shaped by community involvement	• Fear of crime and lack of safety in a particular locality – community safety partnership involving residents, police, local authority, etc. • Improving the life chances of young children in disadvantaged neighbourhoods – Sure Start partnership involving health bodies, schools, local authority, police, residents, families, etc.

The collaborative agenda has a powerful momentum enhanced by the political significance of cross-cutting issues and outcome delivery. In the light of this, it is reasonable to conjecture that partnerships will emerge as the core of public sector activity and that what are currently regarded as mainstream organisations (for example, local authorities, primary care trusts and executive agencies) become their delivery agents. This is because the organising principle informing public bodies is changing. Traditionally it was one of the functionally-defined services delivered through public bureaucracies. The emerging principle is of outcome-defined issues facing particular groups or localities that are tackled through multi-agency

partnerships involving local communities (Table 2.6). The projects undertaken by partnerships involve mainstream public bureaucracies as the delivery agents. For example, Sure Start partnerships fund posts in health, social
services and education to deliver their programmes, thus binding local and
health authorities into a collaborative vision. This inversion of role suggested by our conjecture would place partnerships firmly at the heart of
strategic public policy development and implementation. This has significant implications for democratic and managerial practice, which will be
explored throughout the book. However, in order to do this it is important
initially to examine the theoretical underpinning of collaborative action.
This is the task of the next chapter.

3 Understanding Collaboration

The emergence and form of collaborative activity has been the subject of study for a number of years, and has given rise to a series of theories which seek to explain this phenomenon. As befits a way of working that cuts across traditional boundaries, theoretical perspectives informing collaborative activity between organisations tend to be located in a variety of disciplines, including organisational sociology, political science and economics (Faulkner and de Rond, 2000). In general theories do not seek to provide a comprehensive explanation of the collaborative process. Instead they tend to offer insights into particular aspects of collaboration. However, it is important to note that the predominant perspective in the literature is one that views collaboration as an exception. The narratives of policy development, decision-making and programme delivery are ones in which individual organisations work largely independently in their functional 'silos' (Richards *et al.*, 1999) and where inter-organisational working – or even co-operation between different divisions in the same organisation – are presented as activities that cause difficulties and generate disproportionate transaction costs. Differences in organisational interests, professional agendas and ways of working, the political agendas of ministers, councillors and quango chairs and the tradition of input rather than outcome budgeting all contribute to the erection of a substantial barrier to collaborative activity. The methodology for the analysis of collaboration in public policy therefore places questions of conflict above those of co-operation.

In this chapter, however, we take a broader perspective. We explore a number of theoretical approaches to demonstrate how theory can help us understand:

- *why* collaboration happens – the imperatives and drivers in the policy and organisational context and in terms of key actors;
- the *form* collaboration takes – the way in which the relationship is constituted, for example as a partnership governed by a board or an informal network of loosely connected individuals;

35

- what factors affect the *capacity* and *practice* of collaboration – the professional, organisational and individual resources to develop, sustain and manage collaboration and the relationship with more conventional means of governing, managing and monitoring public services.

We set these theoretical approaches within an overall framework for understanding collaboration that distinguishes between 'optimistic', 'pessimistic' and 'realistic' perspectives. The optimist and pessimist perspectives have previously been applied elsewhere by Challis *et al.* (1988). We have adapted and updated their usage drawing on more recent theoretical developments, and in particular we have added a third perspective – the 'realist' approach (Table 3.1).

Table 3.1 *Theories and approaches to collaboration*

Questions	Optimist	Pessimist	Realist
Why collaboration happens?	Achieving shared vision: *Collaborative empowerment theory* *Regime theory* Resource maximisation: *Exchange theory*	Maintaining or enhancing position: *Resource dependency theory*	Responding to new environments: *Evolutionary theory*
What form of collaboration is developed and why?	Multiple Relationships: *Collaborative empowerment theory* Coalitions: *Regime theory*	Inter-organisational network: *Resource dependency theory*	Obligational, promotional and systemic networks: *Evolutionary theory* Policy networks as meso level or governance instruments: *Policy networks theories*
Which factors affect collaboration?	Individual factors: Reticulist skills and abilities, trust: *Collaborative empowerment theory* Leadership: *Regime theory*	Organisational factors: Culture, bureaucracy, professionalism: *Resource dependency theory*	Institutional factors: The mediation of individual and organisational factors: *New institutional theory*

Drivers for collaboration

Optimist perspectives: exchange theory, collaborative empowerment and regime theory

For optimists collaboration takes place in order that a shared vision may be achieved. This shared vision may be arrived at through prior consensus among stakeholders or may require the negotiation of conflict. In either case the theory that underpins the optimistic perspective is one which is characterised by two key features:

1. that collaboration will result in positive outcomes or improvements for the system as a whole, and
2. that the stakeholders share a level of altruism in relation to collaboration, that is, that future positive outcomes for the system override the desire for sectional gain by the participating organisations.

Exchange theory, developed by Levine and White (1962), is an important early contribution to understanding collaboration. Their study highlighted the way in which service users with multiple problems needed to engage with a highly fragmented and specialised array of health and social welfare providers. The difficulty users faced in negotiating the system prompted the drive to collaboration. Levine and White identified the prevention and cure of disease as the orientation of the overall system, and one that therefore informed the objectives of individual providers. However, few individual organisations had access to sufficient of the necessary resources to fulfil their objectives. In reality other organisations in the system controlled resources that were necessary for any individual organisation to undertake its tasks. Hospitals, for example, were reliant on primary care providers for referrals of service users. And these primary care bodies needed to refer on because they did not have the resources to treat such individuals. Scarcity of resources therefore motivated a pattern of voluntary exchange relations between the individual agencies in the inter-organisational network. In Levine and White's words:

> Organisational exchange is any voluntary activity between two organisations which has consequences, actual or anticipated, for the realisation of the respective goals or objectives. (1962, p. 588)

This is a very broad definition of exchange which according to Blau's critique (1964) can lead to a tautological view in which every form of interaction between organisations can be seen as exchange. Nevertheless Levine and White do not see such inter-organisational exchange arising purely on an *ad hoc* basis. They make much of a concept that has become central to the study of collaboration – the organisational domain. This refers to an explicit or implicit agreement between each organisation about their respective areas of operation in the delivery of system-wide goals. However, in a situation of resource scarcity some organisations will control more than others and may use this power to challenge others' domains in order to gain greater security for their own position (this is termed power-dependency or resource-dependency theory, to which we return below). Consequently it can be argued that exchange theory is a special case which applies in organisational systems that have a high normative regard for altruistic behaviour and a strong respect for others' autonomy (for example some systems of religious or charitable agencies).

While Levine and White present an optimistic view of collaboration, others emphasise the socially desirable outcomes that can be achieved. An important contributor to this normative perspective is Himmelman (1996). He understands the value of collaboration as resting with its capacity to 'transform' power relationships in society so as to achieve social justice for communities that have been disadvantaged and discriminated against in the prevailing political environment. For Himmelman power is defined as 'the capacity to produce intended results' (1996, p. 22) and he argues that the sharing of power amongst different stakeholders is the only way to achieve the vision of social justice. However, he identifies two ways in which this power may be shared – through *collaborative betterment* or *collaborative empowerment*. Collaborative betterment occurs when agencies outside the community design and control a process into which the community is invited. He argues that this collaborative strategy 'can produce policy changes and improvements in programme delivery and services, but tends not to produce long-term ownership in communities or to increase significantly communities' control over their own destinies' (p. 29). In contrast, collaborative empowerment is 'the capacity to set priorities and control resources that are essential for increasing community self-determination' (p. 30). The process starts with community organisation, and then spreads out to engage public, private and other organisations in the collaborative activity. Himmelman's framework, therefore, is one based on multi-sector involvement – community, voluntary, statutory and private interests – but with an orientation towards one in which communities and community empowerment are at the heart of the collaborative process. The mutuality that underpins Himmelman's analysis, however, implies a degree of altruism among public and private interests as it is they who would be required to give up control and influence in order to deliver this wider goal.

Finding ways of theorising collaboration between a myriad of different actors is also a preoccupation of 'regime theorists'. However, their focus is the development of a means of governing in a context where governments have limited power and influence. Regime theory fits within the optimist perspective as it 'directs attention to the conditions under which ... effective long-term coalitions emerge in order to accomplish public purpose' (Stoker, 1995, p. 55). This approach to understanding urban governance was developed originally in the US through the work of Stone (1993), but has also built up a series of trans-Atlantic studies including those by DiGaetano and Klemanski (1993), Harding (1994) and DiGaetano (1997). It moves beyond the analysis of the hyperpluralists, who see the vast array of organised interests ranged against weak city government leading to fractured, diffuse and ineffective urban policy-making. Instead they consider 'how in the midst of diversity and complexity a capacity to govern can emerge within a political system' (Stoker, 1995, p. 57). Stone argues that the two traditional roles of the state – as an agency of control and of arbitration – are limited by the structural conditions pertaining, namely the complexity of problems and fragmentation of interests. In order to be effective, government must (in Stone's words) 'blend' its capacity and resources with those of other actors. It does this by adopting a new role as mobiliser and co-ordinator and, as in the case of some major cities world-wide, by building a strategic vision for the urban area in partnership with key actors. The motivation for business interests to join this coalition is in the production of a longer-term strategy for the locality to which all key parties are signatories and involvement in the flourishing regeneration agenda. Reviewing the Leeds Initiative, a strategic public–private alliance, Haughton (1996, pp. 33–4) observes that 'for the private sector, [it] is seen as a powerful voice for the city ... [it] has also served as a vehicle for greater engagement with the regeneration quangos ... which had some early problems establishing credibility and legitimacy'.

Pessimist perspectives: resource dependency and the political economy

For theorists within the 'pessimist' perspective, collaboration takes place in order that stakeholders may preserve or enhance their power, prioritising personal or organisational gain above all else. This perspective derives from resource-dependency theory, which as we noted above can be treated as a more widely applicable perspective than exchange theory.

Resource-dependency theory also has a long pedigree. An early sociological formulation was by Emerson who argued that social relationships commonly entail 'ties of mutual dependence' (1962, p. 32), with A being dependent on the resources controlled by B to achieve desired goals. This starting point is similar to that for exchange theory. But where exchange theory would see the next step being mutually beneficial collaboration, resource-dependency theory adopts the premise that each party attempts to control or influence the other's activities. Power, therefore, 'resides implicitly in the other's dependency' (*ibid.*). This formulation was applied to the study of organisational collaboration by Yuchtman and Seashore (1967), Pfeffer and Salancik (1978) and others. Central to the resource-dependency view is that organisational decision-makers are typically oriented to the acquisition and defence of an adequate supply of resources. This literature, however, is principally about the way in which a focal organisation perceives and responds to its external environment rather than the operation of the inter-organisational network as a unit of analysis.

Benson (1975) provides a rich theoretical analysis which addresses this question and broadens out to consider the political economy of the inter-organisational network as a whole – the fundamental rules that structure interactions within a particular grouping of organisations. Benson's central proposition is that surface-level interactions between organisations, for example to do with co-ordinating service delivery, are ultimately explained with reference to the underlying pattern of resource distribution and acquisition. All organisations need to pursue key scarce resources, that is the authority to perform particular functions and the money to fund necessary activities, and do this by using various strategies. Benson identifies four such strategies:

1. The fulfilment of programme requirements. Organisations will seek order and predictability in their established programmes and will not tolerate practices that interfere with this.
2. The maintenance of a clear domain of high social importance. Such a domain is characterised by one or more of the following attributes: (a) exclusiveness (b) autonomy (c) dominance over other agencies.
3. The maintenance of orderly, reliable patterns of resource flow.
4. The extended application and defence of the agency's paradigm. The organisation and individuals within it promote its view of the world and way of doing things.

The interactions between organisations in the network form the basis of the exchange of scarce resources across the network. The capacity of particular organisations to benefit from such exchange will depend on a number of factors including their position in the network (whether it is nodal or peripheral), how much money and authority they have or need and their significance in the wider environment, that is, the support they can mobilise among different interests. From this perspective the motivation to collaborate is about both realising surface-level objectives to do with service delivery and achieving change in the substructure – the political economy – to secure current and future access to valued resources. Those who do not play this inter-organisational game are destined to decline and eventually cease operations.

Realist perspectives: evolutionary theory

For 'realists' it is the wider environment – or more specifically changes in the prevailing context – that are critical in determining the incidence of collaboration. In this environment both altruism and individual gain can coexist. What is important is how either or both can be achieved through collaborative activity that is appropriate to the changing context. Drawing on private and public sector experiences, Alter and Hage (1993) have developed an 'evolutionary theory' of organisational collaboration that sets out the realist position. Alter and Hage's evolutionary theory suggests that collaboration between organisations is becoming more likely for a number of reasons including changing political and economic objectives, growth in technological capacity and an increasing demand for quality and diversity in goods and services. In order to take advantage of this changed environment, organisations must meet certain conditions for collaboration that combine elements of the optimist (desire for improvement) and pessimist (need for resources) position. However, the extent to which organisations will succeed in their evolution will be dependent upon other contextual factors such as the existence of trust between stakeholders and the complexity of the task. The evolutionary theory of collaboration does not assume that collaboration will occur automatically or that it will ultimately overcome all barriers. Instead it highlights the importance of learning as part of the collaborative process and again cites this as something that can be beneficial both to the individual organisations involved and to the wider society.

Forms of collaboration

The forms adopted by collaborative relationships can be understood from different theoretical perspectives, each of which illuminate particular implications for theory, policy and practice. In this section two perspectives – organisational and political science – are examined. These have been selected because of the interconnections they identify between different collaborative relationships and the issues they raise about how collaborative arrangements impact upon the governance of society.

An organisational perspective

From an organisational perspective the forms of collaboration can be conceptualised as a spectrum. At one end are informal and largely *ad hoc* relationships and at the other highly structured and formalised interactions, which ultimately may lead to the integration of collaborating agencies into a single organisation (Figure 3.1). The continuum essentially captures the degree to which interactions between participants are self-governed or are regulated by some external or overarching structure with explicit rules and points of reference. Organisational and public policy literature refers to informal relationships as a *network*, while various degrees of formalisation which are less than complete integration are termed *partnerships*.

For optimists the idea of a continuum of activity is important as it suggests that more sophisticated and therefore more effective forms of collaboration can be developed from lower-level relationships. For example, Himmelman proposes that collaborative forms exist in the operation of four different relationships (networking, co-ordination, co-operation and collaboration) 'that build upon each other along a continuum of complexity and commitment' (1996, p. 26). While the achievement of the optimal form – collaboration – will not be possible in all cases, it is essential in order to deliver social justice. Implicit in his argument is the optimistic assumption that once stakeholders perceive the benefits of other forms of interaction they will inevitably be driven to seek to achieve collaboration.

Other literatures, however, apply the term *network* in a different way. Benson (1975), as we discussed earlier, distinguishes between the surface-level co-operative interactions between organisations and the deeper structure of the inter-organisational network that shapes them and upon which they are ultimately dependent. For him, network is a phenomenon that expresses the nature of authority and resource relationships between these organisations. It is a unit of analysis in its own right, independently of the study of organisational interactions. For Benson the inter-organisational network is at its most effective when it is in equilibrium, a state that can be

Figure 3.1 *Forms of collaboration and rules of governance*

Form of collaboration	Loose network of informal, *ad hoc* relationships	Limited agreement to share information	Agreement to undertake activities jointly	Agreement to constitute formal governing body	Creation of federal structure in which participating bodies agree to devolve upwards some of their autonomy	Merger of participating bodies into single organisation
Rules of governance	Self-government through mutual norms and obligations and shared values and trust	←———————→			External government through overarching constitution	Hierarchy
Organisational and policy terminology	Network	Partnership			Federation	Integration

discerned from analysis of interactions between organisations at the level of the superstructure. The evidence required to demonstrate this state is:

- domain consensus – agreement amongst participating organisations about the role and scope of different agencies;
- ideological consensus – agreement about tasks and how to approach these;
- positive evaluation – respect by members of one organisation for the value of the work of other organisations;
- work co-ordination – activities programmed between organisations to maximise their efficiency and effectiveness.

Levels of equilibrium can vary without the network becoming imbalanced providing all the dimensions vary in the same way, that is, if domain consensus is low then all other dimensions must be low too. However, variation between dimensions will cause the network to become imbalanced. Usually this is caused by factors acting on the network from outside, for example where a superordinate body such as government legislates that work co-ordination between organisations should be high even though domain consensus is low. This is a familiar scenario in the UK and is described as an *imposed* rather than *voluntary* partnership. It alerts us to the pessimist position that in the search for scarce resources, such as authority and money, organisations may enter into collaborations for which they are not fully equipped.

Alter and Hage are similarly concerned with the inter-organisational network. They propose a sequential model of network development and argue that each stage is an essential precursor of the next (Table 3.2). The embryonic network arises from 'bartering interactions between administrators and workers across organisational boundaries. As problems arise,

Table 3.2 *A model of symbiotic network development*

Type of network	Obligational networks	Promotional networks	Systemic networks
Inter-organisational activities	Almost none; *ad hoc*	Peripheral; segmented	Essential; enduring
Emergent properties	Boundary spanners	Pooling of resources	Division of labour
Goals	Individual; member needs	Supra-ordinate member problems	Supra-ordinate societal problems

Source: Adapted from Alter and Hage (1993, p. 74).

information is exchanged, and the parties concert their action. If a problem is solved, then trust is built, and the basis for further collaboration is established' (Alter and Hage, 1993, p. 75). In this way obligational networks – 'informal loosely linked groups of organisations having relationships of preferred exchanges' – build into promotional networks – 'quasi-formal clusters of organisations sharing and pooling resources to accomplish concerted action' – which lead to a systemic network – 'formal interorganisational units jointly producing a product or service in pursuit of a supraorganisational goal' (*ibid.*, p. 73). However, Alter and Hage emphasise that the value of the systemic network is its capacity to produce products or services that could not be delivered by one organisation alone. If this production capacity is not required then neither are collaborative relationships at the level of the systemic network.

A political science perspective on collaborative form

There are a number of theoretical approaches within the political science literature that seek to understand the forms of collaboration that may emerge between organisational actors in a political system. Those of particular relevance to our discussion are the policy networks approach and regime theory. Policy network analyses fit with the 'realistic' perspective on collaboration. This is because policy networks operate in contexts where the distribution of power is uneven and where different interests are able to influence decision-making for their own ends while also contributing to wider societal goals.

Policy networks as interest intermediation: the British approach

The British approach to policy networks emerged during the 1980s and was formalised in the work of Marsh and Rhodes (1992) and Jordan and Schubert (1992). Marsh and Rhodes conceptualise a policy network as a structured set of relationships between government and pressure groups (which may include producer interests) within which policy is negotiated over time. They see policy networks as a meso-level approach to understanding the exercise of power in policy-making. Their approach draws from neo-pluralism the notion of uneven distribution of power in a liberal democracy and the capacity of organised interests to shape agendas and affect policy outputs, and from corporatism the concept of structured sets of relationships between government, business and other key interests engaged in bargaining and negotiation over policy.

Policy network, however, is a generic term and Marsh and Rhodes distinguish a continuum of possibilities from relatively closed and tightly-knit *policy communities* where participants share a common view or ideology and there is equity of resources to more open and diffuse *issue networks* in which there may be contest between views and differential resource distribution (Table 3.3). The essential hypothesis in the British tradition is that network structure affects policy outcome. For example, Marsh and Rhodes propose that a tightly-knit policy community is likely to demonstrate a high degree of policy continuity while in an issue network there is likely to be variation in policy outcomes because it will be easier for different groups to affect the policy agenda.

However, the policy networks approach has also been subject to a number of criticisms. One concerns the assumption that it is the structural features of the policy network that determine policy outcomes. Dowding (1995) challenges this view and draws attention to the impact of the preferences and bargaining strategies of actors within networks. Similarly Hay (1998) points to a reification of structure and a tendency of policy network analysis to ignore the dynamic processes at work, which may result from the intentions of particular actors. This resolves into the structure–agent problem: to what extent is the agent dependent upon or privileged over structure, and how does one affect the other? As Daugbjerg and Marsh comment:

> The policy network is a political structure which can constrain and facilitate the actions of agents. At the same time, policy networks are the product of patterns of structured privilege, based on access to and control over resources, and are constructed and reconstructed through the actions of agents. (1998, p. 70)

The debate about the value of policy networks continues, with Marsh's attempt to address the structure–agent relationship through a 'dynamic and dialectical approach' (Marsh, 1998; Marsh and Smith, 2000) precipitating further reaction from those exercised by what they perceive to be the inherent weaknesses of the policy networks approach (Dowding, 2001) or the likely contribution of a dialectical model (Raab, 2001; Evans, 2001; Marsh and Smith, 2001).

The relevance of this policy networks approach to an understanding of collaboration and partnership is twofold. First it draws attention to the way in which established and structured sets of relationships persist and are influential in shaping the policy context. These relationships may formally be reflected in working groups or advisory bodies, but equally important is the unwritten assumption of insider status accorded to those privileged

Table 3.3 *Policy networks, policy communities and issue networks*

Dimension	Policy community	Issue network
Membership		
Number of participants	Very limited number; some groups consciously excluded	Large
Type of interest	Economic and/or professional interests dominate	Encompass range of affected interests
Integration		
Frequency of interaction	Frequent, high-quality interaction of all groups on all matters related to policy issue	Contacts fluctuate in frequency and intensity
Continuity	Membership, values and outcomes persistent over time	Access fluctuates significantly
Consensus	All participants share basic values and accept the legitimacy of the outcome	A measure of agreement exists, but conflict is ever present
Resources		
Distribution within network	All participants have resources; basic relationship is an exchange relationship	Some participants may have resources, but they are limited, and basic relationship is consultative
Distribution within participating organisations	Hierarchical; leaders can deliver members	Varied and variable distribution and capacity to regulate members
Power	Balance of power among members; although one group may dominate, it must be a positive-sum game if community is to persist	Unequal power, reflecting unequal resources and unequal access; a zero-sum game

Source: Adapted from Marsh (1998, p. 16).

players and their informal and interpersonal interactions with government officials and ministers. Secondly, the policy networks approach points to the relationship between the structure of the network and the nature of policy outcomes. This relates directly to questions about the composition and membership of partnership boards and the wider network of relationships within which they are located. Theoretically, a more inclusive (that is, plural) network should lead to a policy outcome that gains wide support. However, this may be a lowest common denominator solution which is potentially suboptimal in terms of a longer-term conception of the public interest. Therefore understanding the ways in which informal and interpersonal linkages operate in and around the pieces of organisational structure in which relationships formally reside and exploring whether and how networks can be actively led towards public policy goals are both important aspects of an appreciation of the dynamics and sustainability of collaborative forms.

Policy networks as a mode of governance: the continental approach

While the British approach has emerged to create a meso-level understanding of interest group intermediation, the German and Dutch literature has traditionally been more concerned with policy networks as an emerging form of governance in contemporary developed societies. Their focus is the manner in which the steering and regulation of societies takes place given the multiplicity of organisational actors, highly differentiated policy sectors and absence of centralised authority. The unit of analysis is the pattern of inter-organisational relationships as a whole – the linkages and their intensity, standardisation and so on. These constitute the structure of governance – and a new structure of governance compared with the centralised authority that forms an essential part of traditional conceptions of public administration. From this continental perspective, the policy network comprises:

> All actors involved in the formulation and implementation of policy in a policy sector. They are characterised by predominantly *informal* interactions between *public and private* actors with distinctive, but *interdependent interests*, who strive to solve problems of collective action on a central, *non-hierarchical level*. (Börzel, 1998, p. 260; italics in the original)

Consequently this notion of network can be contrasted with that of market and hierarchy. This is a position taken by Lowndes and Skelcher, drawing on the work of Kooiman and van Vliet (1993), Kickert *et al.* (1997) and others. They offer the view that:

> The network mode of governance arises from a view that actors are able to identify complementary interests. The development of interdependent relationships based on trust, loyalty and reciprocity enables collaborative activity to be developed and maintained. Being voluntary, networks

maintain the loyalty of members over the longer term. Conflicts are resolved within the network on the basis of members' reputational concerns. (Lowndes and Skelcher, 1998, pp. 319–20)

There are, as Börzel notes, differences between the German and Dutch literatures. The former tends to address broader questions to do with the relationship between the state and civil society and the emerging problem of ungovernability. This includes the problem of defining appropriate forms of legal instruments to enable the state to steer increasingly autonomous and self-referential societal subsystems. In contrast the Dutch literature, especially reflected in the work of Kickert *et al.* (1997), Klijn (1996) and colleagues at Erasmus University, deals more with questions of strategy and management. A central concern in their work is the problem of the effective and efficient operation of a policy network, and the literature thus adopts a more managerial approach in contrast to the legal-political interests of the German school. Their relevance to our discussion relates to the potential role and capacity of government in acting to steer and guide the network towards wider public policy outcomes.

Regime theory – capacity to govern

As indicated above, regime theorists specify a role for government in mobilising actors into a particular type of collaborative relationship – a coalition. While these coalitions may comprise members of peak bodies, these are not the only types of coalition envisaged in regime theory. For example, Stone (1993) discusses various regime types, including lower-class, opportunity expansion regimes. Smith and Beazley (2000) examine this particular regime type in the context of recent UK regeneration policy and, drawing on Himmelman's collaborative empowerment model, argue that community involvement in a governing coalition should go beyond access to resources to take up 'lower-class opportunities'. For them:

a community coalition would be explicitly grass-roots generated, not a top-down imposition (albeit initiated and enabled by top-down funding). Moreover, it would, in a normative sense, be based on the *involvement* of communities in making strategic choices about regeneration in their localities. (2000, p. 858)

Here government's mobilising role is confined to provision of policy and resource opportunities in recognition of the imbalance of power between government and community sectors and the need to create an environment where communities are able to dictate the agenda.

Factors influencing the capacity and practice of collaboration

Individual factors

Building and maintaining collaborative relationships requires particular capacities. Optimistic perspectives point to the fundamental importance of human resources in relation to the capacity and practice of collaboration. The attention they pay to the need for specific skills and abilities to facilitate collaboration is borne out in studies of collaborative practice where success factors invariably include reference to key individuals who bring particular skills and play particular roles in collaborative effort (Friend *et al.*, 1974). These individuals are often referred to as reticulists, people who are able to bring networks together and help others identify relevant linkages between them and other actors. For Himmelman (1996) there are a number of different roles that may be played by reticulists, among them convenor, capacity builder and catalyst. However, each of these roles requires individuals to understand and be able to work network relationships. Reticulists may also have a role to play in more active facilitation of the collaborative. For example, Sink (1996) identifies that personality factors may get in the way of collaboration between people who have all the requisite skills. In this case Huxham (1996) suggests drawing on the skills of a facilitator to help putative networks determine how they may work together and what kinds of attribute they need within the collaborative if it is to work well.

One vital attribute of successful collaborations is trust. Himmelman identifies a basic level of trust between parties as essential both to begin a collaborative venture and to sustain and deepen the collaboration over time. However, trust can also be undermined or limited in practice rendering the nature of the collaboration correspondingly limited. So Alter and Hage, while affording priority to the role of trust in the evolution of collaborative efforts, understand that the propensity towards trusting relationships is context specific and possibly culturally specific. Identifying the key elements of trusting contexts is important in supporting their development and reproducing these relationships in the future. Similarly examining more closely exactly what is meant by trust is important if it is to be helpful as part of a framework for analysis (Luhman 1979; Coulson 1998).

The final factor that is essential among the human resources for collaboration is leadership. This capacity combines the attributes of the reticulist with the ability to develop and communicate a persuasive vision of the future and a strategy for achieving that vision. Leadership may be the domain of a particular actor, for example regime theory specifies the contribution of the state as strategic leader mobilising necessary resources (Stone, 1993). However, it may also be considered as necessary across all organisations and sectors involved in the collaboration if a particularly difficult goal is to be achieved. Leadership may also be necessary at particular points in the collaboration. For example, Benson (1975) refers to the need for strategic intervention in relation to conflict resolution in order that an inter-organisational network may maintain or retain its balance. This example signals the need for the leader to be considered as someone with the necessary authority to intervene and also to be sufficiently trusted by the other collaborators to resolve any emergent conflict.

Organisational factors

Attention to specific skills and roles among individuals, though important, is insufficient if it is not supported by a wider commitment to developing new ways of working and organising for collaboration. This is because the capacity of individuals to act will be partially informed by the organisational context within which they operate. Pessimist perspectives on collaboration identify two very important reasons for being sceptical about collaborative efforts. In the first place collaboration will require the organisation to lose some of its independence and secondly collaboration will require the investment of resources with no certainty about the degree of benefit that will result. In public policy contexts where resources are always insufficient and autonomy of action is highly prized by key actors, for example professionals, organisational cultures have emerged that reinforce this scepticism about collaboration (Hudson, 1987). The professional bureaucracy that characterised the public sector up to the late twentieth century contributed to these cultures an emphasis on professionals being able to exercise their own judgement drawing on upon a set of values that underpinned their capacity to practise, coupled with a focus on process to demonstrate the core public sector values of probity and accountability.

In the current climate, where new public management has wrought massive change to professional bureaucracies, the warnings about the dangers of collaboration have been heightened as government enthusiasm for collaboration has increased. For example, the recent contribution of Barton and Quinn (2001) highlights the way in which mandating health and criminal justice professionals to work together to deliver a new drug treatment programme attempts to integrate two professional groups with different value bases and different discourses about the recipients of the programme. It is not possible to blend these two discourses which is why they have never voluntarily sought integration, so ultimately either one discourse will dominate or there will be continuing conflict. Barton and Quinn argue that professionals and practitioners need to become more involved in the policy process in order to try and mediate these impulses towards sterile collaborations.

The role of culture, therefore, is central to the development of collaborative capacity within organisations and thence across sectors (Newman, 1994). However, in order to develop this culture, there must be a widespread understanding of the concerns of particular actors combined with the appropriate leadership and strategic intervention in order to secure the required culture and organisational ownership of collaboration as a way of working (McGann and Gray, 1986).

The contribution of new institutional theory

The need for collaborative capacity is not matched by any certainty that this capacity will grow within organisations or across sectors. This is exemplified through the 'realist' perspective of Alter and Hage who emphasise that evolution towards effective collaborative arrangements is not a linear process of improvement. Even if stakeholders have maximised their learning and developed the relevant skills, abilities and relationships necessary at different stages, this does not mean that further development is inevitable. A way of explaining this emerges from an examination of new institutional theory.

Particular theorists have relevance here. The work of Scott (1991), Meyer and Rowan (1991) and Clegg (1990) focuses on the role of 'myths' or 'symbols' present in the wider institutional environment in shaping organisational structures and cultures. These 'myths' are drawn from a range of sources and combine to form 'institutional templates' to which organisations adapt. The power of this emergent belief system about organisational design and orientation overtakes any consideration of the effectiveness of prevailing organisational arrangements (DiMaggio and Powell, 1991; Meyer and Rowan, 1991). In addition the legitimacy afforded to organisations that adapt to the dominant 'templates' is accompanied by access to greater resources, thus helping to secure the organisation's existence (Lowndes, 1996).

What this theory alerts us to is the importance of institutional factors in creating a normative environment for collaboration. However, the extent to which they become embedded depends upon the strength of other local factors to dilute or resist their impact (Clegg, 1990). Among those factors are the logics of appropriate behaviour that determine how things are done in particular environments (March and Olsen, 1989). These give rise to rules and norms that are routinised, giving organisations stability but also enabling them to adapt to changes in the wider environment. Daugbjerg and Marsh's earlier comment (1998) on the operation of policy networks is reflective of these features. Logics of appropriateness can change over time but the process of change can result in the coexistence of 'old' and 'new' ways of doing things (Lowndes, 1997).

The idea of logics of appropriateness help explain the persistence of particular ways of doing things in the face of the development of new and sometimes legally sanctioned ways of working. Their power can be seen all the more readily if one considers the alternative that March and Olsen put forward, the logic of consequentiality. This logic drives behaviour towards desired and anticipated outcomes and focuses on ends rather than means. Applying this logic to collaboration one might expect a greater take-up of collaborative activity in order that the benefits of the desired outcomes may be realised. However, in reality this may not be the case. Logics of appropriateness compete with and may win out over logics of consequentiality. The reasons why this might happen and the conditions that might pertain to allow for the development of logics of appropriateness that complement collaborative ways of working will be explored later (Chapter 6).

Collaboration and public policy

The collaborative endeavours discussed in this book are focused on public purpose. Governmental bodies at various levels are key players. Public money – in some cases of a considerable scale – is directed at them. Elected politicians, appointed quango board members and senior public servants sit on their boards. Consequently we must consider the extent to which such collaborations address the underlying concerns of good government and the traditional agenda of public administration.

A central concern is the operation of power relationships between citizens and public service providers. Here the tensions between the optimist (power as social production) and pessimist (power as an instrument of control) perspectives are played out directly in the practice of collaboration. The issue is important because of the increasing attention paid to involving citizens in the design and delivery of public services. However, notwithstanding the recognition of the role of the citizen, politicians and service providers find it very difficult to realise this new relationship and often use their resource power to frustrate the active participation of voluntary and community members. The experience of citizens and communities in collaborative ventures and the significance of power in informing these experiences will be discussed in more detail in Chapter 9.

Linked to the issue of power is that of governance arrangements within collaborations: specifically who governs and how. For optimists, broadening the range of actors involved in the collaboration can improve governance by enhancing the process of accountability, while for pessimists actors' leverage over the instruments of governance is directly linked to their authority in the network and the external environment. These reference points are important because they secure particular lines of accountability, for example to government or professional associations. An important question here is the extent to which traditional governance values can be maintained or developed through collaborative arrangements and what the role of government is in the prevailing context. These issues will be explored in more detail in Chapter 8.

Finally, with collaborative activity so widely practised and government policy increasingly reliant upon the operation of partnerships to deliver policies and programmes, some investigation of the contribution made by collaborations is essential. There is little in any of the theoretical contributions discussed above that relates directly to evaluation. However, the different perspectives do alert us to some lines of enquiry for evaluation of collaboration. Optimists, in their focus on the achievement of positive outcomes, signal the need to evaluate progress toward those outcomes from the perspective of the different actors involved. Pessimists, in their focus on the difficulties associated with collaboration, suggest a need to examine the efficiency of the collaboration, that is, examining the costs as well as the benefits of working in this way. Finally, realists point to the need to consider the context within which collaboration is happening, as this will influence both the forms and subsequent ambition of the collaborative venture. Recent developments in evaluation have given rise to evaluative frameworks that specifically address the significance of context (Connell and Kubisch *et al.*,

1995; Pawson and Tilley, 1997). Their respective contributions to the evaluation of collaboration will be considered in Chapter 10.

Conclusion

This chapter has examined some of the theoretical underpinning for collaborative activity. Recognising that there is no single tradition of collaborative theory, but rather theories that speak to different aspects of collaboration, we have not sought to provide exhaustive coverage of the possible contributions. Instead we have identified key theoretical perspectives that illuminate the challenges and opportunities presented by collaboration and also explain the continuing pull of collaboration despite its associated difficulties. Our discussion of theory has concentrated upon explaining the emergence of collaborative action, the forms that such action might take and the factors that affect the capacity and practice of collaborative efforts. However, the theoretical discussion has also alerted us to some of the key outstanding issues that need to be addressed by collaborators operating in a public policy environment, specifically how to secure the good governance of collaborative endeavours and how to achieve improvement in collaborative practice and outcomes. Each of these themes is explored in more detail in the following chapters.

4 Collaboration on Cross-cutting Issues

Cross-cutting issues are those which have a fundamental effect on citizens' sense of well-being, yet continue to defy the actions of governments and others to address them. In part this is due to their nature. Issues such as environmental sustainability, fear of crime and social exclusion require concerted action by numerous actors from across the public, private, voluntary and community sectors. They cannot be tackled successfully by a single agency, nor will disjointed action have any real effect. Collaboration therefore has become the accepted mechanism for implementing public policy on cross-cutting issues.

Necessity, though powerful, is not the only motivation in play. Collaborative action with regard to cross-cutting issues is frequently directed at achieving a vision of the future. Environmental sustainability is perhaps the best example since it involves clear vision for a global environment that to be achieved requires action at international, national, local and individual levels. Overcoming health inequalities and promoting good health is another cross-cutting issue that operates at all these levels and has a bespoke organization, the World Health Organisation, to promote and protect the international vision for health improvement. Achieving a shared vision is also evident among other initiatives that are seeking to address cross-cutting issues closer to home. So Jacobs' (1999) work describes the importance of 'vision' in European and American cities attempting ambitious regeneration programmes.

There are other powerful motivating factors that drive action in relation to cross-cutting issues. For example, in the UK the National Strategy for Neighbourhood Renewal (Social Exclusion Unit, 2001) is one part of the government's programme to tackle social exclusion. A key feature of this strategy is the emphasis on 'joining up' existing service providers' activities better in order to maximise the application of resources available to address social exclusion. Elsewhere the work of Milward and Provan (1998) illustrates the difficulties associated with attempting to bring the maximum resources to bear on health and social care services in an environment where a cross-cutting issue is made more complex by the fragmented nature of service delivery. This focuses attention on the significance of context (see Chapter 3) in informing the nature and extent of collaborative activity.

In the UK partnerships have become the preferred collaborative form, building upon three decades of initiatives that have sought to join up policies and services to deliver benefits for the community. This chapter traces the development of collaboration on cross-cutting issues, examining the way in which the underlying imperatives and resulting approaches have changed and developed and paying particular attention to the interplay of imperatives and context. We focus on three of the many policy areas in which collaboration is now widespread. The first is regeneration policy, whose thirty-year history illustrates the centrality of collaborative activity to initiatives intended to overcome spatial concentrations of disadvantage. Community safety is the second policy area. This is chosen as a more recent and legislative-led collaboration. It is also one which touches on fundamental questions of concern to individuals and communities. The third policy area we examine is collaboration between health and social care, with a particular focus on NHS–local authority relationships. This has always been an area where the boundaries between the responsibilities of the various parties have been indistinct. The result has been concern about overlaps, gaps and a lack of co-ordination in services. We include it also because it is of high priority to the post-1997 Labour government, and has been subject to a number of initiatives to improve working across boundaries.

Partnerships in urban policy

The fundamental imperative driving UK regeneration policy for the last thirty years has been a vision of revitalised urban areas where poverty, poor health, low educational attainment, high crime and joblessness are things of the past. Closely associated with this has been the need to maximise the resources that can be brought to bear to help deliver regeneration. However, the way in which regeneration policy has been operationalised to respond to these imperatives has varied significantly depending upon the prevailing political and policy context and the role adopted by central government.

EPA, CDP and policy for the inner cities

During the 1960s there was a growing awareness that levels of poverty and inequality were still unacceptably high. A consensus emerged that the creation of the welfare state and government intervention in national and regional economic policy in the previous two decades had not met the objectives of its designers. Significantly the explanation for the persistence of inequality and poverty, which up until that point had been attributed to individual and collective pathology, began to be expressed more in terms of unresponsive public organisations and a lack of co-ordination and co-operation between them. This interpretation reflected a wider debate across government informed by ideas about corporate planning and management from the US (Friend, Power and Yewlett, 1974) coupled with new roles for professionals that developed in community-based projects initiated by the voluntary sector (The Community Work Group, 1973.).

This debate led to the creation of education priority areas (EPAs) and community development projects (CDPs), time-limited partnerships which employed an action-research methodology to develop and test initiatives to combat urban poverty. EPAs directed additional central government resources into education and related provision in areas with poor levels of achievement, experimenting with different strategies and evaluating the results. The 12 CDPs employed a similar approach but across a wider range of issues. They were vertical partnerships between central government, a local authority and a local university. The projects were grant-aided by the Home Office, with an action team based in the local authority and a research team located at a nearby university. The critical analysis of capitalism and the role of the state developed by the CDP teams, and the strong association of some with local struggles, led to tensions in their relationship with both their employing local authority and the Home Office (Loney, 1983; Mainwaring, 1988) – prefiguring the questions of identity, loyalty and accountability that have been present in partnerships subsequently, although generally not at such a pronounced level.

Notwithstanding reservations about the value of CDPs, governments have maintained a commitment to partnerships as a means of addressing urban policy problems. The 1977 White Paper *Policy for the Inner Cities* (DoE, 1977) identified the need for a co-ordinated approach at central government level, one of the gaps highlighted by the CDPs. Despite this stated intention, urban regeneration policy has primarily been seen as the remit of a single department. Stewart (1994), echoing an earlier analysis by Lawless (1981), concludes that the result has been a series of fragmented and overlapping initiatives emerging from, and controlled by, central government. Even the regional offices of government created in 1994 were, until 2001, principally arms of DETR with limited input from other relevant departments (Mawson and Spencer, 1997). The lack of integration by central government is not reflected at local level, however, where there has been considerable innovation across the boundaries of the plethora of bodies involved.

Emerging regeneration partnerships

Partnership has been a key feature of regeneration programmes since the 1970s (Table 4.1). It is built on the premise that success would only come through the effective co-ordination of all those with an interest in regenerating the inner city (Bailey *et al.*, 1995). However, the nature of the partnership and definition of the partners has changed over time in response to developing political perspectives. Among the earliest regeneration partnership initiatives was the Inner City Partnership Programme (ICPP), created as a result of the 1977 White Paper. The stated intention was to establish a cross-sector partnership in each designated local authority area, but in reality they were a continuation of the vertical partnership relationship between central and local government begun with CDP in which there was detailed ministerial involvement in agreeing the specific projects included within each authority's annual programme (Bradford and Robson, 1995). Although voluntary sector bodies benefited from the local partnership by gaining access to funding, neither they nor the private sectors were

Table 4.1 *Government initiatives for regeneration partnerships, 1977–2001*

Date	Initiative
1978	Inner City Partnerships and Programmes (ICPP) established through Inner Urban Areas Act
1981	Task Forces established
1985	City Action Teams (CATs) established; Estate Action (EA) implemented
1986	First Urban Development Corporation (UDC) set up
1988	Action for Cities including announcement of Housing Action Trusts (HATs); Welsh Valleys Initiative; New Life Partnerships in Scotland
1991	City Challenge 1st round. TECs and LECs established
1992	English Partnerships and Government Offices for the Regions (GORs) announced
1993	Single Regeneration Budget (SRB) introduced; City Pride in Birmingham, London and Manchester
1997	New 'zonal' initiatives, e.g. HAZs, EAZs
1998	New Deal for Communities (NDC) 1st round
2000	Neighbourhood Renewal Fund announced; Local Strategic Partnerships announced
2001	National Strategy for Neighbourhood Renewal Action Plan published

permitted to challenge the core central–local governmental relationship (Barnekov *et al.*, 1990).

Conservative governments after 1979 initially presented a radically different approach to regeneration. Here visions of revitalised inner cities were accompanied by a much stronger focus on maximising the resources available to regeneration by drawing on private sector leverage. The Conservatives also moved away from vertical relationships with local government, instead choosing to introduce a number of powerful single-purpose agencies to lead aspects of regeneration. Urban Development Corporations (UDCs) were the first to be created, powerful local quangos dominated by private sector interests and with a primary focus on physical regeneration. Training and Enterprise Councils (Local Enterprise Companies in Scotland) (TECs/LECs) were established in 1990 with responsibility for employment and business development. Again private sector interests dominated, holding two-thirds of each TEC board's membership. Finally, in the early 1990s, Housing Action Trusts (HATs) were set up in six localities to undertake physical, social and economic regeneration with a clear emphasis upon increasing the mixed economy of provision in housing. HATs are governed by a board appointed by the Secretary of State and ownership of the housing is transferred to this board for the duration of the initiative subject to a vote by the affected tenants. The constitution of these local quangos did not fit easily with a philosophy of partnership. Bailey *et al.*, for example, view UDCs as embodying 'a particular phase of New Right ideological thinking about how best to institutionalise processes of urban regeneration, the interests to be included and supported, as well as those to be excluded and bypassed' (1995, p. 53). However, HATs have generally adopted a more inclusive approach to their work, actively involving tenants on their boards (Chumrow, 1995).

Subsequent initiatives continued to prioritise the involvement of the private sector but broadened the focus of regeneration to include economic development in addition to physical regeneration. Consistent in various policy initiatives was the desire to reduce the burden of responsibility upon the state, marginalise the role of local government and increase opportunities for enterprise. This led to a steady stream of initiatives in the 1980s and early 1990s. For example, in 1985 the Estate Action programmes encouraged the involvement of housing associations in the management of social housing, the use of private sector leverage to support government grant and the diversification of tenure in housing estates, and in 1986 the Inner City Task Forces brought together civil servants with local private and public sector representatives to focus attention on improving enterprise and employability among populations in targeted areas of disadvantage.

The City Challenge initiative in 1991 marked a sea-change in the constitution of partnerships. Although established as local regeneration companies, the board composition was more inclusive with membership extended to all relevant parties – including local government, health bodies, the police, residents and the private sector. Local government was brought back centre-stage through its key role as the enabler of the collaboration – although it was still a minority partner in the City Challenge company board. The scale of local government funding was an important factor here, following a recognition that sustainable regeneration required the influencing and bending of its mainstream programme resources. However, the fortunes of City Challenge and the extent to which the involvement of local stakeholders were effective was mixed, in part because it was pioneering a new approach to partnership in which a much wider range of interests than ever before was involved in making decisions on programmes to revitalise a local community. Inevitably there were differences of perspective, ways of working and values which sometimes hindered the process (Mabbott, 1993; Russell *et al.*, 1996).

The introduction of City Challenge was part of a broader re-framing of urban policy. An Audit Commission review described it as a 'patchwork quilt of complexity and idiosyncrasy' (Audit Commission, 1989, p. 9) and recommended a more co-ordinated and wide-ranging approach which would emphasise strategic intervention and improvement across localities rather than focus on specific neighbourhoods within them. Evidence of this can be found in Scotland and, to a lesser extent, Wales. The work of the Scottish Development Agency from 1975 and the Scottish Enterprise Agency and Scottish Office in the 1980s in co-ordinating major regeneration programmes such as Glasgow Eastern Area Renewal (GEAR) and *New Life for Urban Scotland* (Scottish Office, 1988) had facilitated a 'greater sense of strategy through partnership' (Bailey *et al.*, 1995, p. 59) in Scotland than was apparent in England, as had 'Urban Development Wales' – a similar strategy established in the Principality in 1991.

As a consequence a number of changes were made to the organisation of policy implementation for regeneration in England. In belated recognition of the complexity of the regeneration task, the Government Offices for the Regions (GORs) were established to improve co-ordination of central government activity in the regions and provide a more sensitive interface between local partnerships and Whitehall. 'City Pride', a voluntary initiative bringing local strategic players from all sectors together to develop and monitor progress towards a vision for the future, was established in three cities. At the same time the introduction of a new 'catch all' regeneration programme – the Single Regeneration Budget (SRB) – integrated a multiplicity of existing spending programmes into a single pot in order to maximise resource flexibility. SRB also introduced further significant changes. It fulfilled the Audit Commission's recommendation that local authorities should be allowed to lead local regeneration strategies and it also placed greater emphasis on economic and social regeneration delivered as a result of partnerships with the targeted communities. However, the context had not changed entirely. SRB bids for funding were competitive and central government (through the GORs) retained a key role in approving spending and monitoring the performance of local partnerships. Between 1994 and 2000 there were six rounds of SRB, giving rise to over 900 partnerships (see Appendix 2). Although there will be no new SRB rounds, local regeneration partnerships can clearly be said to have come of age.

Regeneration partnerships and New Labour

There were three main changes in regeneration policy following the 1997 general election. First, competition for funds was largely replaced by targeting spending on key areas based upon indices of deprivation, for example through the Neighbourhood Renewal Fund (NRF) which allocates resources to the 88 local authorities with the highest levels of deprivation. An element of competition remained in other initiatives such as Health Action Zones where localities had to make a case for being awarded HAZ status in competition with other areas. Second, partnerships *with* communities gave way to the idea of partnerships *led* by communities, as in the New Deal for Communities (NDC) initiative which prioritised the capacity building of community leaders as members of neighbourhood partnerships prior to any decision-making about spending NDC resources. Third, regeneration policy was recast to strengthen joined-up action in key policy areas – namely education and employment, health, crime and the physical environment. This was initiated in NDC but expanded under the National Strategy for Neighbourhood Renewal so that 'joining-up' occurs within neighbourhoods and also across localities. This will be facilitated through the establishment of a Local Strategic Partnership (LSP).

Notwithstanding the significant influence of central government, partnerships for regeneration in localities did not exclusively arise as a result of central policy or invitation. Bailey *et al.* (1995) show that partnerships for regeneration took a myriad of forms, only a small proportion of which were initiated in direct response to central government (Table 4.2). Smith and Beazley (2000) identify an additional type of local regeneration

Table 4.2 *Forms of regeneration partnership*

Type	Genesis	Area	Partners	Remit	Examples
Development	Local	Small area, town centre	Private developer, housing association, local authority	Joint development	Foyer schemes
Development trust	Local	Neighbourhood	Community with others	Community regeneration	Community Trusts
Joint agreement, coalition, company	Local but may be response to national policy	Discrete area	Public, private, voluntary, community	Strategy preparation; implementation often via third party	City Challenge, SRB, NRF
Community regime	Local	Neighbourhood	Community-led with others	Community regeneration	NDC
Promotional	Local	District wide	Private sector led; Chamber of Commerce	Place marketing	City Pride
Agency	National legislation	Urban, sub-regional	Public sector sponsor, private sector appointees	Terms of reference from sponsoring agency	UDC, TEC, LEC, HAT
Strategic	Regional, local	Sub-regional, metropolitan	Multiple	Strategy for development	Local Strategic Partnerships

Source: Adapted from Bailey *et al.* (1995, p. 30).

partnership – the community regime. This highlights the growing importance of community leadership in regeneration partnerships. Prior to 1997,
community-led regeneration partnerships remained the exception, although
there were successful examples. For example, the Balsall Heath Forum in
Birmingham is a community-led neighbourhood forum that has led the development of a local regeneration programme, securing private sector sponsor-
ship and accessing national (SRB) and European (URBAN) funds. However,
post-1997 the increasing emphasis upon community-led partnerships is likely
to encourage more collaborations to emerge and to take the lead in regeneration under the National Strategy for Neighbourhood Renewal umbrella.

Central government-initiated partnerships may be a small proportion of
partnerships for regeneration but they have tended to be the most influential
because of the resources they bring to localities. This resource power has
enabled central government to exercise considerable influence over the shape
and nature of regeneration partnerships. It has also enabled central government to exercise increasing influence over what priorities are met and how,
through the monitoring and evaluation processes that regeneration partnerships are required to adopt. The role of the superordinate body has therefore
been crucial in operationalising regeneration policy, and in interpreting how
the imperatives of achieving a vision and maximising resources are to be met.

Partnerships for community safety

Community safety is acknowledged as a key 'cross-cutting' issue for government (Bright, 1997; Clarke and Stewart, 1997; Richards *et al.*, 1999).
The concept emerged in the early 1980s from a recognition that the attainment of 'cross system goals' in the criminal justice system was limited following changes in the system itself and the social, economic and political
environment within which it was located (Davies, Croall and Tyrer, 1995).
This critical acknowledgement of the scope and complexity of the community safety task prompted collaborative action at national and local levels.
Increasing public fear of crime together with a heightened awareness of its
impact and its consequences for victims drove a political agenda that prioritised a vision of safer communities. At the same time concern at the
costs associated with maintaining the criminal justice system fed a desire
to join up the activities of the various community safety organisations to
improve their efficiency and effectiveness. The imperatives resulted in a
variety of partnership initiatives to promote community safety (Box 4.1).
However, the extent to which these partnerships have been effective has

Box 4.1 *The development of collaboration on community safety*

1976 Home Office publication outlines measures for crime prevention, especially 'situational' crime. Emergence of Community Policing, including actions to involve communities and reduce fear of crime as well as developing crime prevention methods.

Early 1980s Neighbourhood Watch established.

1983 Home Office Crime Prevention Unit established, to develop policy initiatives with other agencies.

1987 National Association of Victim Support Schemes receives government funding of £1.5million.

1988 Crime Concern, a Home Office and private sector funded charity established. Develops crime prevention projects. Safer Cities initiative begun, with 20 projects funded through Home Office linked to regeneration agenda for inner cities. Crack Crime government programme established.

1990 25 per cent of all police forces have neighbourhood policing as part of community policing approach. Victim's Charter published. Drug Prevention Initiative – 20 teams in 'at risk' localities. Increased reporting of 'vigilante' activity in 1990s.

1991 Morgan Report recommends local authorities should have statutory responsibility for community safety.

1993 Creation of National Board for Crime Prevention, a multi-agency body including local and central government, police and probation.

1994 130000 Neighbourhood Watch Schemes established. Home Secretary propose to extend citizen involvement in police work, patrols, special constables and parish constable/warden scheme. Single Regeneration Budget introduced and Government Offices of the Regions established with a member of Home Office staff seconded to each.

1996 *Misspent Youth: Young People and Crime*, Audit Commission study published. LGMB study of Community Safety activity at local authority level published.

1997 Labour Government, Crime and Disorder Bill published. Audit Commission Review of Community Safety work begun. Drugs 'Tsar' appointed.

(continued)

1998 National Drugs Strategy produced. Crime and Disorder Act passed. Her Majesty's Inspectorate of Constabulary Report, *Beating Crime*, published.

1999 Crime and Disorder Partnerships led by local authorities and the police initiated in England and Wales to develop local strategies for crime reduction. Community safety partnerships in Scotland. Crime Reduction Programme funding created for England and Wales.

been mediated by prevailing central–local government relationships and underlying tensions between key local agencies.

Early initiatives

There are three key components of community safety:

1. Perceptions of fear of crime, regardless of incidence.
2. Social factors increasing the risk of criminal acts being committed.
3. Situational or physical factors that provide an opportunity for crime to take place.

Early activity by the Home Office in the 1970s and 1980s did much to popularise the concern with situational crime prevention. It focused on 'target hardening', environmental improvements and redesign and use of surveillance. It aimed to involve the active citizen in Neighbourhood Watch local partnerships between residents and the police in which the former monitored the area for potential criminal activity. In 1983 the Home Office Crime Prevention Unit was established to develop preventive programmes in conjunction with other government departments and potential private and voluntary partners.

In the 1980s voluntary partnerships were formed between key statutory and non-statutory service providers across the UK to address both the social and situational aspects of community safety. Very often these were initiated by local authorities anxious to take action over an issue of such pronounced public concern. Such developments were not always welcomed by the police who frequently saw local authority initiatives as a distraction from the core business of preventing and detecting crime. Undaunted, local authorities pressed ahead and Community Safety Strategies became increasingly common. These took a broad view of the problem and identified ways in which local authority departments and other bodies could work together to reduce the opportunity for, incidence of and fear about crime. However, relationships with the police were frequently tense reflecting the underlying conflict between these two key organisations about whose domain this was and who should lead with respect to issues of community safety.

Voluntary partnerships were increasingly supported by access to government funding. The Home Office's Safer Cities Programme funded local partnerships to find ways of creating safer cites where economic enterprise and community life could flourish. The principle of the programme was that there could be no central blue-print and local activity should be managed through multi-agency partnerships. However, the Conservative Government's lack of faith in local government meant that the funding regime for the programme and parallel evaluation sought to maintain Home Office control over its broad direction. In practical terms, however, the Crime Prevention Unit was not equipped nor able to retain extensive central control. This resulted in what Tilley described as 'local autonomy combined with a weak centre' (1993, p. 50), giving rise to 'emergent outcomes' that may have been very different to the intentions of the central policy-makers. In fact Tilley's evaluation shows how the local partnerships' initial emphasis on situational crime prevention changed as a result of community concerns to embrace social aspects of crime prevention, for example in relation to racial harassment, and those which occurred in private rather than public spaces, such as domestic violence. Conventionally these 'social' aspects of the community safety agenda were far less likely to receive direct funding and there was frequent conflict between stakeholders about the nature of community safety priorities which often marginalised issues such as domestic violence. However, increasing attention began to be paid to domestic violence and the role of statutory agencies in supporting what had long been a voluntary sector agenda. This coming together of interests resulted in the development of the 'Forum' movement, multi-agency partnerships established to focus on tackling domestic violence through a variety of strategies (Dobash and Dobash, 1996a, 1996b; Hague *et al.*, 1996; Hague and Malos, 1996, 1998).

Developing a strategic approach

The Morgan Report, a key review of community safety activity, was published by the Home Office in 1991. It emphasised the multifaceted nature of the issue:

> We see community safety as having both social and situational aspects, as being concerned with people, communities and organisations including

families, victims and at-risk groups, as well as attempting to reduce particular types of crime and the fear of crime. Community Safety should
be seen as the legitimate concern of all in the local community. (Home
Office, 1991, p. 13)

The Morgan Report was strongly supportive of local partnership working,
arguing that a strategic multi-agency approach was necessary to enable
effective co-operation between individual agencies in all aspects of community safety (Figure 4.1). It also placed local government firmly at the
centre of the debate by recommending that it should have statutory responsibility for the issue.

The response to the Morgan Report was not universally positive. The
Home Office rejected the proposal to place a statutory responsibility on
local government as it believed there were sufficient examples of positive
partnership working arising voluntarily. The Association of Chief Police
Officers (ACPO) expressed concern at the potential threat to their operational independence (Jones *et al.*, 1994). Research also suggested that
giving one organisation the formal 'lead' in partnership working in community safety would be detrimental as it would undermine the problem-
solving focus provided by collaboration (Liddle and Gelsthorpe, 1994).

As a consequence voluntarism prevailed, at least in the short term.
However, the absence of direct funding for community safety activities
meant that other sources of funding were increasingly being used to
resource programmes. Benyon and Edwards' (1999) analysis indicates that
a great deal of local crime prevention activity was funded through more
general urban regeneration programmes in the 1990s. However, this
brought its own problems. According to Benyon and Edwards:

- The co-ordination and coherence of regeneration partnerships was poor
  with no national strategy to frame action and local strategy undermined
  by time-limited project funding. Community Safety activity continued
  to be peripheral to core business for most partners.
- Accountability of activity was partial with a policy elite determining and
  evaluating performance. Local stakeholders had limited involvement and
  the prevailing partnership structures were not sophisticated enough to
  facilitate wider involvement.
- Durability of partnerships was unlikely, tied as they were to funding and
  suffering from an absence of skills among partners to create sustainable
  partnership relationships.

Figure 4.1 *Potential activities for community safety partnerships*

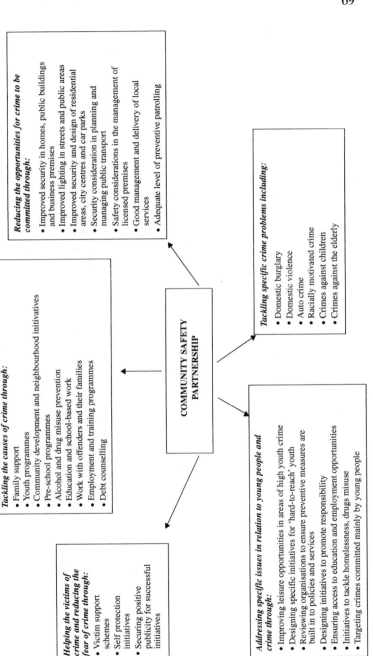

Reducing the opportunities for crime to be committed through:

- Improved security in homes, public buildings and business premises
- Improved lighting in streets and public areas
- Improved security and design of residential areas, city centres and car parks
- Security consideration in planning and managing public transport
- Safety considerations in the management of licensed premises
- Good management and delivery of local services
- Adequate level of preventive patrolling

Tackling the causes of crime through:

- Family support
- Youth programmes
- Community development and neighbourhood initiatives
- Pre-school programmes
- Alcohol and drug misuse prevention
- Education and school-based work
- Work with offenders and their families
- Employment and training programmes
- Debt counselling

Tackling specific crime problems including:

- Domestic burglary
- Domestic violence
- Auto crime
- Racially motivated crime
- Crimes against children
- Crimes against the elderly

COMMUNITY SAFETY PARTNERSHIP

Helping the victims of crime and reducing the fear of crime through:

- Victim support schemes
- Self protection initiatives
- Securing positive publicity for successful initiatives

Addressing specific issues in relation to young people and crime through:

- Improving leisure opportunities in areas of high youth crime
- Designing specific initiatives for 'hard-to-reach' youth
- Reviewing organisations to ensure preventive measures are built in to policies and services
- Designing initiatives to promote responsibility
- Ensuring access to education and employment opportunities
- Initiatives to tackle homelessness, drugs misuse
- Targeting crimes committed mainly by young people

Source: Adapted from Home Office 1991, p. 32.

Notwithstanding this apparently limited success, a Local Government Management Board (1996) survey found that 62 per cent of local authorities were in multi-agency community safety partnerships, over half had a budget for community safety work and one third had appointed an officer responsible for community safety. According to the survey the key factors that were perceived to restrict further development included the unhelpful attitude of central government and the lack of statutory authority for local government's role.

Statutory partnerships

Shortly after the 1997 election the Home Office published *Getting to Grips with Crime – A new framework for local action*. This marked a significant shift in the political and policy context for community safety. Its proposals were enacted in the Crime and Disorder Act 1998 – a wide-ranging piece of legislation making provision for new approaches to policy implementation in several areas including youth justice, anti-social behaviour and racially motivated crimes. Partnership is evident throughout the provisions, for example with the creation of Youth Offending Teams in each locality comprising a range of relevant professionals. However, the centrepiece of the legislation is the statutory requirement for local authorities and police authorities in England and Wales to work together to devise and implement new approaches to tackling issues of crime and disorder (there are similar community safety partnerships in Scotland). The two institutions are required to jointly lead a strategic crime and disorder partnership for the locality comprising all the relevant stakeholders in the public, voluntary, private and community sectors. Each Crime and Disorder Partnership is required to:

- produce an audit of crime and disorder in the locality;
- identify key crime and disorder objectives for the locality;
- develop a crime and disorder strategy for the locality;
- identify a programme of evaluation to assess the progress of the strategy towards specified outcomes;
- ensure all activity is underpinned by wide-ranging public consultation to secure broad ownership of the initiative.

No additional resource was made available to implement this aspect of the Crime and Disorder Act although partnerships are able to bid into the new Crime Reduction Programme fund for support for specific projects, including closed circuit television (CCTV).

This move from voluntarism to statutory duty marked a significant shift in central government's approach to community safety. In firmly establishing partnerships as the key vehicles for the delivery of the desired policy outcomes it echoed the recommendations of others, for example, Home Office (1991). It also sought to use a formal partnership arrangement as a way of resolving the conflict between the police and local authorities about whose domain this was. While the statutory duty was welcomed it is important to note that evidence from other policy areas such as regeneration suggests that formal sanction alone is not sufficient to facilitate a changed approach (Hall *et al.*, 1996). It is therefore significant that active support to the new approach was forthcoming in the parallel publication of the review of Her Majesty's Inspectorate of Constabulary (1998) and the Audit Commission (1999). Finally and significantly, at the same time as the Crime and Disorder proposals strengthened local responsibility for community safety, the introduction of new funding programmes and the establishment of the Home Office as monitor and evaluator of local Crime and Disorder Partnerships also strengthened the hand of central government in influencing the shape and priorities of the local partnerships.

Joining up health and social care

The NHS at a local level and social services departments have been subject to constant change, often in an effort to improve effective service delivery across the boundaries between them. These boundaries are organisational and to a large extent functional, although there are areas of overlap, for example both services provide walking sticks, Zimmer frames and other equipment to individuals. However, there are also professional boundaries, with tensions between the medical and social models of care reflected in different organisational cultures and modes of working (Hudson, 1987). The political boundaries between the services are also significant. The NHS is a hierarchical organisation with local delivery of services ultimately accountable through a management structure to the Secretary of State. Local authorities are responsible for social services functions, and through councillors to the local electorate. Collaboration between health and social care therefore requires negotiation of a number of sensitive issues.

Working across the health and social care boundary has been on the political and professional agenda for some considerable time. In the early years of the new millennium it was heightened by the criticism of social services departments' lack of capacity to deliver community care or collaborate with health providers (May and Brunsdon, 1999). There was also public concern about hospital waiting lists and the apparent inability of hospitals to release older people into the community once they were medically fit because of an absence of sufficient social service support (the so-called 'bed-blockers'). In theory UK health and social care services fit well into Levine and White's (1962) model of exchange (see Chapter 3). Both services have shared goals relating to the promotion of health and independent living and each service area needs the other in order to deliver this effectively. However, in practice the extent to which the logic of exchange prevails depends on a variety of other contextual factors including political and professional roles and relationships.

Developing co-ordination

The interplay of imperatives and context for collaboration in health and social care occupies three distinct phases. In the late 1960s and during the 1970s the focus was on the co-ordination of relevant policy development and implementation at both national and local level. This emerged from a national policy preoccupation with the application of rationality in decision-making and was characterised by the publication of 'A Joint Approach to Social Policies' (JASP) by the Whitehall Central Policy Review Staff in 1975 (Challis *et al.*, 1988). Here 'co-ordination is seen as the rational response to the complex, untidy sprawl of social boundaries and responsibilities and to the problem of resource scarcity' (*ibid.*, p. 2). Co-ordination was deemed necessary at the level of information analysis, decision-making and service delivery. According to Challis *et al.*, a vital assumption underpinning JASP was that co-operation would replace competition between Ministers and departments:

> If a 'joint' and more coherent approach to social polices is to have any chance of succeeding, departments and Ministers must be prepared to make some adjustments, whether in priorities, policies, administrative practices, or public expenditure allocations. For example, a study of a problem area might show that short-run remedial measures (department A) were ineffective unless supported by long-run preventive policies (department B); this might require a shift of resources within B, or from A to B, or to B from elsewhere. (JASP, quoted in Challis *et al.*, 1988, p. 3)

Following the 1974 reorganisations of health and local government, co-ordination at a local level was through joint consultative committees

(JCCs) and joint finance arrangements. JCCs were to undertake service planning across organisational boundaries, and could bid into the joint financing pot for resources to help bring collaborative schemes to fruition.

The mixed economy of care

In the second phase 'the rationality of politics, had ... triumphed over the politics of rationality' (Challis *et al.*, 1998, p. 20). While the early policy documents, for example *Care in Action* (Department of Health and Social Security, 1981), continued to stress the need for local co-ordination to maximise use of resources, this was to involve a wider range of providers. The new agenda was about reducing public provision and involving the voluntary and private sectors more fully, thereby maximising the application of resources to health and social care through a 'mixed economy' of provision. At a broader level this involved the introduction of market mechanisms to challenge the dominance of the public sector and new management techniques to challenge the dominance of the professionals. The introduction of the internal market in health meant that contractual relationships became commonplace between purchasers and providers of services and in some cases new providers of services were sought from the private sector, for example for cleaning and catering contracts. This purchaser/provider split was replicated in social services with an increasing emphasis on commissioning service provision from the independent sector. For some this emphasis on market creation and competition between providers may have accentuated the need for local co-ordination, but in practice it diminished the possibility for collaboration between professionals and others across the sectors (Flynn, 1997). In the NHS this policy reached its nadir with the announcement of Public Private Partnerships (PPPs) – an initiative to involve the private sector in the building and leasing of hospitals, building on the earlier Private Finance Initiative (PFI) (see Chapter 5).

One of the defining policies of the Conservative governments in relation to collaboration between health and social services was the NHS and Community Care Act 1990. Although community care had been articulated by national governments years before the passage of the 1990 Act (including in Department of Health and Social Security, 1971 and 1978), its development proceeded slowly and an Audit Commission (1986) study concluded that services were still primarily delivered through institutions or hospitals. The recognition that resources were not being transferred from institutional settings to community settings to support community care, coupled with the increasing level of social security payments necessary to support people in residential care, provided an urgency for reform (Hadley and Clough, 1996). The White Paper *Caring for People* (Department of Health, 1989) outlined the government's aspirations. Community care was about:

> providing the right level of intervention and support to enable people to achieve maximum independence and control over their own lives. For this aim to become a reality, the development of a wide range of services provided in a variety of settings is essential. These services form part of a spectrum of care, ranging from domiciliary support provided to people in their own homes, strengthened by the availability of respite care and day care for those with more intensive care needs, through sheltered housing, group homes and hostels where increasing levels of care are available, to residential care and nursing homes and long-stay hospital care for those for whom other forms of care are no longer enough. (1989, p. 9)

Delivering this kind of commitment required the drawing together of health and social services providers in order that care could be provided in an integrated and seamless way. The Griffiths Report (1988) recommended that social service departments should be given the lead role in managing community care. Having responsibility for cash-limited budgets, they would oversee the preparation of 'assessment and care packages' for those who wanted to make use of the service. Social services departments would purchase care but not provide it, acting as enablers in the process with the majority of funded care to be provided by the voluntary and/or private sectors. The 1990 Act added requirements for the publication of community care plans and the establishment of arm's-length inspection units. The urgency of reform was reflected in the timescale for implementation, which was initially envisaged to take place over three years. Therefore, by 1993 it was expected that new inspection and complaints procedures would be set up, local authority and health plans would be ready, new assessment and care procedures would be established and social security funds transferred. However, it was later accepted that the system would take longer to establish and an incremental approach was adopted (Wistow *et al.*, 1994).

The Community Care policy has been criticised from a number of angles, including the problem of demand outstripping supply, thereby rendering the assessment process impotent if insufficient funds are available to meet care needs (Grant, 1995), and opportunities for preventive work being removed

(Lewis *et al.*, 1995). The process was also criticised for jeopardising rather than facilitating collaboration through the application of 'top-down' requirements for change. As Hadley and Clough observe:

> One of the lessons to be learnt from the systems imposed on public services by the Conservatives is that collaboration and co-operation cannot be taken for granted when changes are imposed. They are by-products of wider systems in which people find that it is worthwhile and possible to work with others. (1996, p. 210)

Supporting strategic collaboration

The election of the Labour government in 1997 resulted in a significant change in emphasis in relation to the organisation and management of both the NHS and social services departments. This represents the third and latest phase which draws on the value of rationality from phase one and the use of market approaches from phase two, overlaying both with a focus on developing and rolling out a pragmatic solution to improving service delivery and outcomes. Labour has done little to alter the purchaser/ provider principle that underpins service delivery in health and social care. However, it has overlaid this with an emphasis upon working within a strategic service delivery framework across agencies and has encouraged collaboration between stakeholders to improve service delivery (Corby, 1999; May and Brunsdon, 1999). Central to this agenda in England is:

- *Saving Lives: Our Healthier Nation* (Department of Health, 1998). The government's health strategy for England articulates the significance of health inequalities to people's life chances. It advocates a 'joined-up' approach across central government and locally though partnerships, including Health Action Zones.
- Health Improvement and Modernisation Programmes (HIMPs). These are strategic frameworks devised in partnership between health and other partners that identify local needs, establish targets for delivery and describe monitoring and accountability arrangements between partners for the delivery of health and social services.
- Primary Care Groups (PCGs) – bodies for commissioning primary health care, working closely with social services. PCGs are evolving into Primary Care Trusts (PCTs), free-standing bodies responsible both for commissioning and delivering primary health care services and accountable to strategic health authorities.

The Health Act 1999 was a 'top-down' instrument but one that sought to respond to the demands of local professionals in relation to the development of collaborative working to improve service effectiveness. The Act placed a statutory duty of partnership upon the NHS and local authorities, removed some of the legal obstacles to joint working between them and made available a new partnership grant. Since April 2000, pooled budgets, lead commissioning and integrated service provision have all been available to health/local authority collaborators. This support for collaboration was further endorsed and extended in the NHS Plan (DoH, 2000).

The impact of this approach was illustrated in a Local Government Association (2000) survey: 80 per cent of local authority respondents reported a positive relationship with the local health sector, and almost 9 out of 10 indicated that their relationship had improved since 1997; 71 per cent of authorities reported joint arrangements with the health sector for the provision and/or commissioning of local services; 88 per cent of respondents were either making use of the new powers under the Health Act or had plans to do so. Of those employing the Health Act flexibilities: 43 per cent of authorities were involved in pooling budgets, 33 per cent were involved in lead commissioning arrangements and 56 per cent were involved in developing integrated provision.

Table 4.3   *Contextual analysis of community care and the Health Act flexibilities*

Contextual factors	1990 community care	1999 Health Act
National policy	Focus on co-ordination of market mechanisms involving purchasing and providing across public/private/voluntary sectors	Commitment to collaboration based upon application of a variety of mechanisms
Role of superordinate body	Imposed via legislation	Flexibilities offered to health and social services to collaborate; voluntarism encouraged
Local environment	Suspicion and mistrust of untested mechanisms; market creation required organisational change in social services and development of new relationships with independent sector	National context has 'caught up' with local demands; 'Partnership in Action' consultation paper paved the way

The Health and Social Care Act 2001 strengthens the legal framework for collaboration by introducing a power to create a new statutory body called a Care Trust. Care Trusts will allow for the further integration of health and social care commissioning and/or service delivery. They are described as partnerships by the Department of Health, but will be NHS bodies created on application to the Secretary of State by the relevant NHS Trust or PCT and local authority. The DoH sees them as partnerships which 'create a stable organisational framework for long-term service and organisational continuity' and which have distinct governance arrangements built upon a Care Trust Board (Department of Health, 2001, p. 2).

The case of health and social care illustrates the limits of 'top-down' approaches to collaboration which are perceived as negatively affecting professional interests and conversely their capacity when they are seen to be 'going with the grain' of professionals' aspirations. This is exemplified in Table 4.3 which presents a comparative analysis of the contextual factors at play in the Community Care Act 1990 and the Health Act 1999.

Conclusion

The case studies reveal five main imperatives that drive action towards collaboration. These are:

1. Achieving shared vision;
2. Maximising the use of available resources;
3. Addressing complexity in policy or service environments;
4. Maximising power and influence in relation to a policy or service area;
5. Resolving conflict.

An understanding of these imperatives is supported through reference to the theoretical explanations for collaboration discussed in Chapter 3. Regime theory, for example, places weight on the development of multi-agency cross-sector coalitions which can merge resources to deliver a vision. The case of regeneration policy highlights the power of 'the vision' in driving collaborative activity, and the development over time of new partnership forms illustrates the way in which a more integrated approach to planning and resourcing urban interventions has developed. A specific recent focus is the greater role of communities, about which Himmelman's (1996) 'collaborative empowerment' model has insights to offer. Alter and Hage's (1993) evolutionary model of collaboration stresses the impact of new environments, reflected in the emergence of community safety as a new policy goal. They draw attention to the significance for collaboration of contextual factors, and especially the development of learning between participants. In the case of community safety this was supported by the voluntaristic approach to collaboration which was retained despite the recommendations of the Morgan Report. However, the Report clearly indicated the way in which policy might develop and the cross-party significance of the issue, enabling the relevant actors to adjust their positions and be able to respond positively to the legislative framework for collaboration introduced in 1998. Finally, the example of health and social care replicates the empirical case from which Levine and White (1962) developed their model, namely one in which overall system goals are only realisable through collaboration to exchange resources. However, we argued in Chapter 3 that exchange could be seen as a special case within a wider resource dependency perspective, and that such dependencies, following Benson (1975), structured surface-level interactions. The nature of the political and professional differences between the health and social care subsystems reveals how activities to promote exchange relationships can be thwarted when the autonomy and domain of particular interests are threatened.

The case studies also reveal that in practice no single imperative will dominate the direction of activity. The potency of the vision in regeneration was usually accompanied by a desire to make best use of all available resources. Occasionally this was an ideological imperative, for example the government's desire to reduce the role of the state, but it was also a pragmatic response to circumstances in which there were insufficient resources to address the problem. Pragmatism was also evident in the case of community safety where the appointment of the police and local government as joint holders of responsibility for community safety was as much designed to address the conflict between them as it was by a conviction that this was the best way to achieved a shared vision of community safety.

However, the case study examples also revealed that the extent to which these imperatives are translated into successful collaborations depends very much on their interaction with various contextual factors. There are three significant factors to take account of. The first is the national policy context. Imperatives towards collaboration will be influenced by national policy-makers' perception of this particular policy instrument. If the logic of collaboration is not highly regarded at national level, then policy is unlikely to facilitate its operation. Conversely, if policy-makers view it as a key means of delivering outcomes then they will be motivated to amend policy rules and requirements that might be experienced as obstacles to collaboration, for example by introducing the Health Act 1999 flexibilities. The national policy context can also inform how collaboration is pursued, for example whether the emphasis is upon collaboration through the use of market mechanisms or pooled budgets. Secondly, and linked to the above, is the way in which key bodies (superordinate bodies) influence the operation of collaboration. The most obvious example is the use of legislation by central government to impose partnership relationships. However, there are other bodies that can shape the successful development of collaborations. These include national professional organisations such as the Association of Chief Police Officers (ACPO), who had a key role in opposing some elements of the Morgan Report, and regional bodies such as the Government Offices of the Regions (GORs) that advise government on the performance of local regeneration partnerships. Finally, however strong the imperatives for collaboration, an insufficient capacity at the local level will frustrate the development of successful partnerships. Local partners need to accept that working collaboratively will support their particular purpose and consequently to accommodate exchanges across organisational, political and sectoral boundaries with different cultures and forms of accountability. These issues are particularly acute in relation to multi-agency cross-sector regeneration programmes introduced in the 1990s, but also illustrated in the complex history of health and social care collaboration.

This chapter has focused on the way in which the interplay of imperatives and contexts can influence the genesis of collaborations to address cross-cutting issues. It has highlighted the capacity of particular actors to influence the form taken by collaboration, and in this regard central government is particularly significant given its policy initiation, funding and legislative resources. The next chapter explores this issue in greater detail by focusing on the way in which the drive to partnership in the UK has been played out in public–private and public–voluntary sector collaborations and within a multi-level system of governance.

5 Collaboration Across Sectors

The underlying purpose of public policy collaboration is to add value to activities that either would not occur or would not be as effective if left to an individual organisation. Collaboration, from this point of view, becomes a means to an end and therefore stands outside ideological debates about the role of the state and the involvement of non-public organisations in shaping, managing and delivering collective objectives. Whether the resulting partnerships are with business, the voluntary sector or other public bodies is of no relevance; what matters is whether collaboration is the best means to deliver the stated policy. Yet we are bound to question this pragmatic approach and ask whether a focus on consequences entitles us to ignore the means that are used, especially in relation to issues of public policy.

It is the widespread use of public–private partnerships that has generated most debate. Ranson and Stewart (1994) and others have argued that it is important to ground discussions about the application of public and private management techniques in their specific context. For example, governmental activity is premised on the value of transparency and service in the wider public interest. This is in tension with the secrecy inspired by the commercial values of the business world and its orientation towards private benefit. From this perspective there are inherent difficulties in government–business collaboration to deliver public policy goals. The debate about the relationship between the public sector and the voluntary sector is more muted. This is partly because of a greater degree of compatibility in their underlying values, but also because in some nations the state has played a major role in funding the delivery of public services through the voluntary sector. With intra-public sector partnerships one might assume a close compatibility of values, yet there too tensions can be found between differing political agendas, professional perspectives and hierarchical relationships. Partnership can become a virtuous symbol designed to rally otherwise divergent public bodies – or perhaps to conceal significant differences behind the appearance of unity. These issues are particularly salient in relations between tiers of government where questions of autonomy, control and authority for action come to the fore.

These are the concerns that we explore in this chapter. Our intention is to examine the politically contested nature of collaboration for public purpose and to show that this is far from being a neutral technique of the modernised post-ideological state. Rather, its employment is rooted in matters of value and interest. The chapter initially considers the development of public–private collaboration, examining its form and utility in the UK. Secondly, we consider voluntary–public sector collaboration, exploring the development from relatively simple grant and contract arrangements to longer-term and more sophisticated forms of relationship. Finally, we discuss the multi-tiered collaboration between levels of government, considering the impact of the European context and the development of governmental institutions in the nations and regions of the UK.

Public–private collaboration

Public–private partnership is not a new departure. Boyle (1993), for example, demonstrates a continuing relationship between state and business in managing the economy of west central Scotland in the period from the 1930s. Governments world-wide have also frequently employed the private sector to deliver public infrastructure projects, whether this is building a motorway or new hospital, and to provide specialist services where it did not have the skills or capacity, for example in the field of engineering and information technology. However, collaboration between government and business in public service provision has developed considerably as a result of the changing intellectual, political and managerial climate since the 1980s (see Chapter 2). This process has continued apace in the UK in recent years, stimulated by the pragmatism of the post-1997 Labour governments who expanded the Conservatives' earlier experiments with the private financing and management of public projects.

The distinctive feature of recent government–business relationships are the increasing complexity of collaborative arrangements and the involvement of the private sector in the direct delivery of public services. Underlying these developments are both ideological considerations about the respective place of state and market and political judgements about risk and how it is to be managed. The rushed privatisation of British Rail and subsequent history of Railtrack plc's bankruptcy, together with the failure of private companies to deliver satisfactorily the contracted-out housing benefit service in a number of councils, shows that the use of the private sector is not a panacea. It may bring benefits, but equally government is left to solve and pay for problems that arise (Commission on Public Private Partnerships, 2001).

Contracting-out

Contracting-out the delivery of public services was counter to the norms of the UK state in the latter half of the twentieth century, although some smaller local authorities did make limited use of private companies for refuse collection and grass-cutting. In the early 1980s the political profile of contracting-out was raised when a handful of Conservative-controlled local authorities offered refuse-collection and street-cleansing services for competitive tender. Legislation subsequently introduced compulsory competitive tendering (CCT) for basic public services. Where a council wished to retain the option of in-house provision, this choice had to be tested against the market. The intention to enhance the scope of contracting-out to local government support services was voluntarily adopted by some councils before the policy agenda was overtaken by the Best Value regime. Contracting-out was also adopted in the NHS, especially in hospital laundry, catering and cleaning services, and in central government through its 'market testing' strategy (Newman, Richards and Smith, 1998).

Problems of principal–agent relationships

Public–private relationships which emerge where business wins a contract are typically termed client–contractor or (in care services) purchaser–provider. Both are essentially principal–agent relationships in which the public authority (the principal) specifies the service to be delivered, including any necessary service standards, policy obligations and legal requirements to be met and the contractor (the agent) agrees to deliver these in return for a fee. But this apparently simple relationship contains significant complexity. Problems arise because in a competitive market there are strong incentives on the contractor to minimise their costs and maximise their revenue. For example, the client will require regular monitoring information on performance and will make payments on this basis. However, the contractor is better able than the client to know the reality of performance against specification, leading to the problem of information asymmetry. The ability of a contractor to control (at least partly) the quality, quantity and timeliness of the data provided to the client is a powerful resource in the relationship. As Walsh comments:

> Where there is perfect ... information, then there is little difficulty because the principal will be able to monitor the agent's performance and design an effective set of sanctions and incentives ... Without perfect information ... the principal may not be able to tell whether or not there has been a failure, or, if there has, whether that failure is the result of the actions of the agent ... for example, shirking. (1995, p. 36)

An additional problem is the length of the principal–agent chain. Those letting the contract, normally middle-tier managers, are acting as the agents of senior management who in turn act for politicians or board members. They in turn are the agents of an electorate or appointing body (for example a Minister) and ultimately the public as a whole. Similarly the contractor as agent may sub-contract with other providers or deliver the service through semi-autonomous business units. Finally, there is an enduring problem of specifying in a contract the qualitative aspects of a service. Considerable intellectual energy has been devoted to this problem and various solutions developed (Stewart and Walsh, 1994). However, the nature of the service can make this a very difficult enterprise, for example where service users are ill-defined (as in the case of recipients of a street-cleansing service) or not able to offer an opinion (such as those in receipt of a highly technical or professionalised service such as community legal advice). This remains an elusive area and one in which there is endless opportunity for inadvertent or deliberate under-performance by the contractor.

Developing long-term partnerships

Contracting-out is typically based on relatively short-term contracts. There is thus an incentive for contractors to maximise their revenue and minimise their costs during this period, accentuating the principal–agent problems. However, there has been a gradual development of longer-term public–private collaboration since the mid-1990s. This has been informed by the notion of relational contracting which is premised on the idea that the formal legal agreement is less important than the commitment of the parties to work together (Coulson, 1998; Walker and Davis, 1999). Those advocating relational contracting argue that trust and mutuality will replace the suspicion and divergence of interests found in traditional short-term contracting. Partners are in the relationship for the long term, and thus require a more open and transparent engagement with each other. There may be formal contractual elements to a longer-term collaboration, but the intention is that this should be subsumed within a wider vision. Klijn and Teisman express this as the difference between 'contracting-out' and 'partnership' (Table 5.1):

> Contracting-out is characterised by a principal–agent relationship in which the public actor defines the problem and provides the specification of the solution ... Partnership, on the other hand, is based on joint decision making and production in order to achieve effectiveness for both partners. Relational transparency, or in other words trust, is crucial. (2000, pp. 85–6)

However, the notion of longer-term relational partnerships should be subject to careful analysis. Despite the rhetoric of common interest there are also important differences of value and motivation. Relational contracting offers a soft language to conceal what is in reality a significant business

Table 5.1 *Comparison between contracting-out and long-term partnership*

Contracting-out	Long-term partnership
• Government and company in principal–agent relationship	• Government and company involved in joint decision-making and production
• Government defines problem, specifies solution and selects company to deliver	• Both parties develop joint products that contribute to their interests
• Benefits are efficiency	• Benefits are effectiveness
• Key to success is unambiguous specification	• Key to success is developing processes for interweaving goals, efforts and products
• Project managed with strong monitoring of contractor	• Process managed with strong emphasis on dialogue and joint problem-solving
• Contractual transparency, including rules covering tendering, selection of company, service delivery and inspection and monitoring	• Relational transparency, involving building enduring relationships which integrate organisational actors' efforts to work towards common goals

Source: Adapted from Klijn and Teisman (2000, p. 86).

strategy based on an assessment of market conditions and driven by considerations of competitive advantage. The ability to gain first mover advantage by establishing an early foothold in a new or expanding market for public services provides companies with an opportunity to create a more secure business environment. Such long-term public–private collaboration is in its infancy. However, public–private partnerships (PPPs), the successor to the private finance initiative (PFI) introduced in 1992, begin to develop the new terrain of longer-term relationships with business to deliver a complex package of activities.

Private finance initiative/public–private partnership

The written contract is a key instrument in PFI/PPP schemes, but relational elements are also important. They provide a means of developing a longer-term partnership between government and business. PFI/PPP also offers an alternative means of funding public investment projects. Traditionally government would borrow the money required to build a project, thus adding to the Public Sector Borrowing Requirement. Under PPP/PFI, government contracts-out the funding, building and operation of the scheme to the private sector. The private sector company or consortium accesses the necessary capital finance itself, recouping this in fees charged to the government for its use of the facility. The added attraction of PPP to post-1997 Labour governments is the belief that it will stimulate an injection of private sector creativity and thus aid the modernisation of public services. If there is an ideological edge – which is a matter of debate given Labour's avowed pragmatism – it is that it reflects the notion of a stakeholder society in which a variety of interests are brought into the governmental process (Falconer and McLoughlin, 2000). However, an alternative perspective would suggest that the process is more one of neo-corporatism with a strategic alliance between the state and capital at national level being reflected in a range of local-level public–private partnerships from which the public and workforce are largely excluded.

Forms of PFI/PPP

Fully-fledged PPP engages the private sector as an integral part of the design, building and financing of the project as well as the subsequent management and delivery of that service. This is termed DBFO (design, build, finance, operate). However, there are also lesser variants, including

BFO and DBF. For example, in the building of a new school:

> The appointed consortium will be expected to provide a range of
> services including: maintenance of the school building and grounds;
> power, heating and lighting; janitorial, cleaning and security services;
> insurance; and catering services .... The Council will continue to provide
> all teaching, administrative and technical/clerical services. Around twelve
> Council staff could transfer to the appointed service management
> company. (Hall *et al.*, 2000, p. 165)

Similarly in 1997 the Prison Service let two 25-year contracts to
Securicor/Costain and Group 4/Tarmac to build, maintain and operate
prisons. The estimated contract cost of £513 million is expected to offer a
10 per cent saving compared with building prisons using public funding
and then contracting-out their operation. The deal is also expected to produce faster and more innovative construction. The contractors are responsible for all custodial and ancillary services in the new prisons, including
catering, education and medical care (National Audit Office, 1997). The
PPP package therefore has two significant differences compared with
contracting-out. The first is that the public sector client is encouraged by
government to define its requirements in output terms, thus potentially
enabling the private sector partner to identify innovative solutions. The
second is that there has to be a significant transfer of risk from the public
to private sectors. However, whether government would let a particular
project fail is a matter of debate.

The projects undertaken through PPP have become more ambitious. One
of the most complex involves the upgrading of London Underground's
infrastructure and rolling-stock. This business will be separated into a
publicly-owned service delivery company and three privately owned infrastructure companies. The former will be responsible for planning and operating underground services, including drivers and station staff, and for
safety on the whole system. The infrastructure companies will have responsibility for upgrading and maintaining the track, tunnels, signals, stations,
lifts, escalators and trains in a group of underground lines under a 30-year
contract. The assets will revert to the public sector at that point.

Evaluating PFI/PPP

The evidence on PPP as a stimulus to innovation is mixed. Hall *et al.*
(2000) observed that in the case of a new high school the public sector

client had a pre-existing view about location and design. Competition was therefore on price rather than innovative design. In contrast, an evaluation of two prison PFI schemes identified innovative solutions in relation to construction and the control and monitoring of prisoner movements (National Audit Office, 1997). The Commission on Public Private Partnerships (2001) considered the evidence on the value-for-money impact of PFI/PPP. They note the Arthur Anderson study for HM Treasury which estimated 10 to 20 per cent savings through PFI/PPP with reference to the public sector comparator (the figure used to evaluate private sector bids). However, the assumptions built into the calculation of the Public Sector Comparator may be adjusted within a single PPP scheme or between schemes. For example, in the case of the Channel Tunnel rail link the Department of the Environment, Transport and the Regions (DETR) made several changes in its methodology for estimating the benefits of the project. Its final calculation excluded the benefits to non-UK resident passengers and included an amount for regeneration benefits. The latter figure comprised £500 million: 50 per cent of the difference between the expected cost to the public sector and the anticipated benefits (National Audit Office, 2001b). The quantification of costs and benefits of PPP schemes are more akin to art than science and careful attention needs to be paid to the assumptions underlying the figures. The value for money benefits of PPP also appear to vary across the public sector with prisons achieving an estimated 10 per cent net benefit compared with hospitals where benefits compared to the public sector comparator are generally marginal. One explanation is that prisons are full DBFO schemes for a single client while in hospitals the service providing activity is restricted to property management and maintenance functions, and medical and related services remain the responsibility of the relevant NHS trust.

Strategic partnering

New forms of longer-term public–private relationships developed in the early years of the new millennium. These are termed strategic partnering and focus on a complex package of relationships between a public organisation and a company or consortium. The leading companies in the field include Hyder Business Services, BT and Capita. The package typically has a number of elements including contracting-out of council services, private investment in council business processes and IT, and call-centre and business park development. In Middlesbrough, for example, the local authority established a 10-year strategic partnering agreement with Hyder Business Services in 2000. The purpose of the partnership is defined as sustaining jobs in the council, generating extra jobs locally, reducing costs and producing efficiency savings (Foster, 2001; Middlesbrough Council, 2000). It involves the council in a £260 million contracting-out exercise which transfers 1000 staff involved in property management, finance and procurement, housing benefit and education awards to Hyder management. In return, Hyder invests in a call-centre for customer enquiries and relocates 490 jobs to Middlesbrough from their existing contracts, involving £150 million of business. There is the prospect of an additional 750 new jobs over the 10-year period and a partnership with developers is planned to create a £19 million investment in a regional business centre. There will also be a £20 million investment in information technology to produce a major improvement in the council's processes and systems. The partnership will be managed by a board comprising senior councillors, the chief executive of the council and senior managers from Hyder.

Strategic partnering is likely to develop significantly in future years. The models are available and are being tested, especially by local authorities (Filkin *et al.*, 2001). The political and managerial climate is more encouraging of business involvement at a level greater than the relatively simple CCT-type contracts. The Byatt report (Byatt, 2001) argues for the development of a more sophisticated and strategic approach to the procurement of goods and services by local authorities and a greater willingness on the part of business to understand and invest in the development of local government services. The Commission on Public Private Partnerships report (2001), however, argues that PPPs should not be seen as the sole means of producing or delivering public services. It is critical of the way in which PFI/PPP has been presented as the only option and the poor performance of some such partnerships. It also argues for the need to have a much stronger stakeholder involvement.

Public–Voluntary Sector Collaboration

The voluntary and charitable sector was instrumental in developing many of the services that became an accepted part of the UK's welfare state, including education, health care and social services. Davis-Smith (1995) demonstrates how, during the past two centuries, the voluntary sector has become increasingly interwoven with the activities of the state but has also retained a degree of flexibility and autonomy from what is now a highly significant source of its funding. It has also continued to provide services in fields that are beyond state activity and actively campaigns for changes in legislation and government policy. This underlying variety in the nature of the voluntary sector is illustrated in the mapping undertaken by Kendall and Knapp (1996). They estimate that there are somewhere between 200 000 and 400 000 voluntary organisations (depending on definitions used) spending some £30 billion, of which 40 per cent arises from government funding, and with almost one million paid employees. However, a distinction must be drawn between those more formally constituted bodies (the 'voluntary' sector) and local residents and citizens' groups (the 'community' sector) (Chanan, 1991). Typically, it is the former rather than the latter who tend to have a service delivery function. The highly differentiated nature of this 'third sector' therefore means that collaborative relationships with governmental bodies vary in their form, intensity and tenure.

Traditional forms of relationship

Historically, some broad patterns of public–voluntary sector collaboration can be identified. The classic position – a minimal form of collaboration – is characterised by Deakin (1995, p. 43) as 'pioneer, supplementer of state provision and candid friend'. Here voluntary and state sectors operate in parallel, with the voluntary sector initiating new forms of service that the state may adopt – as it did, on creating the NHS, with those hospitals run by the charitable sector – or filling gaps in public provision, sometime supported in this role by government grants. Leach and Wilson found that elements of this approach remain in relationships between some local authorities and their voluntary sector. They typify this as the 'traditional/incremental' orientation in which authorities 'have over the years chosen to support a range (often a limited range) of voluntary organisations, and continue to do so through tradition and precedent rather than as an expression of a more explicit view of their value' (1998, pp. 8–9).

The contract culture

However, a more directive and instrumental form of collaboration emerged during the 1970s and 1980s. This had two apparently contradictory stimuli.

The first was the creation of major public programmes which, in part because of the target groups they were designed to reach, required the active involvement of the voluntary sector in their delivery. These included the employment creation and training initiatives arising from the Manpower Services Commission and its successor bodies (for example TECs and Learning and Skills Councils – LSCs), the Community Programme which at its height in 1988 accounted for 15 per cent of all funding to the voluntary sector (Deakin, 1995), the Urban Programme of the 1980s and SRB in the 1990s. This instrumental approach was also evident in local public policy, where some Labour-controlled councils targeted funding to voluntary organisations whose objectives advanced their economic development, anti-poverty and equalities agendas (Lansley *et al.*, 1989; Leach and Wilson, 1998). The second factor in the changed collaborative environment was the reformulation of the role of the state. The search for alternative service providers and value-for-money in public spending resulted in a recasting of the collaborative relationship. General grants that supported an organisation's core costs and service delivery were replaced by more focused contractually-based funding for defined services to given performance levels. What quickly became known as the 'contract culture' marked a major watershed in collaboration between voluntary and state sectors. It reconstituted the voluntary sector as an adjunct to the state in a flexible labour market where voluntary organisations competed for contracts against other potential providers.

Yet the discourse employed still echoes the earlier form of relationship and conceals the essentially instrumental and contractual basis of the new regime. 'Contracts' with voluntary sector bodies are called 'service level agreements' and the form of collaboration is described as 'partnership' rather than 'contracting'. The undesirable impact of the contract culture combined with more clearly defined national and local policy objectives was identified by Gutch, Kunz and Spencer (1990, p. 3). They argued that the voluntary sector was in danger of 'becoming the agent of local government – functioning more like a department of the local authority than an independent agent'. Nevertheless this particular collaborative model has subsequently been maintained and extended. It has found a philosophical justification in the idea of the enabling local authority which supports others to meet community needs (Clarke and Stewart, 1988). National schemes have also been important, including the quasi-markets found in Community Care and Supporting People as well as the range of area-based initiatives. This economic incorporation of the voluntary sector has been augmented by a political incorporation through the norm of reserved seats on partnership boards.

From contracts to compacts?

The relationship between the state and the voluntary sector is now under-going a reconsideration. There have been concerns about the longer-term implications for the voluntary sector of the replacement of grants by con-tracts and specifically the prioritising of financial viability above the core values of the organisation. The stronger orientation to service delivery challenges voluntary organisations' independence from the state and their ability to advocate for specific interests. There is also a wider debate about the contribution of the voluntary and community sectors to generating and maintaining social capital (Putnam, 1993; Etzioni, 1995, 2000). This res-onates with the post-1997 Labour governments' concerns to stimulate active citizenship, and hence opens up a new agenda for public–voluntary sector collaboration.

Commissions on the Future of the Voluntary Sector in England and in Scotland reported in the mid-1990s (National Council for Voluntary Organisations, 1996; Scottish Council of Voluntary Organisations, 1997). They called for a compact with national government that would set down the basic principles of the relationship but would also establish undertakings that would bind the partners to a more equitable working arrangement. This idea was developed further after the election of a new government in 1997, and compacts have been agreed with administrations in the nations of the UK (for example Home Office, 1998). There have been parallel developments at local level, with councils for voluntary service (CVSs) and local authorities negotiating their own compacts to express and regulate the principles guid-ing their overall relationship (Craig *et al.*, 1999; Ross and Osborne, 1999). It remains to be seen how these strategies to deliver a new form of collabora-tive framework will impact upon the day-to-day relationships between the voluntary sector and the state, and to what extent the imperatives of money, policy and expediency will undermine them (Deakin, 2001). Nevertheless this appears to mark a significant new phase in public–voluntary sector collaboration.

Vertical collaboration: multi-level governance in the European context

Any examination of collaboration for public purpose should address not just the horizontal linkages between agencies operating at approximately the same geographical scale but also the vertical connections between tiers of government. Citizens of the UK can find up to six tiers of government impinging on them (parish or community, district, county, region or nation, UK, European), in addition to the countless partnership bodies, quangos and arm's-length agencies. Analysis of and debate about multi-level governance is well developed in states with federal systems of government where questions about jurisdictional integrity and the constitutional right of superior bodies to intervene in the affairs of lower tiers are matters of academic, political and legal interpretation (Sartori, 1997). The UK, however, has a pragmatic and informal constitution and a tradition of political centralisation. Its politics, unlike a number of European neighbours, is built on an aggressive adversarialism and an absence of multiple membership of different tiers of government by individual politicians. This reduces the capacity of political leaders to build alliances between these tiers compared, for example, with France (John and Cole, 1999). In this context it is not surprising to find a paucity of domestic debate (particularly in England) about multi-level governance and vertical collaboration. Despite this there are a number of developments that are forcing this issue on to the agenda. We explore three that are of particular import, namely the European institutions, devolution to Scotland and Wales, and the regional debate in England.

The impact of European institutions

Two processes are focused on the European political institutions. The first is the transmutation of the independent nation state into a quasi-autonomous actor located within a wider political structure. As European institutions have evolved their role, so they have constrained the powers of national decision-makers across a variety of fields – from employment law and procurement practice to state industrial aid and agricultural policy. If there is a debate in the UK about multi-level governance, then it is structured in terms of the balance of power between nation and Europe as exemplified in the saga of Britain's accession to European Monetary Union. For central government, therefore, the issue is less one of collaboration with the supra-national tier and more one of retaining autonomy in the face of expanding policy domains where the boundaries between national and European authority are not always clearly defined (Schmitter, 1996). Siedentop puts it like this:

> For a nation so long used to self-government, and identifying itself so completely with parliamentary sovereignty, it is bitter, indeed almost

intolerable to forgo the satisfactions afforded by self-government. (2000, p. 41)

The second process is one by which European programmes have reached down and directly engaged with sub-national government. The structural funds are particularly important in this respect. These provide assistance to accommodate the impact of industrial and economic restructuring. Central government and its regional outposts are involved in the procurement of such schemes and the provision of matching funding, but delivery is through local or sub-regional partnerships in which local authorities have a key role. Consequently local authority awareness of the ways in which European policies and programmes can support their communities and augment their own economic development strategies has stimulated some to open direct contact with the European Commission and Parliament, in some cases by retaining officials based in Brussels (Chapman, 1995; Martin and Pearce, 1999). The creation of the Committee of the Regions has supported the expression of sub-national governments' voices at the European level. Benington and Harvey (1998) contextualise these developments in terms of the difficult period of central–local relations during the 1980s and early 1990s when UK local authorities by-passed Whitehall to do business with more sympathetic institutions in Strasbourg and Brussels. These vertical linkages have been supported through a growth of transnational networks between local authorities within Europe.

Devolution to Scotland and Wales

The question of political devolution from the Westminster Parliament to new institutions in Scotland and Wales has been debated with more or less enthusiasm for some considerable time. The Labour government elected in 1997 fulfilled its manifesto commitment to devolution and legislation was enacted in 1998. The provisions in Scotland are more extensive than those in Wales because it had had a pre-Union parliament and subsequently retained a separate legislative, legal and educational system. The Scottish Parliament has full legislative responsibility for a range of devolved functions and also has the ability to vary the rate of income tax charged in Scotland by up to three pence in the pound on the basic rate. It has a powerful committee system which has the authority to initiate legislation as well as scrutinise the work of the Executive. In Wales the settlement did not include powers for the Assembly to instigate primary legislation nor to raise revenue. Consequently the form, functions and financing of local government in Wales is dependent upon legislation passed at Westminster. However, the Assembly has power in relation to 'secondary' or 'subordinate' legislation within aspects of these Westminster Acts. It is also has a specific duty to 'sustain and promote local government in Wales' and must create a Partnership Council to that effect, a feature not found in the Scottish legislation.

Local government is one of the key functions allocated to the new national institutions and this creates a different dynamic in multi-level governance. There is the potential for a closer and stronger relationship between local and devolved decision-makers than was possible when the Secretary of State was essentially the arm of the UK Executive in the nation. Indeed the Welsh Assembly and the Scottish Parliament and Executive have made local government one of their key priorities. Each has only a relatively small number of councils under its remit – 32 in Scotland and 22 in Wales – and the scale of the two nations in population and policy terms means that the policy networks are relatively small and close. Emerging evidence reveals that the vertical relationships between local authorities and the national institutions in the two countries are close and that there is some difference in policy intent and the policy instruments being deployed compared with that of the UK government in terms of English local authorities (Boyne *et al.*, 1999; Jones and Trystan, 2001; Midwinter and McGarvey, 2001). In Scotland, for instance, the introduction of streamlined political management arrangements is being undertaken through a co-operative process rather than by the use of legislation as in England and Wales. Similarly the Best Value regime for improving service performance has been phased out in Wales and was never introduced in Scotland, although a somewhat different system does apply there. Differences are also evident in education, health and other fields. And, as we demonstrate in Chapter 2, the partnership arrangements sponsored by the two national bodies are somewhat different from each other and from those in England.

Regional governance in England

While Scotland and Wales have gained political bodies, the regional level of government in England has largely experienced devolution of administrative activity. The one exception is London, with its elected mayor and strategic Assembly. Elsewhere there has been a gradual growth in central government's presence in the regions. Eight government offices of the regions (GORs) were created in 1994 when the separate regional presences of the Environment, Employment, Education and Trade and Industry departments were merged and made accountable to a regional director. Subsequently other departments (for example, the Home Office) have become part of the GOR structure. This initiative in Whitehall collaboration was stimulated by the inability of compartmentalised government departments, some of which had little or no regional presence, to respond effectively to the problems of inner cities and depressed regions. The way in which EU programmes reached directly to the sub-national level was also important in promoting the strengthening of central government in the regions. GORs play a key role in relation to a number of government initiatives delivered at the sub-national level, including a wide range of partnerships. This has enabled some GORs to develop a range of formal and informal collaborative relationships with public agencies, business and the voluntary and community sectors, thus stimulating networks to contribute to multi-level governance within the region (Ayres and Davis, 2000; Mawson and Spencer, 1997).

There was a step change when the Regional Development Agencies (RDAs) were created in 1999. These are quangos with appointed boards whose task is to advance the economic regeneration, business competitiveness and skills agenda in the regions. RDAs have a significant and growing potential to influence sub-national public policy in England, especially through their duty to prepare a regional economic strategy. These provide a context for the plans of other agencies operating in the regions, as well as the delivery of national and European programmes. A Regional Chamber or Assembly has been created in each region. Their role is to provide input to the RDA from stakeholders in the region and to monitor and hold the RDA to account. Local authority members are in the majority in each chamber, but seats are also reserved for business, trade union, voluntary sector, educational and other interests (Dungey, 2000). In addition there is a growing tier of regional and sub-regional partnerships, quangos and government bodies, for example Learning and Skills Councils and Regional Cultural Consortia (Skelcher *et al.*, 2000).

The regional level in England therefore presents a complex mosaic when viewed either down from national and European levels or up from localities. An analysis of the role of central government at regional and local level found that there was no overall understanding of the cumulative impact of policies at the regional level and that regional networks of government bodies were fragmented. It also highlighted how what came to be called 'initiativitis' – the rapid deployment of a series of area-based initiatives – resulted in overlapping and unco-ordinated activities that reduced their effectiveness and created burdens for local organisations (Performance and Innovation Unit, 2000). The main response by government was to create the Regional Co-ordination Unit (RCU), an interdepartmental body at central government level with the remit of acting as the 'head office' for the GORs, engaging more departments with the regional dimension and co-ordinating policy initiatives with a local or regional impact. It has a particular role in vetting proposals for new area-based initiatives prior to decision by a cabinet committee.

It is interesting to observe that this solution employs a piece of Weberian bureaucracy to centrally manage a fragmented set of networks. Yet these networks provide a means of undertaking multi-level governance within the region in a way that accommodates the complex pattern of jurisdictions exercised by different elected, appointed and partnership bodies. An example is provided by Ayres and Davis' (2000) research on the West Midland RDA network. They demonstrate that this network is highly inclusive in terms of the clusters of public activity that are represented in it. This inclusiveness, they argue, generates a potential for entrepreneurial behaviour to bridge structural holes – the gaps between those clusters of activity that when linked produce synergy and added public value. This insight leads to a different solution to the issues raised in the PIU report. It suggests that individual boundary-spanning activity motivated by public purpose can provide a means of steering and enabling multi-level governance. This individual activity would need to be referenced back to a legitimising forum – whether this is the RDA, regional chamber or local strategic partnership. But it is likely to be more successful as an approach to managing complexity than a return to bureaucratic hierarchy. Networking is a developmental, opportunity-seeking process; bureaucratic organisation merely offers static co-ordination.

Conclusion

The cross-sectoral and multi-level collaborative arrangements discussed in this chapter provide an important counterpoint to those concerned with specific policy fields (Chapter 4). There, inter-organisational theory provided insights to explain the nature of the collaborations that emerged and the issues they faced. The material in this chapter, however, is at a different level. It concerns fundamental questions about the distribution of power and authority between major groupings in society. In the case of public–private sector partnerships, we see a gradual engagement by the state with the idea that the private sector has a role to play in achieving public purpose. This poses a challenge to the principle of sectoral differentiation which has become ingrained into the British psyche since the creation of the welfare state. The contrast with other European nations is stark. In France, for example, there is a longer tradition of the state contracting-out tasks that it did not have the capacity to implement, although within a more technocratic form of public administration (Nelson, 2001; Teisman and Klijn, 2000). The emergence of public–private collaboration in the UK could be analysed in terms of resource-dependency theory, but this would be to miss the underlying political and cultural dimension that is specific to this national context. What is being witnessed is a transformation of institutional patterns through the forcing of this new practice by central diktat.

The position in relation to state–voluntary sector collaboration is somewhat different. Here resource dependency does seem to offer a sound explanation. Resource flows into the voluntary sector are constrained and thus the state has a powerful means of shaping patterns of activity. The case illustrates the voluntary sector's transition from parallel provider to agent, at least as far as social welfare services are concerned. While the discourse is structured in terms of a partnership of equals, the reality of service-level agreements as contracts suggests an alternative relationship.

Finally, the discussion of multi-level governance focused on the impact of institutions and policies at the European, Scottish and Welsh, and English regional level. Here the issues are centrally about the jurisdiction of nested tiers of government, and in particular the challenge to the UK government which is located in a society without a tradition of constitutionally defined territorial division of powers. This challenge comes from a strengthening European sphere of activity as well as from domestic pressures, in particular the claims for greater national and regional autonomy within the UK and the complexity of networks through which governance is now exercised. This reflects a tension between two approaches, which Pierre and Peters (2000, p. 82) distinguish as 'state-centric' and 'governance':

> The main difference between the two perspectives is that in the conventional view the centrality of the state is taken for granted whereas in the governance perspective the state is a *primus inter pares* actor whose capabilities are contingent on its ability to mobilise other societal actors for its purposes.

The UK government operates on the former model, yet its environment demands the latter. The emergence of regional governance in England illustrates that collaborative networks have a powerful dynamic and that state-centric approaches with their bureaucratic predilections do not generate sufficient requisite variety to enable the system to be guided. An alternative to the state-centric or networking dilemma is to create powerful political institutions at the regional level. These are common in other European states, yet London is the only example of a tier of English government intermediate between locality and nation. The formal powers of the Mayor and Greater London Authority are limited to strategic matters, but the body does have a capacity to bring together a variety of actors to address metropolitan-wide issues. Such inclusiveness has been the strategy of Ken Livingstone, the first Mayor, and it presents a model of the way in which a degree of institutionalisation can combine with a governance approach to address complex public policy problems in a decentralised environment. These are matters of building collaborative capacity, and it is to these that we turn in the next chapter.

6 Building Capacity for Collaboration

The increasing scope and scale of collaborative action places greater demands on potential partners to develop their capacity for working in concert with others. Capacity for collaboration can be characterised in a number of ways all of which are important for effective joint working. It is necessary amongst individuals, in the form of specific skills and attributes that enable them to work across agency boundaries. It is also essential within partner organisations in the guise of a culture supportive of collaboration. Finally, capacity for collaboration needs to be present within the strategies and processes of the collaborative activity itself. Capacity building is an activity most frequently undertaken with communities who lack the skills and resources to enter into collaboration with statutory and private sector partners. In the UK dedicated funding for community capacity building has been a key element in area-based regeneration programmes since the early 1990s. Community capacity building is also evident elsewhere. For example, the municipal government of Versalle, Colombia is facilitating the involvement of communities in determining priorities for a local health strategy (Millan and Acosta, 2000), while the Centre for Urban Research and Learning (CURL) in Chicago is one of a number of agencies in the US dedicated to the development of community capacity through collaborative action research programmes (Nyden *et al.*, 1997). Latterly, however, the focus of capacity building has moved beyond communities to embrace other sectors, and particularly voluntary sector organisations whose resources are frequently more constrained than those of major public sector institutions (see Chapter 5).

Building collaborative capacity is not easy. It requires a clear commitment from collaborators and needs to be supported by a significant investment of resources. This chapter examines the components of collaborative capacity and, underpinned by the theoretical insights provided in Chapter 3, reviews the empirical evidence of building individual, organisational and collaborative capacity. We consider the individual skills and roles required in collaborations and the significance of organisational culture in fostering or hindering 'ownership' of collaboration. In addition, we pay particular attention to the importance of trust in relationships that risk failure in an attempt to develop new ways of working and the importance of leadership in this context.

Individual capacity for collaboration

Boundary-spanners and reticulists

Individuals who exhibit the necessary combination of skills and attributes for collaboration are frequently termed boundary-spanners or reticulists (Alter and Hage, 1993; Friend *et al.*, 1974). These are people who are skilled communicators, able to 'talk the right language' in whatever forum they find themselves. They have excellent networking skills giving them the ability to gain entry to a variety of settings and to seek out and 'connect up' others who may have common interests or goals. Their capacity to empathise enables them to see a situation from a variety of points of view which, combined with their communication skills, makes them effective negotiators. In addition to these particular skills, boundary-spanners or reticulists have other attributes which inform their capacity to collaborate. They are people who can 'see the big picture' and understand how different partners can contribute to achieve shared goals. They are able to understand the constraints and opportunities provided by different organisational contexts and how these might affect individual behaviour. Finally, they are individuals who are able to think laterally and creatively and to use these capacities to problem-solve and to take risks to achieve their goals. To this end they are self-managers who possess sound organisational skills (see Box 6.1).

Boundary-spanners and reticulists are able to play a number of different roles to establish, facilitate and co-ordinate collaboration. Their communication and networking skills equip them to act as a link person between putative partners at the beginnings of collaboration. Combining these skills with their organisational and negotiating abilities means that they are able to manage collaborative action at different stages, for example acting as a project manager during the initial phase of partnership creation or developing transitions into new collaborations at the end of a time-limited initiative (see Chapter 7). Their ability to see the place and contribution of collaboration within the wider context, alongside their problem-solving and negotiating skills and their preparedness to take risks, means that they can take a leadership role in the collaboration. Finally, their ability to empathise means that in addition to bringing partners together at the

Box 6.1 *Required skills and attributes of reticulists*

- **Critical appreciation of environment and problems/opportunities presented**
- **Understanding different organisational contexts**
- **Knowing the role and playing it**
  - Co-ordinator/facilitator – link person
  - Leader
  - Manager
  - Supporter
- **Communication**
  - Verbal – 'dealing with all sorts' and being able to translate messages
  - Non-verbal – body language, listening skills
  - Getting and sharing information
- **Prescience**
  - Capacity to accurately anticipate and adapt behaviour
- **Networking**
  - Knowing who the 'right' people are and being able to access them
  - Having 'political skills'
  - Adopting a common code
- **Negotiating**
  - Understanding the other side(s)
  - Garnering the level of support for particular propositions among partners
- **Conflict resolution**
  - Focusing on the 90 per cent
  - Dealing with the 10 per cent
  - Interpersonal capacities – diplomacy, mediation
- **Risk-taking**
  - Dealing with uncertainty
  - Making trade-offs
  - Accommodating the unexpected

(continued)

- **Problem-solving**
  - Limits of authority
  - Creative/lateral thinking
- **Self-management**
  - Time management
  - Ability to prioritise

Sources: Gaster, 1995; Hague and Malos, 1996; Skelcher *et al.*, 1996; Wilson and Charlton, 1997.

beginning of the collaboration, they are able to provide ongoing support to different partners throughout. These individuals exist in all organisations and across all sectors. Very often their role is not codified. However, as partners begin to appreciate the individual capacities they need to facilitate successful collaboration they may seek out such individuals and employ them with a specific remit to design and develop collaborative activity.

Trust

Individuals with reticulist skills are valuable to collaborations because they are trusted by a variety of partners. Trust is a vitally important component of capacity for collaboration and is a key feature of those informal inter-personal networks that underpin formal inter-organisational partnerships (Skelcher *et al.*, 1996). Trust provides a way of coping with risk or uncertainty in relationships with others, features that may be particularly evident in collaborative contexts where partners have not traditionally worked together (Lane and Bachmann, 1998). There is a wide variety of literature on trust from a number of different disciplines, including sociology, political science, organisational behaviour and philosophy. This material highlights the different levels at which trust operates, from micro-level interchanges between individuals to the behaviour of organisations and institutions. These latter aspects of trust will be discussed in the next section. Here we focus on the role of trust in building and cementing relationships between individuals.

Mayer *et al.* (1995) suggest that there are three key antecedents to inter-personal trust. These are:

1. Ability – confidence in the trustee's skills, professional expertise and knowledge. This may be particularly important in those collaborations

where the truster comes from a different background and has limited knowledge of the necessary technical skills.

2. Benevolence – belief that the trustee is altruistic and working in the wider public interest. This is important in collaboration where there are opportunities for individuals to make personal gains without necessarily contributing to the wider goals.

3. Integrity – belief that the trustee will adhere to a set of moral principles. This reinforces benevolence and reflects the inherently individually and organisationally risky nature of collaboration. It emphasises the need for collaborators to be confident that they have shared 'rules of behaviour'.

This emphasis on the goodness and reputation of the reticulist is shared by other writers on trust. For example, Lane and Bachmann (1998) regard the moral basis of trust as comprising a belief system that is based on honesty and an absence of self-regarding behaviour. Similarly Rousseau *et al.* (1998) emphasise the way in which individuals make rational choices about who to trust in part based upon information about their skills and attributes. Rousseau *et al.*, also draw attention to the dynamics of trust between individuals, the fact that repeated interactions can build trust if characteristics such as reliability and dependability are consistently exhibited. Jones and George (1998) also highlight the dynamics of trust in collaboration. They suggest three key variants – conditional trust, unconditional trust and distrust. This is particularly helpful in relation to collaboration as it draws attention to the fact that ability, benevolence and integrity may not in fact all be present prior to a collaboration (particularly in imposed collaborations) and so will need to be developed over time. The extent to which individuals can obtain the necessary level of trust between each other to collaborate effectively will be informed by the dynamics of the relationship, positive experiences increasing trust and negative ones diluting it (Chapter 7).

Leadership

Leadership has a central place in collaborative endeavour. However, it represents something of a challenge to traditional approaches that focus on the role of the formally designated 'leader' that others then follow. In collaboration it may not be possible to easily discern a 'formal' leader as matters of leadership may be contested. Instead leadership needs to be exercised through the employment of personal skills such as persuasion, through the application of processes and activities that nurture and facilitate co-operation between individuals and organisations and through the use of personal authority to access necessary resources to contribute to the collaborative venture (Feyerherm, 1994; Huxham and Vangen, 2000a). Very often what is needed to catalyse collaboration are individuals who are able to 'champion' particular causes and motivate others to take collective action. Such people may not necessarily belong to one of the most obviously powerful partner bodies but may instead have sufficient personal capacity to draw others together and facilitate a changed approach. Sometimes these 'champions' may be religious figures, while on other occasions they may be business people with a particular passion for an issue or a city. What such figures also have in common is that they are most often trusted by partners from all sectors and so can act as 'honest-brokers' in bringing potentially antagonistic bodies together.

In practice, UK government-sponsored collaborations tend to designate a formal leader, for example, health authorities in the case of HAZs, local authorities and the police in the case of community safety. While organisational in focus, the leadership role becomes associated with key individuals, such as the chief executive, chief constable or a senior local councillor. These leaders find themselves applying their leadership capacity in a new environment, one where hierarchies have been replaced by networks and inter-organisational reliance and it is not possible to lead simply by virtue of one's formal authority in a unitary bureaucracy. Luke (1997) argues that we have moved from a 'modern' to a 'post-modern' environment whose key characteristic is collaboration. Here what is needed is 'catalytic leadership'. This is exhibited by individuals with certain core skills: the capacity to think and act strategically, interpersonal skills that can facilitate productive working amongst members of the collaboration and an underlying character that exhibits a desire to achieve results, is able to relate to others and comprises strong personal integrity.

Further contributions to individual collaborative capacity

Whether people have the right skills and attributes to work across boundaries and lead collaborations is only part of the picture. Hudson *et al.* (1999) suggest four further dimensions that need to be considered as contributors to individual capacity to collaborate. These are:

1. the roles individuals play and the extent to which they can identify these roles as important in an environment where collaboration is increasing;
2. individuals' ability to adapt to the increased permeability of boundaries within and between partner bodies;

3. how individuals assess collaboration as contributing to their career and to meeting the needs of their client group or service area;
4. the complementarity or 'fit' individuals perceive between the philosophy of collaboration and a public service environment.

They suggest that the way in which individuals reconcile the tensions and dilemmas within the above dimensions will impact on collaborative capacity beyond the micro-level of individuals working together to the meso- and macro-levels. It is to these levels that we now turn.

Organisational capacity for collaboration

Collaborative culture

The contribution of individuals to collaboration is insufficient if it is not supported by a wider commitment of agencies and groups to developing new ways of working and organising. The discussion in Chapter 3 suggests that collaboration requires partners to subscribe to common values, which in turn underpin a culture of operating that engenders the development of new activities, roles and relationships. It requires complementarity among partners in terms of roles and functions and the need for the host organisations to resource and support the development of a collaborative culture through the decentralisation of decision-making and access to necessary infrastructure (Alter and Hage, 1993). Himmelman (1996) goes furthest in suggesting the need for a 'transformative' culture leading to shared ownership and decision-making.

Newman (1996) suggests that the kind of culture that will be facilitative of collaboration is one which is strategically 'adaptive' and 'responsive'. Organisations with this kind of culture are sufficiently confident to devolve decision-making down to the front-line and have a strong external orientation. The key characteristics of such organisations are:

- a strong focus on the community;
- senior managers that can connect well with other stakeholders;
- effective modes of involving service users;
- strong strategic partnerships with other agencies;
- mechanisms for connecting with diverse communities;
- staff at all levels that can work across boundaries;
- decentralised service delivery;
- strong links with international and other bodies.

The potential dangers to such an organisational culture are that its flexibility runs the risk of limiting effective internal control and accountability for actions and that its external orientation results in the organisation becoming fragmented and losing a sense of internal coherence. While there will always be tension between flexibility/control and fragmentation/integration, the organisation must be able to maintain a balance in order to operate effectively. This requires an appreciation of the importance of learning to improve and sustain the organisation. Newman concludes that organisations are poor at learning, notwithstanding the significance attached to 'learning organisations' in recent years. She argues that if organisations are to build requisite learning capacity they need to make a point of engaging in structured learning activities and processes and that this needs to take place throughout the organisation, with an emphasis on the strategic level and through activities with users and partners.

Learning in collaborations

This emphasis upon learning is evident in the policy programmes of post-1997 Labour governments and is particularly apparent in the development and implementation of local collaborations. The Area-Based Initiatives (ABIs) are required to build local evaluation into their programmes as well as participating in national evaluation programmes to aid learning from experience and to help identify and replicate 'what works' in relation to particular policy questions. In some cases, evaluation is conducted on the whole programme, such as Sure Start, while in others, for instance Crime and Disorder, evaluations relate to specific activities such as burglary reduction schemes. Government has also established central units with a remit to explore and disseminate learning from policy in practice. These can be departmentally specific, such as the Partnership and Systems Branch of the Department of Health, or may exist to serve the whole of government in relation to a particular issue, for example the Social Exclusion Unit and the Neighbourhood Renewal Unit.

However, the extent to which this has contributed to a 'learning capacity' within collaborations is doubtful. For those engaged in local partnerships, external evaluation remains an irrelevance because it serves the interests of the commissioning department in central government rather than the collaborations themselves. Given the dynamic policy environment of government, such evaluations do not keep pace with the changing agenda and are sometimes so long-term that their result do not appear within the lifetime of the collaboration. There is *ad hoc* internal evaluation and learning with some collaborations allocating a specific proportion of their budget to local reviews to support learning. For example, some health action zones have attempted to build learning into their collaborative processes. In the initial stages of the Manchester, Salford and Trafford HAZ, a consultant attended all partnership board meetings and provided structured events for the partners to learn how to improve their ability to work together more effectively.

Organisational leadership

While organisational capacity may flower in a culture of adaptive and responsive strategic processes, it will need support if it is to be sustained in balance over time. This returns us to the subject of leadership, this time in relation to building the capacity of the organisation to act in collaboration. Here leadership is necessary to secure organisational ownership of and commitment to the collaborative endeavour. This is vital, as without it flexible organisations will run the risk of losing coherence as collaborative activities fail to cross-fertilise and learn from each other. It is also important in helping to support an organisation in developing a capacity to innovate, take risks and try out new approaches. Leadership to support new ways of doing things can came from a number of sources. The Department of Health created special funds which HAZs could access. These were intended to emphasise the significance of HAZs as 'trailblazers' for change in the NHS and the development and delivery of health policy. Leadership was also essential from among the key partners to the HAZ, including the health authorities and local authorities involved. However, matters of leadership can be complicated where partner bodies do not see themselves as equal partners. For example, Crime and Disorder partnerships need to be established at the district council level of local government, yet police services operate to wider county or sub-regional boundaries. The statutory leadership of these partnerships is shared between local government and the police. However, problems can arise where local authority chief executives see their opposite number as being the chief constable of the wider police authority, rather than the chief superintendent or equivalent officer with responsibility for the command at district council level.

Inter-organisational trust and principled conduct

Our earlier discussion dealt with the issue of trust between individuals. However, trust pertains both to individuals and organisations, although in the twenty-first century the extent to which any long-standing UK institutions are considered trustworthy is a moot point (Coulson, 1998; Giddens, 1991). In terms of collaboration, the organisational aspect of trust is important as most collaborative programmes that involve the allocation of resources from central government require an accountable body to manage the funds and ensure that they are accounted for appropriately and not misused. Only certain institutions are considered appropriate for this task, largely because they have sufficient organisational capacity to accommodate the necessary systems and because they have the legal constitution and recognition by central government that permits them to handle such funds. The National Strategy for Neighbourhood Renewal, however, introduces a further criteria. It proposed the establishment of neighbourhood management schemes within localities. The scheme will co-ordinate local service provision and ensure that service providers deliver an appropriate level of service to meet local needs and achieve agreed targets. Responsibility for leading neighbourhood management schemes will be assigned to organisations that have sufficient resource capacity to deliver and have credibility with the local community. In these collaborations, therefore, trust needs to be secured with the local community as well as with central government.

Lack of trust is frequently cited as one reason why collaborations are less effective than they might be in achieving their goals through joint working (Huxham and Vangen, 2000b). Cropper (1996) is cognisant of this and suggests that in order to begin to build trust, partners need to agree modes of 'principled conduct' in order to provide the parameters within which partner bodies can work. These cannot replace the development of trust through the experience of working together, but can initiate communication and understanding between partners about their respective beliefs and values and the extent to which they are shared. Cropper argues these exchanges will help to promote 'a sense of inclusion, of predictability or dependability, and of unequivocality in relationships' (1996, p. 96), which others have determined as essential to maintaining commitment to collaboration (Ring and Van de Ven, 1994). The elements of 'principled conduct' are 'fair dealings' in relation to the outcomes of collaboration, namely the distribution of benefits and 'fairness in procedure'.

The way in which benefits are distributed is a major issue. Partners must feel confident that their respective contributions to the partnership will be valued appropriately and that the collaboration will honour its obligations to the partner by way of allocating benefits. It is in the timing of the distribution of benefits that many collaborations experience difficulty and often it is the least powerful partners who perceive the inequity. For example, the experience of the authors in working with regeneration partnerships in the mid-1990s was that community representatives invariably felt that the community was the last stakeholder to benefit from regeneration funding. What they observed in the setting up and development of regeneration partnerships was the major partners securing resources to themselves, either for the purposes of partnership administration or, more significantly, for 'pet projects' that organisations could not fund in any other way. Changes to the management of regeneration programmes have perhaps made this less likely, but evidence of unequal distribution of benefits is apparent in other collaborations. For example, in one collaboration we studied recently we observed that it was much harder for voluntary and community sector partners to access funding to develop projects than it was for statutory sector players. Statutory bodies were allocated significant sums of money almost without question, while voluntary sector bodies had to make numerous applications and fulfil a variety of criteria before being able to access much smaller amounts.

The distribution of benefits therefore relates closely to fairness in procedure. Cropper emphasises that collaborations need to be able to agree ways of making decisions and working in collaboration that are acknowledged to be equitable by all partners. At one level Cropper suggests 'fairness in procedure' will help make clear who has access to information and who can influence decision-making. However, at another level he suggests that it can also help to facilitate changed expectations among partners about how open they can and should be with their partners about their imperative and objectives, so enabling them to better understand the potential of collaboration and the ways of behaving that will help realise this. This is exemplified in many partnerships, where a collaborative culture develops and participants talk about their particular way of doing things that has been engendered through the experience of working together. This phenomenon implies that partners understand the value of collaborating and have a shared understanding of how to facilitate collaborative relationships so as to achieve positive outcomes.

This discussion has demonstrated the significance of both individual and organisational capacity to the development of collaborative capacity. It has focused so far on those skills, attributes and components that need to be present if capacity for collaboration is to be built. However, despite the increasing incidence of collaboration in the field of public policy, the capacity of the various stakeholders to take joint action remains questionable rendering collaborative effort either consigned to the margins or destined to overreach itself (Benyon and Edwards, 1999; Hall *et al.*, 1996;

Hudson *et al.*, 1999). One of the reasons for this is the inability of collaborations to overcome the individual and organisational barriers that are placed in the way of building the requisite capacity for collaboration. These barriers are identified and discussed below.

Barriers to collaborative capacity

Barriers to building collaborative capacity are rooted in the practices and cultures of organisations and professional groups. These can prove to be insurmountable obstacles, suggesting that in some cases there is a limit to the contribution of collaboration in achieving public policy goals. They arise because organisations are structured and managed through overt formal rules and implicit informal norms of behaviour (Ostrom, 1986; March and Olsen, 1989; North, 1990). Very often these informal patterns of behaviour are so ingrained in the organisation that they are seldom recognised or even considered as potential obstacles to collaboration with others. However, the extent to which collaboration is possible will be influenced by the degree of commonality or complementarity of these rules and norms between partners. Organisational rules that may be problematic include the manner in which staff address each other (for example, by the use of first names or titles), dress codes and the protocols that govern decision-making. Norms that may be less immediately evident but are just as potent include expectations about membership of a trade union or professional association in a particular occupational area (McKeganey and Hunter, 1986).

Our analysis of a Sure Start partnership provides an example. Sure Start works through local partnerships which bring together childcare professionals and specialists from a range of public and voluntary sector bodies. In one Sure Start partnership, ground rules were agreed with ease, including the provision of adequate childcare at partnership meetings so that parents could attend. However, in practice the staff from the partner organisations found it difficult to work together because of differing approaches and norms. There were differences between the statutory and voluntary sector about how many staff needed to be present during a home visit to families receiving the service. Tensions emerged about the decision of when the home visits service should begin, with statutory bodies wanting to wait until a clear strategy for action had been agreed while voluntary sector representatives believed it was important to 'get out on the patch' and make contact with local people. The role of staff representatives on the partnership group was also disputed. Some professionals saw it as a way of liaising with the partnership body in order to match the actions of the programme to partnership objectives, while others saw it as having a semi-trade union function whereby staff interests and issues were represented at partnership and management meetings. The assumptions of commonality by the partners, based on the fact that all were childcare specialists, proved to be inadequate. There were very different rules and norms between the organisations and professional groups represented and imbalances of power, particularly between the statutory and voluntary sectors. These power relationships were based on differential assumptions of status, authority, expertise and legitimacy within the initiative. The combination of these factors effectively undermined the capacity of the collaboration to act.

Underlying different protocols and practices may be very different sets of values. One way of illustrating this is to consider the way in which citizens and communities are perceived by different stakeholders and the language that is used to describe them. Some professionals still consider their service users primarily as clients, with the balance of power in the relationship resting with the professional. This is particularly pronounced in services with significant regulatory powers, including trading standards, customs and excise, and the police, where service to the community often means the detention and punishment of particular individuals who have broken the law. For these professionals collaboration can represent a threat to existing power relationships. For others who eschew the 'professional' label, such as community development workers, services users can be the whole community. Here the targeting of 'clients' is avoided because of its potential to stigmatise and the service is operated on as universal a basis as possible. However, this can cut across programme objectives. Finally, collaboration may be perceived as a threat to the role of particular groups of staff if there is a re-branding of the service. In the Connexions service, for example, the ethos of working on a one-to-one basis with young people predominates. This reflects the careers service approach, rather than that of their partners in the youth service who tend to employ group-based interventions.

These different values bring professionals into conflict with each other and may limit the desirability or possibility of collaboration regardless of central government edict (Barton and Quinn, 2001). On occasion such value differences will also exist within as well as between organisations, providing significant difficulty for collaborative effort. For example, the Crime and Disorder Act 1998 created 'anti-social behaviour orders' (ASBOs), a tool for excluding certain individuals from particular areas, for example shopping centres or housing estates. Among police and local authority housing professionals ASBOs represent a significant instrument for reducing the fear of crime experienced by people in particular neighbourhoods. However, among youth and community workers, also employed by the local authority, ASBOs represent a challenge to individual liberty and human rights. In some local authorities failure to agree on the values underpinning community safety work has meant that it has not been possible to establish an approach to the employment of ASBOs within the locality.

If partners are not able or are not prepared to devote sufficient resource to making the collaboration work, then insufficient collaborative capacity will be built. A common complaint amongst partners in collaboration is that their respective contributions are not equitable and invariably partners feel that while they devote sufficient resource others lag behind (Sullivan, Barnes and Matka, 2000). Often this stems from a lack of appreciation of the different kinds of resources partners from different sectors bring and an assumption that those with the most financial or political resources will exercise the greatest influence in the partnership. So for voluntary and community sectors it is their expertise and legitimacy with communities that may need to be set against the physical or monetary resource that other partners can supply. In recognition of the different tensions and challenges that exist in building capacity for collaboration, recent initiatives have sought to develop particular strategies to attempts to maximise the components of collaborative capacity and overcome existing barriers.

Realising collaborative capacity

Building capacity is necessary at different levels of collaboration and realising it at each level requires the employment of particular processes or activities. It is possible to discern five levels at which collaborative capacity is necessary:

1. Strategic capacity – to develop and define the collaborative vision and key themes;
2. Governance capacity – accountability upwards to any superordinate body and outwards to partners and communities;
3. Operational capacity – the organisational structures and processes to deliver new activities;
4. Practice capacity – the exercise of specific skills and abilities among workers;
5. Community and citizen capacity – the cultural, material and personal resources to take part in change processes (Barnes and Sullivan, forthcoming).

Linked to these levels are a number of processes and activities to promote or deliver collaboration. At strategic level partnership bodies that bring together the key partners are common. However, a number of organisational arrangements are possible:

- Partnership Board with wide-ranging membership. A single board comprising all key partners to the initiative, including voluntary and community sectors, with decision-making power and responsibility for initiative oversight.
- Steering Group/Executive split. The two bodies exist in parallel. The steering group comprises wider representation and is concerned with strategic direction while the executive focuses on operational activity. These bodies can either be composed entirely of officers or a mixture of officers and elected members, non-executive directors and chairs of partner bodies.
- Stakeholder groups with joint management team. Deliberation and discussion about the initiative is conducted in the stakeholder groups, which may be locally focused and/or organised to represent particular user interests. Delivery and accountability for the initiative is contained within an officer joint management team.

Experience suggests that some key partners are either poorly represented or not represented at all at this strategic level, including communities, user group and voluntary sector representatives. Therefore each of these options may be augmented by linkage to a community/voluntary sector forum for the purposes of consultation and/or to a wider strategic partnership charged with oversight of well-being in the area as a whole.

At the governance level, partnerships have developed systems for joint performance management and accountability. For the most part these continue to exist in tension with other organisationally specific performance mechanisms and collaborative assessment measures that require achievements to be traced back to a particular funding stream, although in reality outputs and outcomes are often the result of the interaction of a variety of initiatives (Chapter 10). Partnerships have not been particularly successful at accountability downwards to communities (see Chapter 8). However, attention is increasingly being paid to the ways in which partnerships communicate what they do to the communities they are intending to benefit, for instance through newsletters, open days and use of local radio. What is also important is that collaborations have the capacity to communicate and interact with those middle managers and front-line workers in the partner organisations whose activities may be influenced by the collaboration. Without any sense of connection back into the mainstream, those actively involved in delivering new initiatives will feel marginalised and those in the mainstream will begin to question the value and contribution of the collaboration.

Below the strategic level a variety of arrangements pertain. Most collaborations have some form of organisational support, for example a co-ordinator and key staff to resource the work of the collaboration. At an operational and practice level there are a variety of processes used to alter the way in which mainstream organisations plan and deliver services, including:

- Pooled budgets;
- Joint planning and commissioning of services;
- Integrated delivery;
- Sharing information across relevant partners organizations;
- Formal agreements between organisations such as contracts to deliver services;
- Informal agreements between organisations where people simply agree to take on new tasks or do things in a different way to test out what impact these new ways of doing things have;
- Secondments of staff either to new organisations formed through collaboration or to existing partners organisations in order to gain experience of 'what it looks like from the other side'.

The forms of working with communities are equally varied and are predicated upon the definitions of 'community' and 'users' applied in the individual collaborations. Chapter 9 provides a detailed discussion of community involvement in collaboration. Here we summarise the kinds of processes and activities which help build collaborative capacity with communities:

- Bespoke community programmes that attempt to build community involvement into the work of the collaboration through a range of engagement, involvement and capacity-building activities.
- Community development funding that focuses exclusively on building capacity within particular communities of geography, interest or identity targeted by the initiative.
- Public information strategies that inform and educate the whole population.

The degree of collaborative capacity necessary will depend upon the purposes that are intended. An analysis of the 26 local HAZ Implementation Plans reveals a number of common partnership purposes associated both with process and outcomes. These are:

- Achieving health improvements and reductions in health inequalities;
- The joint provision of improved services;

- Systems of governance that are efficient and accountable;
- More successful and embedded cross-agency and cross-sector working (Barnes and Sullivan, forthcoming).

The outcomes that are sought pertain to the creation and release of synergy through collaborative action and the transformation of the 'whole system' of the health economy. Most HAZs find it difficult to describe what the release of synergy will amount to, although at the very least it represents a maximisation of the application of available resources. There is rather more detail available about system transformation with HAZs commonly emphasising the creation of more responsive and flexible delivery of health services, characterised by greater interaction between health and social care professionals, enhanced influence for users and communities and delivery of shared outcomes. As such the transformative aspirations require more than simply a commitment to partnership working. Instead partnership is associated with other characteristics which denote the emergence of a new working environment. A vision of this new environment is set out clearly in the Tyne and Wear HAZ Implementation Plan:

> Our HAZ vision is of all the separate parts of the system achieving a shared and common purpose, converting the current partial networks and partnerships into a self-organising and sustaining system. The governance of this will be rooted in creating conditions in which accountability is not simply to a superior, professional group or organisation, but for contribution to the achievement of health improvement. Accountability for shared purpose cannot be imposed. The system of governance is about new and diverse ways of working together, more than new structure. This form of governance assumes a whole system will only work with clear principles of behaviour, not by controls alone. (Tyne and Wear HAZ, 1997, p. 1)

The extent of ambition of the collaborators will influence the kind of strategies that they develop in order to achieve their outcomes. These strategies will also help to frame the expectations of the collaboration in relation to its collaborative capacity. So for example, the Tyne and Wear HAZ described above is an ambitious strategy which clearly identifies system transformation as essential. As part of this system transformation collaborative principles and practices will become embedded throughout the component parts of the system. Other strategies are less ambitious, with consequent implications for collaborative capacity. For example, many regeneration schemes focused on change within targeted areas. For these, mainstream change would emerge as a result of the development of innovative practices and new ways of working within the collaboration. In such cases collaborative capacity of the whole would only increase if successful ways of doing things were adopted by the mainstream.

Conclusion

This chapter has demonstrated the significance of building collaborative capacity for the development of successful partnerships. It has isolated key components at individual and organisational level and indicated how their development may be hindered by powerful obstacles. It has also drawn on recent research to highlight the ways in which collaborative capacity may be built between partners. However, it is important to recognise that each collaboration is set in its own local context, and will be subject to particular influences as a result. This 'locality effect', introduced in Chapter 4, consists of those unique factors that together characterise the operating culture of a locality. Initial research on this issue has identified a number of factors relevant to the definition of the locality effect:

- Geography – the spatial characteristics of the area, for example the degree and pattern of urbanisation;
- Population – the demographic, socio-economic and ethnic profile of the area;
- Organisational boundaries – the relationship between agencies' operating areas and domains;
- Political culture and relationships – institutionalised norms of decision-making and involvement;
- History of partnership working in the locality (Barnes, Sullivan and Matka, 2001).

These powerful local influences contribute to a shared understanding of 'the way things are done around here' which conditions the approaches and behaviours of local politicians, professionals and communities. It generates a logic of appropriateness in terms of behaviours and processes which are communicated to incomers (see Chapter 3). In this environment, central government's attempts to impose new ways of working such as collaboration may either be welcomed as 'going with the grain' of local action or resisted as an attempt to interfere with established norms. The interaction of these factors means that collaborations will not develop uniformly within localities, even when their parameters are closely defined by central government.

Box 6.2 *Individual roles in a collaboration*

Network enthusiasts – are motivated by the potential for collaboration to open up local governance and cut through bureaucratic systems and constraints

Network activists – see collaboration as a means of defining and managing the delivery of strategic goals

Network pragmatists – view collaboration as necessary to gain access to resources in order to deliver the goals of a particular organisation

Network opponents – regard collaboration as intrusive central direction and an attack on local democracy

Source: Adapted from Skelcher *et al.* (1996, p. 35).

Instead emergent collaborations will be shaped by the interaction of the forces described above (Clegg, 1990; North, 1990). This in turn will dictate the collaborative capacity needs of the emergent relationships and at the same time frame partners' potential to fulfil these needs.

Logics of appropriateness are themselves not singular and uniform. There may be a number of different logics that exist within a locality, reflective of the variety of organisational environments that are present. This helps to explain the way in which 'the way things are done around here' can vary within localities as well as between them. Therefore a prevailing locality effect may coexist with other logics of appropriateness that are particular to certain professional cultures or sectors. Logics of appropriateness can change over time. However, the process of change can result in the coexistence of 'old' and 'new' ways of doing things (Lowndes, 1997; Newman *et al.*, 2000). This helps to explain why partner organisations contain within them people who are stimulated and enthused by collaboration and eager to develop new ways of working as well as people who are concerned that traditional values and ways of doing things are not lost and that new methods are not adopted uncritically (Box 6.2). Collaborations, therefore, are dynamic phenomena and in the next chapter we turn our attention to understanding these processes of change and transformation.

7 The Dynamics of Collaboration

Collaborations are rarely static. Changes in membership, domain, resources and commitments shape and influence their agendas and activities. As collaborative capacity develops, so new possibilities will become apparent (Chapter 6). Sometimes change is intended from the start. A number of time-limited partnerships are found amongst the area-based initiatives stimulated by the UK government. These are created to undertake a particular task and close once their period of operation is complete. A similar dynamic is evident in the case of international relief operations. Here, NGOs and donor governments may establish partnerships with global and local agencies to co-ordinate the provision of emergency supplies and expertise. This temporary structure becomes more limited in its role or dissolves once the crisis is passed or no longer has political priority. Other collaborations are more stable. Those that are constituted as corporate bodies such as companies or joint boards (Chapter 8) will develop bureaucratic needs for order and stability to enable them to function. Such imperatives may arise as much from their own internal needs as the demands of partners for formal accountability in relation to expenditure and performance. Consequently the routines and arrangements of a newly-created partnership become embedded in procedures, organisational structures and role designations.

These dynamic aspects of collaborative relationships are significant but little discussed in the academic literature. Ring and Van de Ven, writing some years ago, comment:

> Relatively little scholarly attention has been devoted to studying developmental processes of IORs (inter-organisational relations). Instead most of the research to date has been focused either on the antecedent conditions or the structural properties of inter-organisational relationships in comparison with other governance forms. (1994, p. 91)

This view still holds. The predominant literature on public policy collaboration and partnerships engages to only a limited extent with temporal aspects of change. The same gap is found in the organisational sociology and management studies literatures. This chapter begins to redress the balance by examining the dynamics of collaboration. Initially we set out different ways of conceptualising change processes that are relevant to an analysis of collaboration. We then employ a life-cycle model to explore the motivation for change. This draws on theories discussed in Chapter 3 and case study evidence in order to develop structural and social process explanations of the change dynamic. The chapter gives particular attention to the process of collaborative closure, a question which is little considered in the literature but is of considerable relevance in an era of time-limited partnerships and governmental restructuring.

Paradigms of collaborative dynamics

There are a number of different ways of conceptualising the dynamic that drives change in collaborations (Van de Ven, 1992). These include the life-cycle of birth, growth, maturation and death, the impact of resource dependencies on the external environment and the operation of social process which are generated around a collaborative activity.

Life-cycle paradigm

Life-cycle paradigms view the development of collaboration as a series of sequential stages, typically ordered in the following way:

1. Pre-conception – where the various parties become aware of the advantages of or requirement for co-operation;
2. Initiation – in which discussions and negotiations build a commitment for co-operative activity;
3. Formalisation – where a governance structure is agreed and the collaboration establishes an identity;
4. Operation – the undertaking of whatever activities are within the remit of the collaborative venture;
5. Termination – the closure, transfer or transformation of the collaboration.

This approach has an intuitive and logical appeal as a way of making sense of a potentially messy process and predicting how it will unfold. It provides a basis for generating research questions about, for example, the way in which transition from one stage to another is undertaken. For policy-makers and practitioners it enables the identification of managerial tasks associated with each phase, and hence the development of good practice guides and performance frameworks. However, the *a priori* assumption of a life-cycle may not hold in all cases. There may be partnership failure at an early stage, or transformation into a new collaboration mid-stage. The superficially attractive explanatory power of a sequential dynamic needs to be tested against other theoretical frameworks.

Resource dependency paradigm

Collaborative activity, when viewed from a resource dependency perspective, becomes the locus of powerful external forces which shape and reshape the venture over time. These tensions may be inherent in the governance structure. For example, the pattern of resource dependency in traditional local authority–voluntary sector collaborations favoured the statutory partner because of their greater access to financial and other resources. The rules of the game in such partnerships changed to some extent as a result of new patterns of public–voluntary sector relationships (Chapter 4). Additionally, the voluntary sector's greater ease of access into disadvantaged communities provided them with a reputational resource which offered the potential to reshape the power balance in the partnership. The dialectical paradigm therefore offers rich ground for researchers to develop explanations of change in collaborative activity. There are clear links with resource-dependency theory and structural theories of societal power (Chapter 3) from which propositions can be derived and tested.

Social process paradigm

A third theoretical insight into collaborative dynamics comes from the observation that such activities are the focus of micro-level social interactions which operate in and around the broader resource dependencies. Ring and Van de Ven discuss this in the context of collaborative business ventures:

> As agents for their firms, managers need to know more than the input conditions, investments and types of governance structures required for the relationship ... The ways in which agents negotiate, execute, and modify the terms of an interorganisational relationship strongly influence

the degree to which parties judge it to be equitable and efficient. These processes also influence motivations to continue, or terminate, the relationship over time. (1994, p. 91)

The social process paradigm therefore engages with both structure and actor variables, and presents a view of collaborations as 'socially contrived mechanisms for collective action, which are continually shaped and restructured by actions and symbolic interpretations of the parties involved' (*ibid.*, p. 96). The collaboration emerges and is sustained and changes through the round of negotiation about motivations, expectations and governance, which generate commitments to work together at legal and psychological (that is, trust) levels and result in executions of those commitments by agents. The whole is mediated by continual or episodic assessments based on judgements about the value of the particular collaborative activity compared with other options (Figure 7.1). From this perspective it is the social process that provides the dynamic to breathe life into the collaboration. It is this process, rather than any temporal unfolding, that comes to the foreground of our interest. It places attention on the interpersonal and political

Figure 7.1 *Social process framework for understanding collaborative dynamics*

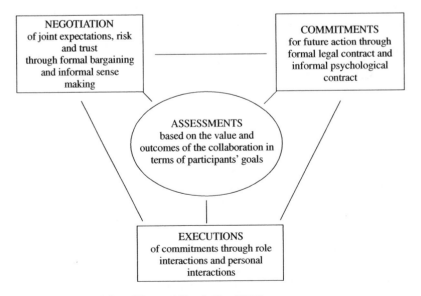

Source: Adapted from Ring and Van de Ven (1994).

skills individual participants bring to the collaboration and the way in which these are deployed at particular moments, and therefore relates back to considerations of collaborative capacity (Chapter 6).

The motivation of change

The three paradigms presented above highlight different determinants of collaborative dynamics. However, it is important to identify how these factors impact over time if we are to explain the realities of change in collaborations. We explore this question by drawing on one of the few longitudinal studies of public policy collaboration (Lowndes and Skelcher, 1998; Skelcher *et al.*, 1996). The research tracked the dynamics of various time-limited partnerships in three localities, enabling the construction of an empirically-derived life-cycle model (Table 7.1). This drew causal connections between the stage of the life-cycle, the mode of governance in the partnership and the relationships between stakeholders. The concept of a mode of governance refers back to the work of Williamson (1985), Powell (1991), Ouchi (1991) and others who distinguish between market, hierarchy and network forms of regulation (although different terms may be employed by particular authors). The relationship between stakeholders refers back to the social process paradigm discussed above. Essentially, the argument in the Lowndes, Skelcher *et al.* work is that the stage in the life-cycle determines the mode of governance which in turn affects relationships between stakeholders. Lowndes and Skelcher describe the life-cycle process like this:

> *Pre-partnership collaboration* is characterised by a network mode of governance based upon informality, trust and a sense of common purpose. *Partnership creation and consolidation* is characterised by hierarchy based upon an assertion of status and authority differentials and the formalisation of procedures. *Partnership programme delivery* is characterised by market (or quasi-market) mechanisms of tendering and contract, with low levels of co-operation between providers. *Partnership termination or succession* is characterised by a re-assertion of a network governance mode as a means to maintain agency commitment, community involvement and staff employment. (1998, p. 321)

What remains largely implicit at a theoretical level in this work is the way in which resource dependencies generated by external funding agencies

Table 7.1 *A partnership life cycle model*

Stage in the life-cycle	Mode of governance	Relationship between stakeholders
Pre-partnership collaboration	Networking between individuals/organisations	Informality, trust and co-operation. Willingness to work together to achieve collective purpose. Differential resources result in emergence of inner and outer networks, with some actors becoming marginalised
Partnership creation and consolidation	Hierarchy incorporating some organisations. Formalisation of authority in partnership board and associated staff	Negotiation and contest over definition of membership and allocation of board seats. Disruption of network as informal balance of power codified. Informal systems and agreements are replaced by hierarchical structure with formalised procedures and decisions
Partnership programme delivery	Market mechanisms of tendering and contractual agreements. Regulation and supervision of contractors. Networking assists in production of bids and management of expenditure programme	Low co-operation between providers. Purchasers' suspicion of over-selling by potential providers. Distinction between inner and outer network sharpens as partnership determines agreed bids and/or fund allocation. Reliance on informal agreements within network to negotiate complexities of contracts. Emergence of trust-based contracting with some organisations.
Partnership termination and succession	Networking between individuals/organisations as means to maintain agency commitment, community involvement and staff employment.	Uncertainty as network stability afforded by partnership comes to an end. Potential for new openness/expansion of links. Trust and informality, with negotiation and contest concerning strategic role of partnership.

Source: Lowndes and Skelcher (1998, p. 321).

provide the motive force driving the life-cycle. Gaining access to resources in turn changes the nature of the mode of governance and stakeholder relationships, as each attempts to bargain into a share of the benefits. We now examine each of the four stages of this life-cycle model, and in the process draw attention to the resource dependency and social process explanations that illuminate the dynamic of the collaboration.

Pre-partnership collaboration

The period of pre-partnership collaborative activity is one in which ideal-type network relationships tend to predominate. The Lowndes, Skelcher *et al.* study found that interactions between potential partners were characterised by informality and weight was placed on the quality of personal relationships. A civil servant from one of the Government Offices of the Regions expressed the way in which social process factors were significant in generating trust and building an infrastructure for later more formalised collaborative activity:

> I have meetings with X on bridges and pavements in the city – he says what the council can do and I say what we can do, then we put it together. Individuals not institutions is what it's all about – individuals can work together and understand what it's all about. (Lowndes and Skelcher, 1998, p. 322)

However, structural factors were also important in providing a context for this individualised exchange relationship. One interviewee observed that where there was little trust between agencies because of conflicts over domains or other resources, only chief executives or senior officers (who the respondent termed 'the heavies') attended inter-agency meetings. When there was greater trust, a wider group of individuals tended to be involved, allowing for a greater variety of inputs, a more efficient use of resources and a broader sense of ownership.

Nevertheless, the propensity to informality, personal relationships and trust in pre-partnership collaboration was regarded negatively by some participants in these embryonic partnerships. Network-style relationships were viewed by those who felt excluded or marginalised as 'cosy', 'cliquey' or 'sewn-up'. The reliance on social contact, friendship and personal trust made it hard for new actors to break in to networks. Information channels were perceived as predetermined with little consideration for new groups, those outside established relationships (who in the Lowndes, Skelcher *et al.* study tended to be women's and minority ethnic groups), or for small or poorly resourced organisations with little opportunity to play the game of networking. A worker in a small Asian women's advice centre commented on the issues involved:

> Whether we get the information or not ... whether it comes in time, seems to be a matter of chance ... You have to be seen around, otherwise you miss out on what's going to happen. (Lowndes and Skelcher, 1998, p. 322)

The research points to the value of brokerage and facilitation both to stimulate pre-partnership collaboration and to reduce some of the misunderstandings and inequities inherent in networks which develop organically. A former city action team project officer described her experience thus:

> We acted like a kind of dating agency – bringing people together. We helped form partnerships that wouldn't necessarily have come together unless someone pushed them together. We took the bottle to the party! We had a Heineken budget – it refreshed the parts other budgets didn't reach! The main outcome for us was not what the partnership produced, but getting it started. (Lowndes and Skelcher, 1998, p. 323)

This discussion links closely with questions of leadership in collaborations (Chapters 6, 9 and 11). The very act of establishing collaborative activity is a consequence of leadership. In some cases it will be about individuals seeing an opportunity that exists and building a network to exploit its potential. Elsewhere it will involve responding to changes in resource dependencies, for example the requirement to create a mandated partnership. Leadership in this context therefore may come as much from personal authority as any formal position in a bureaucratic structure. Evidence of this is provided from research into urban regeneration, where diaries kept by key actors in local networks illustrated the way in which there was a constant search to move an inter-agency agenda forward (Table 7.2).

However, the few studies of the role of leadership in public policy partnerships reveal that this is not an unproblematic issue. Drawing on research in the US, Gray (1996) identifies differences in both the formal authority of the leaders of collaborations and the strategies that they use. She notes, for example, that one partnership was led by a city manager who was able to employ his formal executive authority (and presumably his nodal position in local community networks) to establish a collaboration. In contrast, others were led by individuals who lacked formal positions of authority but had persuasive abilities and a knowledge of the issues. This enabled them to draw participants together and establish a

Table 7.2 *Networking activity by a voluntary sector worker*

Date	Contact with?	How?	Who initiated?	Comments by respondent
Sat	Regional arts/education forum members	Meeting	Forum steering group	Positive. This voluntary group has sprung up in response to the slow death of local education authorities
Mon	Officer in Economic Development Unit, Local Authority	Letter	Me	To update information submitted for the City Challenge bid. Our proposals have been accepted
Tues	Two training managers in Training and Enterprise Council	Meeting	Me	Difficult meeting to negotiate year 2 of funding for training scheme
Weds	Officer in Economic Development Unit, Local Authority	Phone	Me	Contact re. continuation funding for a scheme. No information from them. This is making planning difficult as the official start date is in three weeks
Weds	Project officer in funding body at regional level	Phone	The funding body	Re. funding for next year – told we were being given a standstill allocation and that we should be grateful
Weds	Officer in Environment Department, Local Authority	Phone	Me	Initiated a discussion about funding for next year. They said apply. Positive!

Day	Role	Method	Actor	Comment
Thurs	Officer in Compact – a local education/business partnership	Meeting followed up with phone conversation	Me	Not good news. They have supported us for the past four years and for next year is talking cuts. We await further news before making an application
Thurs	Chair of Leisure Committee, Local Authority	Meeting	The councillor	Called off. Although rearranged, this was a missed opportunity to discuss many mutual issues
Thurs	Regional arts/education forum co-ordinator	Phone	The forum	Exchanged information. An informal supportive network is emerging!
Fri	Local arts forum co-ordinator	Meeting	Me	Positive. This is a voluntary organisation that grew out of work we undertook for City Challenge. It will support the delivery of plans that will also assist us
Fri	Local education project worker	Phone	The project	Very positive. They would like us to deliver aspects of their programme. Paid work for next year!

Source: Skelcher *et al.* (1996, p. 10).

common programme. In the latter case, 'the convenor must have high credibility in order to convince others that the collaborative initiative has some
value for them and that they should join' (Gray, 1996, p. 75). Purdue *et al.*,
in their study of community leaders in regeneration partnerships, comment
on the connection between the propensity to leadership activity and the
governance structure of the collaboration:

> The contract compliance culture of SRB and other regeneration funding
> regimes does not actively encourage dynamic, innovative leaders to get
> involved in partnerships. Participation in partnerships is particularly
> attractive to individuals who are adept at reading account sheets and
> wading through documents. Their time and services are encouraged by
> the bureaucratic procedures and funding element of SRB. It does not
> follow that they will have good leadership skills. (2000, p. 44)

One of the themes that this discussion highlights is the significance of the
membership of a collaboration on its policies, ways of working and governance. At a finer grain of analysis, partners may change the individuals who
attend board or other meetings on their behalf. These individuals may arrive
with a different perception of their role, of the purpose of the collaboration,
or with other experience and contacts and as a result impact on the activity.
As Huxham and Vangen comment: 'There is thus a cyclical relationship
between the nature of the participating organisations and the focus of collaboration, with the participants defining the focus and the focus defining new
participants' (2000c, p. 793). Huxham terms this 'domain shift'. Change at
the organisational and individual levels therefore sets a context within which
leadership of the overall co-operative venture can be exercised.

Partnership creation and consolidation

Lowndes, Skelcher *et al.* observe a clear trend towards formalisation as
pre-partnership collaboration within a network of actors gives way to a
hierarchical and bureaucratised structure. The hierarchical form of governance that emerges – with defined roles, responsibilities and reporting
lines – increases transparency, provides clearer accountability and establishes a means of managing the tasks necessary to bid for resources and
deliver programmes. This mode of governance constitutes the agreement
between partners about the form of the collaboration and the way in which
it will make decisions and be accountable. However, its definition generates a tension with the network mode of governance that underlay the

initial emergence of the collaboration. This tension is experienced particularly by voluntary and community sector bodies who tended to work in less formalised ways than either statutory partners or external funders. The chair of a residents' group who was a member of a regeneration partnership board commented:

> In all the work I've been involved in, it's always us that have had to put the effort in to reach the council's level. We've always had to come up to their level. They've never come down to ours! (Lowndes and Skelcher, 1998, p. 325)

The difference in ways of working was also reflected by the project officer in a small voluntary organisation serving the Afro-Caribbean community:

> I think it's a fallacy that the Black networks are not necessarily there – I think that they're very much there but they quite possibly operate on a different basis. And if they don't conform to the local authority or the City Challenge view then they are not going to see them and they are going to lose out on that potential to support regeneration. (*ibid.*)

Some partnerships resolve this tension by maintaining network-style relationships alongside more formal ways of working and by adopting relatively informal approaches to meetings and decision-making. As a local authority manager commented:

> Informal relationships are important – not necessarily detrimental. They can work better than overarching formal partnerships. It doesn't necessarily mean that if you have a piece of paper that says you're a partnership then you are. You've got to get on with the reality of partnership. In a rapidly changing world, if you get too wrapped up in procedure, you can never change anything. (*ibid.*, p. 324)

Resource dependencies generated by external agencies therefore impact on the mode of governance and social processes within the collaboration. Formalisation is required to assure external agencies of the legitimacy and management credibility of the collaboration in order to maximise success in bidding for funds. It is accentuated by the financial and performance accountability requirements imposed by funders.

The political economy perspective developed by Benson (1975) addresses this point by arguing that change in external resource dependencies affect the pattern of relationships in the collaboration (Chapter 3). Benson proposes four strategies that may be used to achieve this realignment. The first is an *authoritative* strategy in which one actor – who may not even be a formal part of a collaboration – is able to realign network relations by *fiat*. This can involve, for example, the specification of the governance structure for the partnership, priorities and targets, approval procedures and resource allocations. Such mandated inter-organisational relations bind the partners to fulfil certain legal or contractual obligations (Raelin, 1980). This is one limiting case; the other is the *co-operative* strategy. Here change is arrived at through negotiation, compromise and mutual agreement. *Disruptive* strategies occur when the authority and resources of a participant are threatened, hence disturbing the inter-organisational equilibrium. Examples of disruptive strategies include:

1. Domain violation – where the legitimate area of activity of the target agency is invaded by another;
2. Fund diversion – in which funds that might otherwise have gone to the target agency are diverted to another actor in the network,
3. Programme circumvention – where new activities interfere with the target agency's programme effectiveness, thus undermining its status.

Manipulative strategies involve the purposeful alteration of environmental factors in order to realign actors' priorities and behaviours. An example would be the introduction of SRB, which amalgamated a number of separate specific grants and introduced particular criteria in order to submit bids. This generated considerable change in the pattern and nature of collaboration in localities. This formulation helps to explain the way in which the dynamic of a collaboration may be driven by powerful external actors.

Partnership programme delivery

Terms like partnership and network imply consensus and collaboration, yet the research by Lowndes, Skelcher *et al.* underlines the high degree of competition that can occur in inter-agency working. The bidding processes for publicly-funded projects generate competition between partnerships and potentially between the members of a single partnership. There is also a potential for competition for status between agencies as each needs to demonstrate its performance and achievement to current or potential funders. The research demonstrates that network-style relationships associated with partnership are threatened by the imperative to compete. Each agency has to judge whether those bodies they work with are best regarded as a potential competitor or a potential partner. Such judgements are particularly important for smaller agencies and voluntary or community bodies whose survival may literally depend upon gaining access to a winning partnership. Despite the official insistence on community involvement in partnership bids, the competition inherent in some processes has often excluded voluntary and community organisations. An officer from one of the Government Offices of the Regions explained it in this way:

> Unless you're cute and big, the voluntary sector could get squeezed out. Small and specialised voluntary organisations haven't got the clout or understanding or strategic overview required by the... process. These organisations are valuable because they bring enormous energy and commitment, but... you need political clout and strategic nouse to get into partnerships. (Lowndes and Skelcher, 1998, p. 327)

Once established and in receipt of grant funding, partnerships face the challenge of distributing funds for programme implementation. It is at this stage that competitive pressures are manifest as market-style relationships based upon tendering and contractual agreements. Agencies manoeuvre to assert 'ownership' of projects within the partnership's programme. The allocation of funds for programme implementation sharpens the distinction between an inner and an outer network. Consequently tensions between market and network modes of operation become exposed, and particularly the potential for market-style relationships to undermine or impede the development of trust, mutuality and co-operation between partners.

Partnership termination and succession

Collaborative activities end for a variety of reasons. In some cases closure at a particular date may be built into the initial agreement. Employment Zones and SRB are both time-limited initiatives with funding only available for a specified period. However, agencies may wish to maintain the organisational structure of the partnership after this point and seek new sources of funding to continue existing projects or establish new ones. Equally the structure may be reconstituted in a new form, perhaps with changes in the constituent bodies. The question of collaborative closure is one in which there is little theorising or empirical research. The emphasis in academic research and management guidance is biased towards partnership creation; the more difficult problem of collaborative closure often goes unremarked. Yet the growth in the use of public policy partnerships, many of which are time-limited, will undoubtedly make this a significant issue in the future. For this reason we consider the question in some depth. Sullivan and Lowndes (1996) examined exit and succession strategies for time-limited partnerships and identified that powerful social processes were at work. They found three main stances on the part of participants in partnerships. The first was to 'keep the partnership going'. Those who wished to keep a formal partnership in place after funding ceased were driven by a belief either that valuable relationships had been built and should be maintained or that specific outputs from the partnership needed managing and developing into the future or that the locality continued to have pressing social and economic needs which a continued partnership could help promote. The second response was to 'let it die peacefully'. Here actors were happy to see the partnership terminated, stressing the futility of trying to keep a structure and a programme going without a dedicated budget. They also suggested that being prepared to close was a mark of the partnership's success: the goal was to build capacity in the local community and not to perpetuate dependency on the benevolence of an official body. Despite capacity-building activities, a sense of network fatigue was obvious in partnerships coming to the end of a significant programme of work. The final approach was the more pragmatic one of 'support what lasts'. This view represented something of a middle way. It proposed seeking support from the mainstream budgets of local agencies to enable specific projects arising from the collaboration to be sustained.

The parties to a partnership that is not time-limited may decide to cease the collaboration for a number of reasons. In Chapter 6 we discussed the endogenous and exogenous motivations for partnership formation. Endogenous factors included the achievement of a shared vision, adaptation and response to new environments and the maintenance or enhancement of position in a context of resource dependency. Exogenous factors included financial inducements offered by an agency and the normative value accorded to public sector bodies who actively engage in joining up with others (Newman *et al.*, 2000). Success in moving towards these goals builds commitment to continue; conversely failure to progress casts doubt on the partnership's value. However, we might expect the decision voluntarily to cease a collaboration to be mediated by individual and structural factors, which we discuss below.

Individual factors in collaborative closure

Although the academic study of individuals working in collaboration is relatively limited – and focused principally on boundary-spanning roles – it might be expected that the features of a partnership would engender a high level of commitment amongst staff. These features include newness, small size, innovative orientation, often a focus on delivery (and to a well-defined and relatively small community) and distinctive public profile. Dunleavy (1991, p. 200), in his work on bureau-shaping, argues that officials want to work 'in small, elite, collegiate bureaux close to political power centres' rather than large routinised bureaucracies. Newman (2001, p. 122) offers a more measured analysis. She observes the contradictions for public officials involved in partnerships:

> On the one hand many [managers] are cynical about the repeated emphasis on partnership, impatient about the amount of time wasted on often fruitless meetings, and doubtful about the benefits. On the other hand, there has been a willingness to engage with the focus on innovation and to enjoy the new freedoms involved in some forms of partnership activity.

Nevertheless the normative context places a value on those working in a joined-up way. In some sense they are the pioneers, and from this often intense collaborative activity a strong social bond can result. This should not be underestimated as a force for partnership preservation. 'There are powerful social-psychological motivations for preserving relationships' observe Ring and van de Ven (1994, p. 106) 'that entail ... not only economic and technological resources of participating firms, but also the social commitments and entanglements of individual agents'. In other words, individual actors within the partnership provide a force for maintenance in the face of equivocation or a propensity to closure on the part of the partners. However, over time individuals working in partnerships experience creeping bureaucratisation and the undesirable practices identified by Newman. Excessive contractual legality in market modes of governance, over-detailed monitoring of the relationship between the parties, role conflicts, violation of trust and an escalation of commitments in the context of resource decline can all contribute to a de-motivation of actors and their compliance with – or even willing encouragement of – collaborative closure.

Structural factors in collaborative closure

Such individual-level explanations for collaborative closure need to be supplemented by an analysis of structural factors. Here we concentrate on the extent to which a partner considers themselves locked-in to a collaboration. Being locked-in is a function of the dependency between partners and the level of asset specificity in the activity (Ariño, 1997), and we consider each aspect in turn. Dependency is the first issue. Emerson (1962) argues that the level of dependency of an actor A is directly proportional to A's motivational investment in the goals that B will assist in delivering and inversely proportional to the availability of those goals from relationships with other actors (Chapter 3). For example, in the early rounds of the SRB process local authorities had to identify a voluntary sector partner in order to submit a bid. From Emerson's perspective, the local authority (A) was therefore dependent on the voluntary sector agency (B), since without their co-operation a bid would not meet the necessary criteria to gain access to resources. This is a description of the relationship that few in the voluntary sector would recognise. Indeed, various evaluations of the partnership process in these early SRB rounds identified the marginal involvement of the voluntary sector (Mawson *et al.*, 1995). In reality, they were often partners in name only. The tradition of voluntary sector dependency on local authorities for funding, combined with the limited resource they could devote to partnership working, enabled local councils to dominate the relationship even though they were – according to Emerson's formulation – the dependent party. Clearly this theoretical formulation does not reflect reality sufficiently well in other than simple and bounded bilateral relationships. However, before discussing this in more detail, it is important to look at the other contributor to lock-in – namely asset specificity.

Asset specificity concerns the extent to which investment by one or more partners in facilities, resources or equipment may be redeployed to other productive uses. This investment can include tangible assets such as buildings and service-delivery and office technology, for example computers and vehicles. Some of these resources may reasonably be expected to be capable of redeployment to alternative use at the end of the partnership, and thus have low asset specificity. However, there will also be an investment in reputational resources especially where the partnership is high-profile and complex, for example the Millennium Dome or the public–private partnership to renew the London Underground railway system. In both cases there was substantial political commitment to the partnership by individual government Ministers in the face of sustained opposition. Investment in reputational resource should be treated as a sunk cost which it will be difficult if not impossible to redeploy to other uses, unless the partnership proves a significant early success and politicians and other actors can claim credit and kudos. Consequently an organisation's voluntary withdrawal from a partnership is likely to reduce its political assets since it indicates that the wrong decision was made in the first place. The calculus of asset specificity, therefore, leads to a judgement by each partner on the extent to which they are locked-in to the venture and the likely financial and political costs of withdrawal. Because investment is likely to increase as the partnership develops, asset specificity may be expected to become a more significant factor over time.

These two theoretical approaches enable us to formulate a proposition that the greater the level of dependency of A on B and the higher the level of asset specificity, the more A is locked in to the relationship and hence the less willing A will be to terminate it. Conversely, the greater will be the opportunity open to B to engage in opportunistic behaviour to exploit A's dependency. This, of course, makes three assumptions. The first is that B will act in an amoral and individually rational, utility-maximising way rather than considering some wider conception of goodness, for example the benefits deriving to the community served by the partnership. The second assumption is that the relationship between A and B is either unitary, in other words that they do not have any other relationships, or that there are other relationships but that in these A remains the dependent partner. If this latter condition of universal dependence by A on B does not hold, it opens up the prospect of bargaining and trade-offs across the relationships. The third assumption is that B's approach to A's dependency is not moderated by pre-existing relationships between the parties (for example, voluntary sector dependency on local government funding pre-SRB, as noted above). If this assumption does not hold and there is already an institutionalised dependency of B on A, then it opens up the prospect that in the new partnership B will continue to act subjectively as if it were still dependent despite its objective status having changed.

Conclusion

Change is the condition of co-operative activity in many inter-organisational fields. The study of dynamics therefore adds a new dimension to the analysis of collaboration. Questions of power and advantage and of exclusion and inclusion are seen in a new light if they are considered in terms of the changing imperatives faced by partnerships. But as our analysis shows, the explanation of change must be understood at a variety of levels. There are the micro-politics of leadership and interpersonal relations – the social processes discussed by Ring and Van de Ven (1994). These are located within meso-levels of governance structure and membership composition, which in turn respond to the wider pattern of resource dependencies in the environment. The analysis shows how the use of the metaphor of the life-cycle can illustrate the dynamics at work in a collaboration. Some collaborations, and especially those that are time-limited, will broadly follow the pattern of a life-cycle. But different dynamics may be expected in collaborations with a degree of permanence.

We should recognise that the dynamic nature of collaboration is a feature of the contemporary public policy agenda, and especially of the transition from a process of hollowing-out to one in which new integrations are forming and reforming within the congested state. Indeed Cropper argues that our perspective on collaboration and its sustainability should be at the level of the population of organisations rather than individual partnerships. He points out that the process of collaborative endeavour is self-reinforcing:

> Where specific collaborative arrangements are disbanded, traces of organisation are … likely to remain, more loosely formed than before, but potentially capable of generating and pursuing collective strategies. Professional, role and social networks and networking practices, reusable learning about effective procedures and management methods and enhanced understanding of the interests and capacities of others are examples of such traces. (1996, p. 89)

Both informal relationships and the organisational forms adopted by partnerships are embedded in an inter-organisational network which provides the basic substructure for co-operative activity. This is persistent even if individual manifestations of collaboration or partnership are not. That these traces remain and are capable of stimulating new co-operative activity is an indication that – whatever the conflicts, mistrust and tensions in collaboration and partnership – there exists a continued potential for collaborative activity in pursuit of public purpose.

8 The Governance of Collaboration

Governance has emerged as a major theme in the reform agenda for public services globally. It is a complex concept which contains within its usage several different meanings (Newman, 2001; Pierre and Peters, 2000). For some it reflects a critical assessment of the market-inspired reforms during the 1980s and 1990s and the desire to ensure that governmental bodies operate in line with a public service ethos. Even the World Bank, which for many years advocated the use of market mechanisms to deliver public services, now recognises the need for good government in creating a politically healthy community which is capable of improving the life of its citizens (World Bank, 1997). Others use governance to refer to the fragmented public realm and the need to establish processes for guiding and steering societal systems. This sense of the term relates to matters of social co-ordination in relation to public policy objectives, in which collaborations have a clear role to play (Kickert *et al.*, 1997). However, it is the third meaning of governance with which this chapter is principally concerned. This usage is what in the private sector would be called corporate governance:

> The procedures associated with the decision-making, performance and control of organisations, with providing structures to give overall direction to the organisation and to satisfy reasonable expectations of accountability to those outside it. (Hodges *et al.*, 1996, p. 7)

The corporate governance debate in the UK public sector arose from alleged and actual misconduct by Members of Parliament, Ministers and those appointed to quango boards during the 1990s. In the latter case, there was considerable public disquiet about lack of transparency and the substantial ministerial patronage involved in the appointment of board members. A series of managerial, performance and financial failures was exposed, including board members not stepping aside from decisions where they had a conflict of interest, lax arrangements for claiming expenses, ineffective or poorly implemented financial management and contracting regulations and inappropriate personnel and remuneration arrangements (Doig, 1995; Skelcher, 1998). The Public Accounts Committee (PAC) and National Audit Office (NAO) issued a number of highly critical reports on these issues. Public concern about the probity of governmental bodies was a factor leading to the appointment of the Committee on Standards in Public Life (then, the Nolan Committee).

The notion of corporate governance in the public sector returns us to the constituting conditions for public action. These require government that works in the wider public interest, follows proper standards of conduct, is transparent in its decision-making and is accountable to citizens. It is clear to see how this might operate in a single elected body, and even to a more limited extent in an appointed quango board. However, the position in collaborative arrangements becomes more complex because of the different legal forms that partnerships take, the problematic accountability of board members, and the varying requirements placed on them regarding standards of conduct and the rights members of the public have to access meetings and information.

In corporate governance terms, the academic study of partnerships and public policy towards them is in the same state as could be found in relation to quangos in the early 1990s – namely partial and limited. Yet here is a major class of bodies shaping and delivering public policy and spending public money. They are part of the governance of the UK, and this consequently mandates an examination of their corporate arrangements. We commence this process by exploring the different legal forms partnerships take, including joint authorities, company structures and unincorporated associations. This discussion of constitutional arrangements provides an essential basis for the consideration of the conditions for good governance in the public realm and the extent to which partnerships exhibit a democratic deficit. This issue is explored in relation to the public, financial and performance accountability of these bodies.

The constitutional form of partnerships

Multi-organisational partnerships created for public purpose can take a number of different constitutional forms. Each has implications for the roles of board members, the discretion available to the partnership and the wider accountability structure within which the partnership operates. The basic constitutional forms are:

1. Statutory body
2. Joint authority

3. Joint committee
4. Unincorporated association
5. Company issuing share capital
6. Company limited by guarantee
7. Industrial and provident society
8. Trust
9. Charity

The main constitutional forms are exemplified in Table 8.1. These forms have been employed most extensively by local authorities, with long-standing examples of joint committees responsible for specialist services across neighbouring localities (Flynn and Leach, 1984; Stewart, 2000). However, other actors in the public sector are gaining greater flexibility to employ these devices to advance the agenda for joined-up working.

Statutory body

Some types of partnership are constituted as a statutory body. One example is the Education Action Zone (EAZ). The Secretary of State for Education has the power to designate those schools that will form an EAZ 'if it is expedient to do so with a view to improving the standards of education' (s10, School Standards and Framework Act 1998). The Act requires the creation of a corporate body called an education action forum to govern each zone, and defines its statutory purpose as the improvement of standards in the provision of education at each of the participating schools. This body is also an exempt educational charity, which means that it does not have to comply with some of the financial reporting requirements normally placed on charities. However, this does place duties of trusteeship on board members. The membership of the governing forum is defined in the statutory instrument creating each EAZ and invariably includes a wide range of stakeholders, including the local education authority, health and social services interests and business representatives (Figure 8.1). It also typically permits the forum to appoint representatives from other stakeholders should they wish. Designation as a statutory body gives the partnership a legal identity and certain duties and powers. It is therefore able to operate as an independent actor with its own authority, rather than being dependent on functions or resources being delegated from the partners. Consequently it has a number of similarities with the joint authority model, particularly in respect of the corporate rather than representative role of board members (see below).

Table 8.1 *Constitutional forms for partnerships – selected examples*

Constitutional form	Example	Statutory basis	Legal form	Board composition	Accountability of board
Statutory body	Education action zones	Established by Order made by Sec. of State for Education under School Standards and Framework Act 1998	Statutory corporate body and exempt educational charity with 3 year term, extendable by order to 5 years	Members appointed by Sec. of State, governing bodies of participating schools, local education authority (LEA), careers service, LSC, local employers and voluntary organisations	Directly to Sec. of State; as charitable trustees, they are subject to trust law; audit by National Audit Office
Joint authority (or joint board)	Fire and civil defence authorities in metropolitan counties	Created by the Local Government Act 1985	Statutory joint authority	The number of seats on the authority and their distribution between the constituent local councils is defined. Each council nominates its own members to the board	To citizens as council-tax payers and consumers. To Secretary of State, partially through the inspectorate
Joint committee	Joint crematoria committees	Created by local authorities on a voluntary basis using their statutory powers	Single purpose joint committee to which member local authorities delegate their functions under relevant legislation	The number of seats on the joint committee and their distribution between the constituent local councils is defined by the partners. Each council nominates its own members to the committee	To the partner local authorities

Unincorporated association	Crime and disorder partnerships	None, but accepted means to enable county and district councils and chief constables (the 'responsible bodies') to formulate and implement crime and disorder strategies under the Crime and Disorder Act 1998	At discretion of each partnership. Normally unincorporated association with responsible bodies as lead partners	The Act gives Home Secretary power to specify the bodies with whom the responsible bodies must co-operate, and hence offer places on the partnership. These include NHS bodies, schools, voluntary bodies, etc.	Through statutory duty imposed by the Act on the responsible bodies, and to Home Secretary in relation to guidance on the partnership and production of crime and disorder strategies
Company limited by shares	National Exhibition Centre Ltd	Created by local authority on a voluntary basis using their statutory powers	Company limited by shares. The shareholders are Birmingham City Council and the Birmingham Chamber of Commerce	Each shareholder appoints four board directors	To the partners and as required by the companies acts
Company limited by guarantee	Connexions partnerships	Developed autonomously in each locality in response to central government policy initiative	Constituted as company limited by guarantee, the membership being the key partners including the local authority, careers service company, etc.	The members of the company	To central government through performance monitoring; to partners; and as required by the companies acts.

Source: Birmingham City Council (1999); CIPFA (2001); Flynn and Leach (1984); Leach *et al.* (1992).

Figure 8.1   *Potential membership of Camborne, Pool and Redruth EAZ*

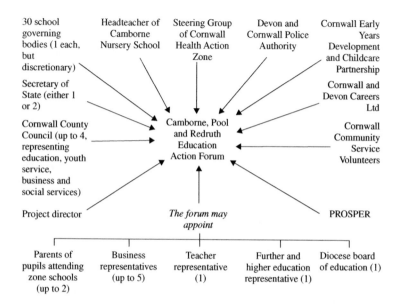

Source: The Camborne, Pool and Redruth Success Zone Education Action Zone
Order 1999, SI 1999/3414.

Joint authority

Joint authorities (sometimes called joint boards) are also statutory partnership bodies. However, the difference, compared with EAZs, is twofold.
First, they undertake a local government function which, for economy of
scale reasons, necessitates integration across several local council areas.
Second, the members of the joint authority are all councillors appointed to
it by the constituent local authorities. A number of joint authorities were
created in the metropolitan areas at the abolition of the metropolitan county
councils in 1986. Then, the county council's police, passenger transport and
fire and civil defence functions were transferred to joint boards (the police
functions were subsequently transferred to separately-constituted police
authorities). Fire joint boards are also found elsewhere in the UK. The value
of the joint authority is that it enables the provision of functions on a cross-
authority basis without the need to rely on voluntary co-operation by the
constituent councils. Indeed joint boards for waste disposal were imposed

in two of the metropolitan counties at abolition because of concern by government that the tensions between district councils would lead to voluntary joint arrangements which would not be sustainable (Leach *et al.*, 1992).

Joint boards are corporate bodies that exist independently of their members. They have a charter and the right to enter contracts, hold and own property, employ staff and be party to legal action in their own name. Their members are appointed in proportion to the party balance on the constituent councils. However, joint authorities are corporate bodies, and consequently when the authority meets to make decisions each member has a legal duty to put the interests of the board above those of his or her own local authority. The members, therefore, are appointees not representatives. Their local electoral mandate and indeed even the policy of their authority towards the joint board's functions (if it has one) should carry no particular weight in their deliberations and decision-making. Consequently Leach *et al.* (1992, p. 138), in their analysis of processes of local accountability in English metropolitan government, argue:

> The system of government which now operates in the metropolitan counties by definition lacks the capacity to operate as representative democracy, as far as the joint boards are concerned, because councillors are not *elected* as members of joint boards, they are *appointed* by district councils to serve on them ... What [this] means is that the direct link between a manifesto promise ... and the capacity to carry out that promise cannot exist in relation to activities which are the responsibility of a joint body.

Joint committees

Joint committees, in contrast to joint authorities, are not corporate bodies. They are not able to hold or control assets, nor to employ staff or engage in legal action in their own name. However, those local authorities and NHS bodies who are party to a joint committee may delegate certain statutory functions to it. In this respect the joint committee acts on behalf of those bodies, but it is the delegating bodies who retain responsibility for the function and the way in which it is exercised. Joint committees may emerge voluntarily, for example to manage and operate specialist facilities and services whose catchment area is greater than that of one authority. Examples include crematoria, trading standards laboratories, purchasing consortia and museums. However, there are also mandatory joint committees, for example the

School Organisation Committees which consider and approve local education authority plans for the provision and closure of schools.

Unincorporated association

The unincorporated association is probably the most commonly used governance arrangement for public policy partnerships. Local strategic partnerships in England, childcare partnerships in Scotland and people in communities partnerships in Wales are all normally constituted on this basis. Unincorporated associations are created on the basis of a memorandum of agreement or similar resolution between the individual member bodies setting out the purpose of the partnership and how it will be governed. Unincorporated associations have no separate legal identity and thus cannot enter into contracts, employ staff or own or control assets. In this sense they are similar to joint committees. However, unlike joint committees statutory functions may not be delegated to them by the partners but they may carry out activities associated with the management of a function, for example they may be a joint client for contracts awarded by neighbouring local authorities or be a joint purchasing body. The advantage that unincorporated associations have over joint committees is the greater flexibility in the governance arrangement. They may include nominees of other bodies, although they are not able to have voting rights, and the members can appoint individuals who are not councillors to represent them provided these individuals would not be disqualified from becoming a councillor and that they constitute no more than one third of the membership (CIPFA, 2001). Individuals on the management committee must act within the constitution and have a duty of care in exercising their powers. They are personally liable for the actions of the association, although they will normally be indemnified by the body they are representing. Unincorporated associations can apply for and be granted charitable status, although this will place additional legal responsibilities on the members of the committee of management.

Partnerships as companies

Partnerships are sometimes constituted as companies. These are independent corporate entities which, like statutory partnerships, can hold property, employ staff, enter into contracts and engage in legal actions. Most public policy partnerships constituted as companies have involved local

---

Box 8.1 *Birmingham City Council – examples of partnerships constituted as companies*

The National Exhibition Centre Ltd
A company limited by shares which manages the National Exhibition Centre (other than Hall 10) on behalf of the City Council. It also owns and operates the International Convention Centre, National Indoor Arena and Hall 10 at the NEC. Shares are held jointly between the City Council and the Birmingham Chamber of Commerce and Industry, and each appoints four of the eight directors of the company.

Birmingham Centre for Manufacturing
A company limited by guarantee which supports small and medium manufacturing enterprises through training and consultancy. Its management board includes representatives from the City Council, Birmingham and Solihull LSC, University of Central England, Birmingham Chamber of Commerce and Industry and small and medium manufacturing.

Birmingham Airport Holdings Ltd
The local authority-owned airport company was restructured to attract private sector investors and enable a major growth in the facility. The company is 49 per cent owned by the seven West Midlands councils (of whom one is Birmingham). The other shareholders include Aer Rianta International cpt, Nat West ventures, John Laing Holdings Ltd, and National Car Parks.

Source: Birmingham City Council (1999).

---

authorities rather than other parts of the governmental system. Birmingham City Council is party to a number of companies created in partnership with the private sector as trading concerns (Box 8.1). The commercial function of these joint ventures and the involvement of private sector players makes the company an attractive constitutional form.

The main forms of company structure are:

1. *Companies limited by shares.* The company issues shares which are held by its members. Assuming a sufficient level of profit, this entitles members to a dividend based on the value and number of shares held. Shares can be traded, and consequently the membership (and thus ownership)

of the company will change. The company may also be susceptible to take-over. The potential for membership to change makes this structure unattractive for partnerships seeking to deliver public policy objectives unless they are trading concerns.

2. *Companies limited by guarantee.* The company's members agree that they will contribute a fixed amount (usually £1) in the event that the company is dissolved. There are no shareholders and consequently the membership of the company is determined by its own rules rather than members' decisions to sell or purchase shares. Any surplus is retained within the company for reinvestment. The attraction of this model is that control is retained within a defined group of members. This may be a particularly important consideration for public policy partnerships.

In either case the management of the company is vested in a board of directors (sometimes termed a committee of management in companies limited by guarantee) who are appointed by the members at the annual general meeting (AGM). The directors may include non-executives who are neither members nor managers of the company. Such individuals may be recruited because of their ability to bring an independent perspective to the company's affairs or particular expertise. However, they may also be appointed to enable the company to develop a link with another organisation or network – in other words, they bring personal and institutional resources that the company would otherwise find it difficult to access (Pettigrew and McNaulty, 1995; Pennings, 1980). Company directors have specific legal duties:

- An overriding fiduciary duty to act in good faith in what they believe to be the best interests of the company.
- A duty to exercise their discretion independently, that is to make decisions informed solely by the facts of the case and their judgement of the company's best interests. However, it is permissible to take into account the interests of a third party which the director represents, but this interest must be declared and must be balanced against the primary duty to the company.
- A duty to avoid placing themselves in a position where personal interest or duties conflict with the individual's duties to the company.
- A duty of compliance to the Company Acts.
- A duty not to make a private profit from their position. (Chelliah, 2001; Wragge and Co., n.d.)

It is the first and second duties which individuals may find creates a tension with their role in respect of the partner organisation that has nominated them to the board. As with members of statutory bodies and joint authorities, so company directors are required to place the interests of that body above those of any other organisation or interest.

There have traditionally been constraints on the legal powers of public sector bodies to create or participate in companies. The legal powers available to local councils generally relate to particular functions, for example forming a company to run a bus operation, own a municipal airport or promote economic development. Where local councils have wanted to establish or take part in companies for other purposes they have relied on s.111, Local Government Act 1972 which empowers a local authority to do 'anything ... which is calculated to facilitate or is conducive or incidental to, the discharge of any of their functions'. There has been considerable legal debate as to the exact meaning and scope of this power, but a liberal interpretation has enabled it to be used as the basis for company creation (Crawford *et al.*, 2000). However, the power of well-being contained in s.2, Local Government Act 2000 enables local authorities to form or participate in companies provided they are intended to promote the economic, social or environmental well-being of the area, and there are likely to be further powers available to form and participate in a range of structures, including companies, to enable the achievement of best value (DETR, 2001a).

Companies created by local authorities or in which they participate are subject to a series of complex statutory controls. In broad terms, the purpose of the legislation is to ensure that local authorities are not able to create companies in order to escape regulations with which they would otherwise have to comply (Crawford *et al.*, 2000). The controls applied to local authority companies include the local government capital finance regime, restrictions on the publication of party political information and the right of members of the local authority who are not on the board to obtain information about the company's affairs in order to undertake their duties as a councillor. Crawford *et al.* conclude that:

> The very complexity of the controls appears to be inhibiting for some local authorities, and for others result in the adoption of less than what they see as the ideal ... The complexity of these controls combines with the uncertainty over the power of the local authority to participate at all to deter the private sector from participating. (2000, p. 147)

Consequently companies have tended not to be employed to any great extent as vehicles to constitute partnerships. However, that picture may be expected to change. It is likely that government will enable greater legal flexibility so that constitutional arrangements do not hinder its objective of improving the performance of public services.

Mutuals and public interest companies

There is now a reawakening of interest in corporate forms whose constitution reflects principles of mutuality. In these bodies individuals or groups with a common interest join together to create and govern an organisation that will deliver this mutual benefit. Collective membership and the rights and responsibilities of members in the governance of the body are therefore central to the organisation's ethos. Mutuals come in different legal forms, but that which is of most relevance to a discussion of partnerships is the industrial and provident society (IPS). These incorporated bodies undertake business activities either as co-operatives or for the benefit of the community, and it is the latter on which we concentrate here. Registration as a 'benefit of the community' society requires the body to demonstrate that its business will benefit those who are not its members and that it has special reasons for being an industrial and provident society rather than a company. These might include operating on the basis of one member, one vote or having a clear social objective. For example, some organisations providing for specific housing needs are registered as 'benefit of the community' IPSs (Registrar of Friendly Societies, 2000).

The IPS legal form has been little used for mainstream public services, other than in the social housing field. However, its basic principles have informed the debate about the idea of the public interest company (Corrigan, Steele and Parston, 2001). The public interest company (PIC) would operate on a trading basis but with strong accountability to members and profits being reinvested or otherwise employed for the benefit of the wider community. By employing such a legal form, Corrigan *et al.* argue, public services would have greater opportunity to innovate, generate income and yet remain accountable to and work in the interest of the community. This is a model that might have advantages for partnerships that wish to incorporate so that they are able to employ staff, enter into contracts and act on their own behalf, yet where accountability to the community is particularly important and the idea of a company limited by guarantee does not seem appropriate.

Trusts and charities

Trust status provides a corporate form attractive to not-for-profit activities and there are a number of examples of trusts being set up to enable local authority–community partnerships, for example in the provision of community projects or to deliver the council's leisure functions. The basic principle is that the assets of the trust are held in common to be used for some specified beneficial purpose. However, a trust has no separate identity from its trustees, compared with a company that has a corporate identity separate from its directors. While a company may be sued and its directors not suffer as a result, trustees are personally liable for their actions and remain liable after they cease to be trustees. However, the trust's constitution may provide for an indemnity to be provided from the trust's assets and liability is unlikely to be found at law unless the trustee acts outside the terms of the trust deed, does not exercise sufficient duty of care, acts in a way that does not protect the trust's assets or makes a personal gain from those assets (Wragge and Co., n.d.). A trust may apply to the Charity Commissioners for registration as a charity if it meets one or more of the four charitable purposes, namely the relief of poverty and human suffering, the advancement of education or of religion, or another purpose for the benefit of the community. This offers certain financial advantages, but also imposes a number of restrictions.

The accountability of partnerships

Conditions for good governance

Underlying the complexities of legal structures and board composition are a set of common corporate governance issues. These issues take a particular form because the partnerships we are considering have been created for public purpose. Ranson and Stewart argue that the essential principles underlying the good governance of public affairs are those of consent and accountability taking place in a context of public discourse:

> In the final resort the authority or legitimacy of public choice rests upon consent ... Consent to the exercise of authority rests upon the processes through which decisions are taken and the quality of public discourse. Consent may usually be given where the processes are accepted even though a particular decision may not be supported. Consent is tested and confirmed through public accountability. Organisations in the public domain are required to account for their actions in the public arena of discourse and there has to be a means by which they are held to account by the public on whose behalf they act. That is the ultimate test of consent. (1994, pp. 93–4)

These issues are familiar in debates about the nature of liberal democracies, for example in terms of the limitations of and alternatives to representative government. However, they are given an added resonance in relation to the preponderance of arm's-length relationships which have emerged since the early 1990s and which introduce more complex principal–agents chains.

Contracting-out, partnership, executive agencies and quangos of various kinds all add intervening variables to the basic relationships between citizen and public decision-maker expounded by Ranson and Stewart. They raise important questions about the way in which consent is given, and indeed whether it is given or merely assumed.

Public accountability: measuring the democratic deficit

Partnership bodies are, by definition, located at arm's length to centres of elected political authority. Elected politicians or their officials may be members of the partnership board, but in this capacity they and the other members are not normally subject to an electoral mandate – the exception being some resident or tenant representatives on regeneration boards. In the light of this structural condition partnerships can be seen as a form of quango – 'quasi-governmental bodies that are appointed rather than elected and have responsibility for shaping, purchasing and delivering ... public policy' (Skelcher, 1998, p. 1). This is not a position that has to date been adopted in the analysis of partnerships. However, there is a strong logic to treating collaborative arrangements as a distinct sub-set of quangos since they share many of the same corporate governance characteristics.

The extensive analysis of quango accountability in the 1990s involved the measurement of the 'democratic deficit' (Weir and Hall, 1994). The democratic deficit refers to the shortfall in the accountability arrangements of a non-elected public body with reference to those applying in the elected sector. This is not just a matter of whether electoral arrangements do or do not exist, but also applies to the other systems that support democratic accountability including access to information and codes regulating standards of conduct. It is possible to quantify the extent of the democratic deficit for a particular class of organisation by measuring them against a set of democratic standards. Those standards applying to local authorities are used as the benchmark since these bodies have the most exacting accountability requirements found in the public sector as a whole.

A survey of 30 SRB partnerships was carried out by Hall *et al.* (1998) to gather data on aspects of their conduct of public business. Subsequently the Robinson *et al.* (2000) assessment of the governance of the Northeast of England analysed 28 SRB partnerships along similar lines. The analysis reveals a variable picture in relation to their presence in these regeneration partnerships (Table 8.2). One quarter of the partnerships surveyed were failing to implement any of the accountability and openness practices that applied to local government, while only one fifth met all the criteria – although it should be noted that election of members was not included. Overall, Robinson *et al.* conclude:

A substantial proportion of [SRB] partnerships do not provide a sufficiently wide range of relevant information on their activities, nor allow opportunities to scrutinise their work, nor provide access to their decision-making processes, nor do they enable the local community to influence their work. (2000, p. 120)

Hall *et al.* reach a similar judgement:

Most SRB Challenge Fund partnerships are at present operating in a manner which is well below the standards of transparency and accountability expected of public service organisations. In each of these respects partnerships fell well short of the practices statutorily required of local authorities. (1998, pp. 61–2)

Table 8.2   *The democratic deficit in regeneration partnerships*

What proportion of partnerships	*Study*	
	Robinson et al. %	*Hall et al. %*
Publish a delivery plan	75	n/a
Publish newsletters	60	65
Publish papers for meetings*	54	47
Have a code of conduct*	46	41
Hold publicly-accessible board meetings*	46	29
Publish an annual report*	43	41
Hold annual general meeting open to the public*	29	n/a
Have public register of members' interests*	21	12
Memorandum of association*	n/a	41
Publication of accounts*	n/a	35
Standing orders*	n/a	35

Note: *Indicates statutory requirement on local authority.
Source: Hall *et al.* (1998); Robinson *et al.* (2000).

The conclusions of the Hall and Robinson studies are supported by an examination of the statutory requirements for public accountability placed on partnerships in fields other than regeneration. For example, EAZ forums are under no statutory obligation to hold meetings in public nor to publicise the dates and places of meetings nor their agendas. Instead this is a matter for the forum itself to decide. The same applies to publication of minutes. The official guidance to fora comments mildly that: 'As a matter of good practice, Action Forums may wish to make public the minutes of their meetings on request, unless there is a good reason for not doing so' (Department for Education and Employment, 1998a, para 2.6.4). The official guidance also comments that forums 'may wish to consider adopting a code of practice to apply to its own members' (*ibid.*, para 2.4.7), but once again this is a matter of local discretion. The only statutory requirement in respect of member conduct is that a member who has a conflict of interest should declare it and withdraw from the meeting of the forum. Contrast this with the position for local councillors. They are subject to a statutory code of conduct which regulates their behaviour in respect of a range of issues, including potential or actual conflicts of interest, relationships with the public and officials, non-disclosure of confidential information and a host of other matters. As with MPs, there is a regulatory body to investigate and hear any alleged breach of the code and sanctions can be applied where members are found to have transgressed (Skelcher and Snape, 2001). Local authorities are, of course, much larger bodies than EAZs and spend considerably greater amounts of public money. Nevertheless there is a case for ensuring at least some degree of consistency between public agencies – especially as the National Audit Office (2001a) found that performance-driven partnerships that are intended to be innovative face particular problems of probity and corporate governance.

In some other partnerships there is a stronger imperative towards assuring public accountability. The non-statutory early years development and childcare partnerships (EYDCPs) provide a contrast to the EAZs. Although their official guidance stresses the discretion available to EYDCPs in their corporate governance, it does provide a mandatory set of requirements (Table 8.3). Of particular note are the requirements for the equal opportunity policy to be reflected in partnership working and planning and – probably uniquely amongst partnerships – that there should be a complaints procedure in relation to partnership members. As with EAZs the decision on public access to meetings is left to the partnership to decide. However, the guidance recommends openness and requires EYDCPs choosing to meet in private to explain their reasons in their Strategic Plan.

Table 8.3   *Corporate governance requirements for early years and childcare development partnerships*

The partnership should:

- Agree and publish terms of reference
- Agree procedures for selecting chair
- Ensure all members involved in decisions and that there is an agreed quorum
- Have a stated policy on expenses for non-local authority members

- Have a written equal opportunities policy which describes how this is reflected in the partnership's working arrangements and planning
- Have transparent contracting procedures

- Agree and record roles of members
- Ensure members receive papers in good time
- Keep agreed written records of all meetings

- Have a written and active policy for monitoring the partnership's effectiveness
- Have a formal complaints procedure for complaints from partnership members and members of the public.

- Make statistical information used in preparing their Strategic Plan public

The partnership must consider:

- Timing of meetings to make them accessible to all
- Whether members should have formal job descriptions
- What training members might need

- Whether decisions should be made by consensus or voting
- Whether meetings should be formal or informal, and open to the public or not; where the decision is against open meetings, the reasons must be recorded in the Strategic Plan

---

Source: Adapted from Department for Education and Employment (2001).

This assessment shows that public policy partnerships are bodies where there is typically a democratic deficit. Yet while we may conclude that the requirements placed on partnerships to provide accountability to citizens appear to be weak, this is only part of the corporate governance framework within which these bodies operate. Consequently we need to explore two further aspects – how performance accountability and financial accountability are delivered.

Performance accountability: delivering outcomes

The motivation for much partnership creation in recent years has been to deliver specific outcomes. As political agendas and organisational structures move out of alignment, so joined-up working through partnerships becomes the means to deliver policy objectives. The changing face of partnership performance management and accountability can be illustrated by comparing the recently established Sure Start with SRB, a longer-standing partnership which is now being phased out.

Sure Start arose from the cross-cutting policy reviews undertaken by the incoming Labour government in its Comprehensive Spending Review (CSR) during 1997 and 1998. One review examined shortfalls in policy and provision for young children or their families who were most in need. It developed the concept of 'Sure Start' – an integrated programme to strengthen the nature and level of provision for this client group (Glass, 1999). There are two fundamental features of the way in which the Sure Start programme has been designed. The first is the attempt to develop a collaborative approach across ministries on this issue, and hence to challenge the deeply ingrained departmentalism found in Whitehall (Chapter 2). In the Sure Start programme political authority is shared between the Secretary of State for Education and Skills as its champion at Cabinet level and in whose budget the expenditure rests and a Minister in the separate Department of Health who has responsibility for overseeing the programme on a day-to-day basis. The Sure Start Unit responsible for managing and delivering the programme is a cross-departmental team which for administrative purposes is located in the Department for Education and Skills.

The second fundamental feature of Sure Start is its integration into the Public Service Agreement (PSA) system. PSAs are a policy management technique developed to implement agreements arising from the CSR. They are essentially a contract between a spending department, which commits to deliver particular policy objectives, and the Treasury, which agrees to make certain funds available. Departments then prepare a Service Delivery Agreement (SDA) which details the way in which they intend to achieve the PSA aims and objectives. Figure 8.2 shows how this process has been applied in the case of Sure Start. The performance management and accountability system inherent in PSAs and SDAs is reflected in the relationship between the Sure Start structure at national level and those local partnerships that are delivering the programme. Each local programme is expected to work towards the PSA and SDA targets, and the plan submitted by each partnership is expected to show how it intends to do this.

Figure 8.2 *Performance management and accountability in Sure Start*

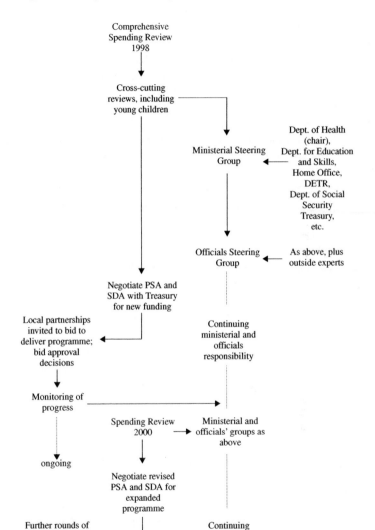

The targets are defined in outcome terms, rather than input or throughput measures that have more conventionally been employed. Monitoring of individual Sure Start programmes is in relation to change from the local baseline in terms of achieving the national objectives and targets. (See also Box 8.2.)

SRB is somewhat different. It was introduced in 1994 as an initiative to target resources on the regeneration of defined localities through the medium of local partnerships (Chapter 4). Unlike Sure Start, SRB has principally been the responsibility of one central government department – originally the Department of the Environment. Government Offices of the Regions play a key role as intermediaries between the department and individual SRB partnerships, but despite their title these have tended to have a stronger presence

---

Box 8.2 *Sure Start's aim and selected objectives, PSA and SDA targets*

The aim of Sure Start

To work with parents-to-be, parents and children to promote the physical, intellectual and social development of babies and young children – particularly those who are disadvantaged – so that they can flourish at home and when they get to school, and thereby break the cycle of disadvantage for the current generation of young children.

Objective 1: improving social and emotional development, in particular by supporting early bonding between parents and their children, helping families to function and by enabling the early identification and support of children with emotional and behavioural difficulties.

PSA target

- To reduce the proportion of children aged 0–3 in the 500 Sure Start areas who are re-registered within the space of 12 months on the child protection register by 20 per cent by 2004.

SDA targets

- All local Sure Start programmes to have agreed and implemented, in a culturally sensitive way, ways of caring for and supporting mothers with post-natal depression.
- One hundred per cent of families with young children to have been contacted by local programmes within the first two months of birth.

Source: Sure Start Unit (*c*. 2000).

than the environment department. The RDAs were created in 1999 and now have responsibility for SRB in their region. Yet this quango was created to advance the economic regeneration, business competitiveness and skills agenda in the regions and thus its remit only deals with part of the broader public policy agenda with which SRB is concerned. Consequently there has been limited interdepartmental ownership of the initiative. Regeneration partnerships have been created at local level, but there is an absence of a complementary collaboration between central government ministries.

The strategic policy framework for SRB is not as clearly defined as that for Sure Start. Hall *et al.* (1998) observe that the process of determining priorities, projects and targets in the first three rounds of SRB was largely the responsibility of those partnerships entering bids, subject to final agreement by the Cabinet's Regeneration Committee. Although a particular round of the SRB might have a theme it was very much up to localities to interpret this in their own context. Performance accountability in SRB is achieved through the delivery plan that each partnership is required to submit and agree with their regional office of government. The delivery plan is in effect a contractual agreement to achieve specified outputs or outcomes. These are specified in terms of pre-defined variables, for example number of jobs created or empty dwellings brought back into use. Overall, SRB can be considered an initiative in which local partnerships have a considerable degree of discretion in defining programmes and targets within a broad and relatively ill-defined national policy context. There is performance accountability in terms of locally-defined targets, but this is not linked to clearly specified national objectives and targets to the extent found in Sure Start.

There are noticeable differences in performance management and accountability between Sure Start and SRB. These are partly a function of the historical moment at which the schemes were devised and the state of performance management technology and political will at that point. However, such differences can also be observed between contemporaneous partnerships. One explanation is to do with the function of the partnership. School organisation committees, for example, have an entirely different role from either Sure Start or SRB. Their purpose is to consider and agree the school organisation plan prepared by the local education authority. Similarly local strategic partnerships are advisory bodies whose decisions can only be implemented through the executive actions of its members or others it is able to influence. Performance accountability in these contexts is a rather different issue altogether. The notion of holding an LSP to account for achievement against targets would be of little value. If a performance accountability system were to be developed it would need to address softer issues of influence over autonomous bodies. This is one of the challenges presented by trying to join up government in a fragmented and decentered context.

Financial accountability: spending public money

Partnerships resourced through public funds have to comply with grant conditions that normally require the partnership to employ particular financial procedures. In the case of unincorporated associations, one of its number must be appointed as the accountable body to act on its behalf in financial transactions. This is often, although not inevitably, a local authority. Unincorporated partnerships will also be subject to a regulatory regime which links accountability for their spending decisions directly back to the public body that made the funds available. In the case of funding from the Westminster Parliament, for example, financial monitoring and accountability procedures link partnerships back into the relevant ministry and through its Accounting Officer to the Minister and hence to the legislature. It is difficult to overestimate how ingrained into the culture of the UK public service is accountability for public money. The accounting officer of a government department is personally responsible for the expenditure of their department, and by convention the Minister is accountable for actions undertaken by officials (including the accounting officer) in his or her name. The Public Accounts Committee (PAC) in the Westminster Parliament exercises considerable authority as the legislature's scrutiniser of spending by the Executive, supported in this role by the National Audit Office. There is close liaison between the two bodies in relation to lines of enquiry, and the hearing held by the PAC will typically be on subjects where the NAO has reported. Ministers and civil servants are required to attend before the PAC, as may senior managers of partnerships. The reports of both the PAC and the NAO can offer trenchant criticism of their ability to manage the expenditure of public money and to monitor and control the actions of their agents – including partnerships. Similar arrangements apply in the devolved legislatures.

The guidance to EAZs makes the point about financial accountability in very direct manner:

> The Permanent Secretary of the Department, as Accounting Officer for the Vote from which funds are paid to the Forum, is accountable to Parliament for the resources which it makes available to the Forum. The Project Director, as the Forum's senior full-time official, shall be held

formally responsible for all financial affairs and for the proper conduct of business ... [and] ... is liable to be summoned to appear before the Public Accounts Committee alongside the Accounting Officer of the Department for Education and Employment when matters concerning the Forum are being discussed. The Project Director may also be required to appear before other Parliamentary Select Committees. (Department for Education and Employment 1998a, Annex L)

Accountability for expenditure is often a matter that is more complex than this guidance suggests. The complexity arises from the various streams of central government expenditure (sometimes from different departments) together with local authority and local NHS resources and in some cases private sector input which flow into partnerships. Determining which funding was used in what ways is by no means a simple task in such an environment of matched funding (that is, one organisation provides funds if another does) and in-kind contributions (for example, human or capital resources being provided in lieu of cash) (Figure 8.3).

Conclusion

Partnerships present a challenge to the principles of public sector corporate governance. They are located at arm's length from the processes of representative democracy yet have a key role to play in delivering improved public services – and especially in relation to individuals and communities who are disadvantaged and where mainstream services have not always been satisfactory. They can have extensive public involvement mechanisms (Chapter 9) but also be governed by boards whose operations demonstrate a considerable democratic deficit. Their legal forms can vary considerably, as can their statutory base and financial relationships. Overall, the governance of partnerships is an area of considerable complexity and potential confusion.

These questions have gone largely unrecognised. Partnerships are regarded as a good thing and as the preferred model to deliver key policy outcomes in the new world of joined-up services. This normative thrust obscures debates which are fundamental to good government – who should make decisions? how should they be made? how should accountability be assured? In the world of partnerships the balance between questions of governance and questions of outcomes has been weighted firmly in favour of the latter. However, the issue of partnership accountability and audit is beginning to be recognised in government. The Sharman Report

160

Figure 8.3 *Education action zones: funding streams and main partnership linkages*

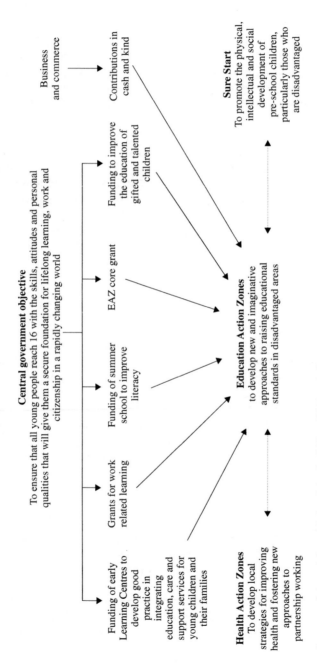

Source: Adapted from National Audit Office (2001a, p. 6).

into central government audit and accountability, commissioned by the Treasury, devotes several pages to discussing the issue. It is treated rather as an afterthought, following extensive discussion of mainstream departmental accountability and audit systems. However, the report emphasises the need for clarity of responsibility and flexibility on the part of audit bodies:

> [The] creation of partnerships and joined-up working does raise a number of issues for auditors. In particular, it increases the need on occasions for different audit bodies to work together. It also presents challenges for the organisation and focus of VFM [value for money] examinations, which in recent years have tended to concentrate on individual departments. It also increases the importance of careful liaison throughout the duration of the project between all parties, and is likely to make the 'clearance' of the report, through which the NAO confirms the facts and their presentation with departments, a more demanding exercise. (Sharman, 2001, para 5.59)

The issue, however, is much wider than the mechanics of the audit process and the politeness of interdepartmental agreement. It is to do with the complexities of ensuring effective financial control in an environment where partnerships are created and see their mission as being about performance, where it is difficult to disentangle who is funding what and where the safeguards of public accountability at the local level are weak. Perhaps if the democratic deficit of partnerships could be reduced there would be more scope for financial accountability to be vested at the local level and to look at the questions of expenditure and performance in the round. In the next chapter we consider community involvement in partnerships and the extent to which this can begin to close the democratic deficit.

9   Citizen Participation and Collaboration

The involvement of citizens in the governance of their societies is a vexed issue in many Western democracies where public participation rates are falling and cynicism about government and politics is a dominant feature. For some the problem lies with the role played by the state. For example, Ostrom (2000) argues that Scandinavian governments exhibit centralising tendencies which turn citizens into 'passive observers' and 'crowds them out' of participation in public policy (p. 12). For others the problem is linked to the state's subjugation to global capital, diluting the act of citizenship to an exercise in making choices about consumption (Monbiot, 2000; Klein, 2000). Another explanation of limited citizen participation points to a wider societal malaise in which economic, social and technological changes have reduced citizens' capacity to participate – what Putnam (1993) terms their 'social capital'. The concern about low levels of public participation are reflective of an underlying unease about the health of Western liberal democracies and the legitimacy of their modes of governance (Daemen and Schaap, 2000).

Paradoxically, in this environment of declining citizen participation in conventional political processes, governments are actively seeking or requiring citizens' involvement as stakeholders in collaborative action. The identification of citizens as partners in the design and delivery of public policy and services alongside public, private and voluntary sector bodies is evident world-wide. In Southern Africa and Asia a programme of 'community-based natural resource management' devolves control of particular resources to local communities working in partnership with relevant public authorities and interests. One of the assumptions the programme works with is that local communities are at least as knowledgeable as professionals if not more so about the management of such natural resources (Fortmann, Roes and Van Eeten, 2001). In the US and the UK local people have long been considered partners in the processes of neighbourhood revitalisation or regeneration. However, their experiences have oftentimes been marred by a recognition that they are not equal partners and that it is their relative lack of resource power that defines their relationship with other more powerful partners (Peterman, 2000; Hastings *et al.*, 1996; Hastings and McArthur, 1995).

This chapter explores the experience of citizens involved in public policy collaborations in the UK. It begins by exploring the particular circumstances that gave rise to the public involvement agenda of New Labour. It then examines the experience of citizen involvement in different types and levels of collaboration, focusing on the issues of leadership, capacity and power relationships. We conclude by considering the impact of citizen involvement in collaboration and identifying ways in which it could be enhanced.

Citizen participation and New Labour

Government initiatives to stimulate citizen participation are not unique to New Labour. In the 1970s the Community Development Projects (CDPs) sought to involve citizens as empowered partners in their dealings with the state (see Chapter 4). The 1980s saw a dramatic shift in emphasis with Conservative governments promoting the notion of the citizen as primarily a customer or consumer of public services. This privatisation of the relationship between the citizen and the state was supported by the contracting-out of local services and the expansion of private provision in key areas of public concern. Lowndes (1995) suggests that this individualised model was recast in the 1990s through the notion of the citizen as 'community member' – an individual with concerns about the impact of the workings of the state and society that went beyond immediate self-interest.

This community member role is present in New Labour's emphasis upon the responsibilities of citizens to each other and to the state. Their agenda contains three key elements:

1. *Revitalising the democratic health of the nation.* Reconnecting the citizen to the state via action to enhance democratic practice by making it more meaningful and relevant to citizens' lives.
2. *Improving public services.* Public services are perceived to be poor and dominated by the professionals that deliver them. New Labour has introduced Best Value into local government – a process of service review that aims to take account of users' views – while in the NHS the Patient Advice and Liaison Services (PALs) will provide a voice for users in NHS service planning (Department of Health, 2001).
3. *Tackling social exclusion.* Specific communities experience exclusion from mainstream democratic, economic and cultural processes in the UK. Variously described as 'hard-to-reach', 'disadvantaged' or socially

excluded, New Labour has targeted specific resources towards creating a more inclusive society, such as the National Strategy for Neighbourhood Renewal. (Social Exclusion Unit, 2001)

The combination of these factors has resulted in the development of a new political ethos where citizens are expected to contribute to the solution of key policy problems in concert with service providers and policy-makers (Barnes and Prior, 2000; Gilliat *et al.*, 2000).

The UK literature pertaining to citizen participation tends to fall into separate but linked categories; material that focuses on citizens' relationship with government, including Lowndes *et al.* (1998) and Leach and Wingfield (1999) and material that explores citizens' experiences in collaboration, including most recently Balloch and Taylor (2001) and Powell, Glendinning and Rummery (forthcoming). While the focus is different very often the purposes identified for citizen participation are common. A recent analysis has identified six such purposes:

1. Citizen participation for governance, that is citizen involvement in development and implementation processes, via the membership of partnerships and/or the setting up and operating of governance and accountability arrangements.
2. Community development as a method of working to achieve objectives.
3. User involvement in decision-making about services, practice and policy development, and in personal service provision.
4. Communication and other strategies to keep the public informed and develop public support.
5. Community and user involvement in generating evidence and knowledge.
6. Citizen empowerment via the operation of programmes to build social capital and/or reduce social exclusion (Sullivan, Barnes and Matka, forthcoming).

These various roles have implications for the citizen's relationship with the state. Representative democracy remains vitally important for New Labour and the restoration of the relationship between citizen and elected representative is evident within the modernisation programmes. However, participative democracy has latterly been popularised as a means of achieving a closer relationship with citizens. Recent collaborative initiatives, such as Local Agenda 21 and Crime and Disorder Partnerships have been associated with the development and application of participative approaches. The most recent addition to the mix is deliberative democracy, a variant of participative democracy but one that privileges informed dialogue and debate between stakeholders on an equal footing in order to produce a collectively agreed and owned outcome (Habermas, 1984; Elster, 1998). Deliberation is evident in some of the recent collaborative programmes such as Sure Start and the peace partnerships in Northern Ireland (Hughes *et al.*, 1998).

This variety of forms is intended to enhance the quality of democracy in modern states. For some (such as Leach *et al.*, 1996; Stewart, 1995) participative approaches are intended to support the primacy of representative democracy. For others however, these forms provide sources of accountability that are parallel or even replace traditional representative forms. This provides a key source of tension in the way in which accountability between citizens, communities and the state is secured in the future, and which we now explore.

Engaging citizens in collaboration

Which citizens?

An early report on the experience of the UK government in relation to cross-cutting issues found that:

> Capacity to involve people in the shaping, design and delivery of public policy and service is an essential component of successfully tackling cross-cutting issues. Desired policy outcomes in these areas usually involve changes in mind and changes in behaviour on the part of citizens, as well as on the part of those who work in, and influence, the public policy system. (Richards *et al.*, 1999, p. 123)

While this conclusion fits with the idea of citizens as active partners it also begs the question: which citizens? The issue of whose involvement is sought goes to the heart of our understanding of citizen involvement in collaboration.

The first point to note is the use of language in public policy. Currently, the term community is preferred. For example, the Department of Health's invitation to bid for HAZ status referred to the need to secure 'community' involvement (Department of Health, 1997). For Etzioni, this usage is vitally important as 'communities provide bonds of affection that turn groups of people into social entities resembling extended families ... they transmit a shared moral culture' (2000, p. 15). So use of the term 'community' may be reflective of an aspiration for society – that 'community' can be fashioned where it may not already exist. Another reason for the use of the term is a desire to promote inclusive public policy in a society where not all of those present have citizenship, for example, refugee communities.

Use of the term 'community' does not, however, resolve all difficulties associated with determining who to involve. For many the nature of 'community' is contested (Hoggett, 1997) and it is now generally recognised that communities in modern societies take a number of different forms including communities of place, identity and interest (Etzioni, 2000; Phillips, 1993). For Etzioni this variety of communities is empowering as membership is based upon a positive choice by an individual to join. However, some see this freedom as being limited to certain members of communities who in their turn will seek to exclude others. For example, Barnes and Bowls' work with mental health users highlights the ways in which individuals may be excluded from place-based communities because of their 'difference' (Barnes and Bowl, 2001). Often exclusion may be unintentional and result paradoxically from concerted efforts to *include* new people in the community. For example, a recent review of a local authority citizen participation initiative found that despite targeting of 'hard-to-reach' groups, the institutionalised relationships that existed between long-standing community activists and the authorities meant that potential new members found it a very difficult group to join (Sullivan, Gaster and Griffiths, 2000).

Overall it is central government that wields the most power in determining which citizens or communities are to be involved in collaboration, not least because it is central government that determines the priorities for collaborative action. A dominant trend apparent through the regeneration programmes of the last two decades is the desire to engage and involve 'deprived communities' in their regeneration. The 'New Labour' focus on social exclusion has led to initiatives that are geographically specific, for example New Deal for Communities, as well as those that target other kinds of 'communities' such as rough sleepers. These initiatives expect that targeted communities will take responsibility for addressing their problems, for example NDC highlights the role of community members in leading sustainable regeneration on their estates. These localised expectations of 'citizen performance' suggest that those in receipt of government funding may need to conform to an aspiration of 'community' that is not expected of other members of society.

Citizen involvement in different levels of collaboration

Collaborative activity can be categorised as taking place at three levels (see Chapter 2):

1. Strategic: activity that is local authority wide or is sub-regional/regional in nature;

2. Sectoral: activity that is concerned with the design and delivery of specific policies or services;
3. Neighbourhood: activity that is focused on a small, geographic community.

Some initiatives may be level-specific, for example neighbourhood management and Community Care, while others may operate across a number of levels, such as HAZ, crime and disorder partnerships and Local Agenda 21 partnerships. However, each level holds specific implications for citizen participation that will determine the nature of the collaborative relationship which develops (Table 9.1).

In strategic collaborations citizen participation may take a number of forms. Very often citizens are not members of the strategic body directing the collaboration, for example crime and disorder partnerships or local strategic partnerships. However, they may be identified as key consultees in the work of the strategic body. So in crime and disorder partnerships, for example, citizens are consulted as part of the process of conducting a crime and disorder audit and developing a local strategy. Where citizens are members of the strategic body directing the collaboration, their role is a representative one. As a result the individuals who participate tend to be 'community leaders', that is people who are recognised as having a legitimate position of authority within their communities. Another way of

Table 9.1 *Levels of collaboration and citizen participation*

Implications for citizens	*Strategic*	*Sectoral*	*Neighbourhood*
Role	Representative – focus on community leaders and umbrella groups	Participative – focus on users and beneficiaries	Representative and participative – focus on users and community members
Proximity to Community	Distant – infrastructure necessary	Close	Close
Remit	Wide-ranging	Focused on specific service	Focused on local well-being
Presence	Citizens one of many stakeholders represented	Users a key stakeholder with providers and commissioners	Citizens one of many stakeholders, but with greatest interest

securing representation is through the formation of an umbrella body to represent the interests of a particular group who then elect or appoint a leader to participate in strategic fora. A number of Health Action Zones have adopted this approach.

The focus on 'representation' and the relatively small number of seats available to citizens on strategic bodies means that they may be offered to individuals who are perceived as reflecting the nature of the local population. For example, Birmingham City Pride – a government-sanctioned strategic partnership vehicle for establishing and monitoring progress towards a vision for the city – initially allocated a number of seats to citizens to reflect the composition of the local population. Such an approach can be problematic. For example, where the number of seats available may not actually reflect the diversity of stakeholders in the population, continued exclusion can result. Where there is no infrastructure to link the strategic body with communities, the capacity of citizen representatives to maintain regular communication may be limited. Finally, where the chosen citizen representatives are not in fact widely recognised by communities as having a connection with them, they may be rejected as appropriate representatives. Regardless of the means of representation, strategic vehicles for collaboration are generally wider-ranging in their remit and comprise the most powerful actors in the locality or region. As such citizen representatives may be able to exercise little influence over the collaboration and may also experience it as inaccessible and only partially relevant to their interests.

Sectoral collaborations are more focused in their intent, requiring the participation of a particular citizen group, usually one that benefits from the service that the collaboration is built around. The focus of the collaboration is clear with an emphasis on improved service design and delivery along with the development of enhanced methods of user evaluation. Service users tend to have a more equal presence in these collaborations as there are fewer partners to involve. Connexions partnerships, for example, actively engage their users (young people) on local management boards (Department for Education and Skills, 2001b). However, in sectoral partnerships professionals, by virtue of their authority, retain considerable influence over decisions and processes (Barnes *et al.*, 1999).

Neighbourhood collaborations are focused on a specific area but are wide-ranging in their remit. They are well-documented in relation to regeneration but are also the focus for environmental sustainability (Local Agenda 21), local service delivery (neighbourhood management) and housing (via estate management boards). It is at this level that citizen participation in collaboration is potentially widest and deepest. The relative intimacy of the collaborative arrangements means that in terms of representation, a wider range of stakeholders can be represented. It also means that citizen participation in the collaboration may be easier and more meaningful because it is close to the respective communities (although this may not be the case where neighbourhood initiatives disregard and cut across communities of identity). The citizen presence in neighbourhood collaborations is significant and under New Labour the emphasis has been on the development of leadership as well as participation amongst citizen members. While the role of citizens as community leaders has become increasingly important, past experience suggests that the development of this leadership capacity necessitates consideration of issues such as legitimacy and accountability.

The role of community leaders in collaboration

The capacity of elected councillors to act as community leaders has been questioned by the diversity and complexity of the prevailing environment (Purdue *et al.*, 2000; Taylor, 2000). Consequently attention has been paid to the contribution of other 'community leaders' who are able to speak with authority and have credibility among other partners. The sources of community leadership are varied but tend to comprise: leaders of communities of identity, such as faith communities or domestic violence survivors groups; leaders of communities of place; and leaders of communities of interest, for example nature conservation groups. Their legitimacy as leaders rests upon a number of factors: authority conferred from elsewhere; specific knowledge; experience of the community; or demonstrable evidence of having benefited the community through their actions.

In a recent study of community care Barr *et al.* (2001) concluded that community leaders made a significant contribution to participative governance in a number of ways. They played a variety of roles, for example acting as convenors for community interests or conduits for ideas and catalysts for change. They brought a range of skills which were complementary to those of partners and reflected their capacity to work with and on behalf of service users and community members and to contribute to collaborative activity. Finally, they had common personal characteristics including commitment, concern for justice and mutuality, perseverance, resilience, awareness of community perspectives and realism. These findings are supported by other studies, for example Purdue *et al.* (2000) and

Anastacio *et al.* (2000). However, while community leadership may now be accepted as a key component in the successful operation of cross-sector collaborations, past experience of collaborative endeavours suggests that operationalising this can prove challenging to both public organisations and community leaders. There are five issues:

1. *The selection of community leaders*: How community leaders are iden-tified and invited into collaborations can be critical in establishing their credibility with the wider community and their impact within the col-laboration. Edwards *et al.*'s (1999) study of partnership working in rural regeneration found that community interests tended to be represented from among a cohort of councillors, community associations and young farmers' clubs. However, they also found that these representatives may reflect the preferences of partnership co-ordinators rather than of local communities. Selecting leaders in this way raises questions about the accountability of the partnership and effectively limits community involvement.

2. *'Making' and 'breaking' community stars*: Participation in collaborative activity can give community leaders access to power and decision-making in a way that they have not previously experienced. While this can prove positive, the prevailing power relationships among the partners may mean that it is short-lived. For example, Barnes *et al.*'s study of the involvement of user groups in community care reveals the way in which 'officials simultaneously held the user group to be legitimate and illegiti-mate, practically useful, and yet useless' (1999, pp. 119–20). One of the most powerful ways in which statutory bodies can silence community leaders is to question their representativeness. Studies have revealed that this can be used as a lever over community leaders where levels of trust between statutory and other partners are low (Barr *et al.*, 2001).

3. *Community leaders, representation and accountability*: Whether and how community leaders can be seen to be representative and account-able is a long-standing tension in cross-sector collaborations. Purdue *et al.* (2000) show that community leaders in area regeneration pro-grammes were frequently only partially representative of communities of identity, that the infrastructure for accountability back to communi-ties was poor and that community leaders often replicated processes of social exclusion leaving some communities with little voice. While these are difficult challenges, at the heart of the debate is a tension about the role that community leaders are expected to play. In some cases user groups have sought to remain aloof from this by refusing to put forward 'leaders' but rather acting as a collective all members of

which need to be participants in the process of decision-making. This can be problematic for state agencies who are anxious to identify a single person with whom they can 'do business'.

4. *Incorporation*: The experience of collaboration can lead to community leaders becoming incorporated into the process of programme design and delivery. Incorporation has been evident through the expectation that community leaders will become 'unpaid community professionals', able to manage the bureaucracy and paperwork associated with the implementation of regeneration programmes (Anastacio *et al.*, 2000; Sullivan and Beazley, 1998).

5. *Sustaining community leaders*: 'Burnout' is a major problem for community leaders in collaborative activity. They are generally under greater time pressures than statutory partners and will invariably experience stress as a result of their voluntary role. This can result in community leaders giving up their role (Skelcher and Davis, 1995). As the breadth of collaborative activities increases there will be greater demand for community leaders and policy-makers need to be aware of the implications of this for individuals.

Citizen capacity in collaboration

The extent to which citizens are able to influence collaborations depends in part upon whether or not they are able to draw upon sufficient capacity to support them. Research into community safety initiatives have identified the significance of community capacity but found little evidence of it (Benyon and Edwards, 1999), while evaluative work in health has emphasised the importance of building capacity for collaboration among communities if health improvement is to be achieved (Sullivan, Barnes and Matka, forthcoming).

Citizen or community capacity is determined by a variety of factors, some of which are individual but others of which are structural (Table 9.2). A great deal of attention has been focused upon developing the capacity of individuals within communities. Area-based initiatives in the UK devote resources to capacity-building programmes that seek to increase the personal skills and confidence of citizens through confidence-building activities and training in practical skills such as running meetings, making presentations and preparing bids for funding. In addition, lack of time and money can limit individual involvement in collaboration and in some cases citizen participants are paid for their involvement. The existence of structural inequalities within society

Table 9.2   *Factors influencing citizen involvement in collaborations*

Individual	Institutional	Societal	Environmental
• Time • Skills • Money • Confidence • Motivation	• Rules – what is permitted • Culture – the way the organisation works and its values • Orientation – the priority afforded citizen participation	• Age • Class • Disability • Ethnic origin • Gender • Sexuality	• Location • Crime • Poverty • Nature of community ties

and the failure of public bodies to address these will also impact upon the extent to which individuals feel able to participate. So when issues of physical access or translation or interpretation are not addressed, or when there is no provision for childcare in partnership meetings, or there are no 'ground rules' specifying intolerance of racist or sexist language in meetings, then participation for many community members becomes difficult if not impossible (Barnes, Newman, Knops and Sullivan, 2001).

The extent to which these challenges will be effectively addressed depends very much on the capacity of local partner organisations. Here other institutional factors will come into play. These factors will determine how the rules for collaboration with communities are established and will be informed both by the culture of the organisations and the consequent priority it affords to community participation (see Chapter 6). Finally, citizen capacity in collaboration will also be informed by wider environmental factors. For example, in an area where fear of crime is high, community members may feel less able to participate in collaborative activity which requires attendance at evening meetings. Similarly the location of meetings may restrict who can attend. For example, Liverpool City Council's Area Forums cover a large geographical area. To enable as many members of the community as possible to attend over a year's cycle of meetings, the meetings are rotated around different neighbourhoods.

An important concept that links individual to wider aspects of community capacity is social capital. Social capital is a relationship-oriented concept that focuses on engagement in civic activity. Putnam (1993) argues that the qualities of trust and reciprocity that are developed in civic relationships create the capacity among citizens to engage in collective action and increase their expectations about the nature of their relationship with the institutions of government. Therefore, action to release or develop social capital within communities has become a concern of many involved in community-based collaborations. However, Putnam's thesis has been criticised by Lowndes and Wilson (2001) and Maloney *et al.* (2000) for neglecting the role of state agency in facilitating or hindering the development of social capital. For example, in relation to community safety, Liddle and Gelsthorpe (1994) illustrate how the anxiety among statutory partners about raising the expectations of communities beyond their ability to respond led to a limited engagement with communities and minimal attempts at capacity-building.

Capacity-building can take individuals to different levels of skill and confidence. In some cases the desired outcome is to enable communities to take the lead in leading and managing their own communities. For example, Taylor (2000) cites instances of local communities that have become managers of their own housing organisations. However, in other cases citizen or community capacity is one of a number of elements that need to be in place if positive outcomes are to be achieved. For example, the Audit Commission (1999) argued that successful local community safety strategies required local organisational support, political commitment, positive media support and dedicated funding as well as community capacity. The extent to which citizens and communities will desire a high level of control over their lives and services will in part be dependent upon available capacity. However, it may also be influenced by the experience of past collaborations and in particular the operation of power relationships within those collaborations. It is to this issue that we now turn.

Power relationships in collaboration

Who has power and how it is measured and employed are important to address if citizens are to be able to exercise influence in collaborative endeavours. Successive evaluations of regeneration programmes and health and social care initiatives reveal the level of frustration experienced by community members who gain a place at the decision-making table only to find that their input is marginal to the outcomes of the programme (for example, Mayo and Taylor, 2001). This power imbalance remains in current initiatives. For example, the national evaluation of HAZ found that while communities were perceived as key stakeholders they were the least likely to be involved in the strategic decision-making (Barnes, Sullivan and Matka, 2001). Even when they were involved, their potential power in relation to the statutory players was limited. In the words of one, 'it's like being Luxembourg in the EU with France and Germany. You know you have a veto but you're not really sure how much difference it makes in practice' (Barnes and Sullivan, forthcoming).

The imbalance in power stems from the fact that statutory bodies have both the authority to act in key policy and service areas and can call upon significant resources to support them. Although resources in collaborations may be held and dispensed by a superordinate body following a process of consultation, the power bases of statutory bodies gives them an advantage in such debates. However, citizens and communities are not without power. Their advocacy may be based upon experiences as a resident in a regeneration area or a service user or a victim or survivor of crime. This experiential power provides a source of expertise that professionals or politicians may not have and gives them credibility and legitimacy with the community and, possibly, with other stakeholders. Ways of redressing power imbalances in collaborations include the allocation of a number of places around decision-making tables for community members to speak on behalf of or about the experiences of specific groups or communities. For Peterman (2000) one of the key issues is how far power is shared in the decision-making process. His study of community-led neighbourhood activity in Chicago identifies three separate uses of the term 'empowerment': as the management of services; as participation in decision-making in government; and as community control involving a transfer of power. His studies of resident housing management programmes reveal that where the focus was primarily on citizens as consumers then little power was shared, and:

> a resident management effort did not result in the residents actually taking control of their development, but instead merely resulted in the transfer of some, or even, in some cases, a significant number of management tasks to a tenant corporation. In these situations, even though there had been resident organising, it had not led to empowerment. (2000, p. 38)

If statutory bodies are not prepared or required to give up power then it remains likely that 'empowerment' will result in the increase of citizen's responsibilities rather than their influence. Latterly the UK government has tried to address this problem by introducing schemes that are predicated on giving communities greater control, for example the New Deal for Communities and Neighbourhood Management programmes. In both cases significant 'empowerment' funding is allocated to support the capacity-building of communities and the explicit intention is that communities adopt leadership roles in relation to the initiative. However, Carley *et al.* (2000) suggest that this kind of strategy will only take real effect if it is accompanied by other measures to devolve the power of statutory bodies down to more local levels so that communities can influence decisions across the board.

Power is a feature not only of formal mechanisms, but also of informal networks between key individuals in collaborations, relationships that are reinforced through familiarity and commonality of interest. As we have discussed earlier (Chapter 6) networks are powerful forces with the potential to exclude. Skelcher *et al.* (1996) suggest a five-point strategy for maximising the potential of networks to share rather than retain power:

1. take positive steps to widen access to potential participants;
2. ensure that those involved have the opportunity to shape the overall process followed by the collaboration;
3. codify certain behaviours, that is, that all participants are heard with respect and all decisions are taken through consensus;
4. ensure that statutory bodies are open to the outcomes of networks and prepared to make changes to accommodate their proposals;
5. develop networks' ability to learn from their experiences and build their capacity to link with others to form a stronger framework.

However, access to decision-making and participation always seems more likely for some community members than others, despite these various attempts to challenge and change the prevailing power relationships in collaborations. The next section will examine the capacity of collaborations to go beyond 'the usual suspects' and draw upon evidence to suggest some strategies for action to involve those groups who are considered 'hard-to-reach'.

Engaging the whole community

There are different terms to describe the citizens that collaborations seek to involve with least success. These include 'marginalised', 'socially excluded', 'disenfranchised' and most commonly 'hard-to-reach'. The question of who exactly is 'hard-to-reach' will vary depending upon the purpose of the collaboration. So, for example, while collaborations based upon communities of place may experience difficulty in involving their disabled members, collaborations that are focused upon disabled services users may have difficulty in involving young disabled people or black or Asian disabled people.

However, there are some differences in the way in which specific groups are perceived for the purposes of collaboration. Those groups that are most frequently highlighted for involvement include young people and black and minority ethnic communities. The focus on the former tends to reflect concern with the apparent alienation of young people from civic and political life and society's wider concern with the incidence of anti-social behaviour (Barnes, 1999; Gaster, 1999). The concern with the latter communities acknowledges their relative disadvantage and social exclusion and the failure of many community-based organisations to represent their interests (Chau and Yu, 2001). Quaiyoom (1993), for example, cites the exclusion of black and minority ethnic tenants from local tenant associations. Other groups are less likely to be sought as potential collaborators either because of their very marginal status, for example travellers, drug users and homeless people, or because of the prevailing attitudes of professionals (Keywood *et al.*, 1999; McCauley *et al.*, 1997).

The experience of involving 'hard-to-reach groups'

Regeneration partnerships with their focus upon poor and excluded communities should provide insights into the involvement of 'hard-to-reach' communities. Early experiences were not particularly positive, as the example of the Single Regeneration Budget in engaging 'hard-to-reach groups' illustrates:

> The SRB has drawn together a range of activities under one funding umbrella, and mixed capital and revenue programmes. Evidence so far seems to suggest that it will be unable to ensure black communities experience meaningful economic regeneration because it provides no guarantee of resources at the end of a demanding and rigorous process. (National Council of Voluntary Organisations, 1994, p. 7)

Subsequent evaluations of black and minority ethnic involvement in SRB bear out this statement (Loftman and Beazley, 1998). Hall *et al.* (1998) show that community access to and involvement in key decisions of the SRB partnerships improved over the first three rounds and leadership of schemes by the community and voluntary sectors increased from 5 to 10 per cent. However, there was an almost total absence of ethnic minority groups being successful in leading schemes and the promotion of projects aimed at ethnic minority groups was cited as a top priority in only 2 per cent of local authority-led schemes.

Government requirements that programmes monitor their activities in relation to their impact upon black and minority ethnic communities meant that it was possible to discern how these communities fared in relation to resource allocation and influence over decision-making. The absence of such requirements in relation to gender meant that even when SRB programmes cited the promotion of women as one of their objectives, their level of success was only evident among the minority of lead bodies that voluntarily monitored such indicators. The lack of focus on the role played by women in regeneration has meant that even less is known about the experiences of women from 'hard-to-reach' communities. Research that has been undertaken reveals consistent themes, including that womens' potential contribution is not supported primarily because their organisational skills, local knowledge and network of relationships are simply not recognised or valued by programme leaders (Riseborough and White, 1994; Kitchin *et al.*, 1994). A similar point is made by Lowndes in relation to the way in which the understanding of social capital is gender-blind and does not acknowledge the kinds of social capital women develop (Lowndes, 2000). This failure to acknowledge the potential contribution of women in the community is compounded by women's own lack of self-confidence in their ability. According to Riseborough and White this means that unless there is a focus on supporting the contribution of women from all backgrounds, their contribution will not be picked up.

The experience of 'hard-to-reach' communities is little better in those collaborations that are specifically targeting their concerns. For example, a Home Office (1991) report into early initiatives to address racial attacks concluded that community involvement in such initiatives was crucial but that initiatives had struggled to involve and retain community members because of the lack of trust between communities and statutory organisations and scepticism on the part of communities that statutory bodies were serious in their intent to address racial attacks. The Macpherson Report (1999), almost a decade later, identified little progress in this regard. Another report evaluating the experience of a specific multi-agency initiative found that community involvement was limited because the mode of selection of community members on its Steering Group led to the domination of statutory partners and left key groups under-represented (Saulsbury and Bowling, 1991).

A study into multi-agency approaches to addressing domestic violence found that only a very small number of the survivors they surveyed had any awareness of the initiative in their area (Hague *et al.*, 1996). While the vast majority believed that they should have an input into the activities of domestic violence fora, not least because of their experience in relation to the issue, there was often a reluctance to do so because of the power relationships between 'professionals' and survivors participating in the fora and the potential for conflict to arise. Survivors also feared that statutory bodies would use them to give the forum credibility and legitimacy.

Most recently a study into the involvement of service users (particularly ethnic minority and older users) in commissioning decisions for the provision of health and social care services found that commissioners remained unaware of basic access issues for users, including wheelchair and British Sign Language facilities, as well as the religious and cultural observances of specific service-user communities (Lindow, 1996). While the researchers concluded that training and support was needed to facilitate collaborative decision-making, professionals did not always accept this. Ethnic minority service users' past experience of discrimination may also make them less trusting of professionals and in some cases their involvement is limited by the protective role played by some voluntary organisations, for example in relation to ethnic minority, mental health service users.

Strategies for action

The experience of 'hard-to-reach' groups appears to show common traits regardless of the context. Therefore it is possible to identify common actions that will help to improve their involvement in future collaborations (Table 9.3). A factor that commentators agree upon is the need to involve 'hard-to-reach' communities from the beginning of the process. Without this evidence of commitment, later attempts at targeting involvement will be diluted through lack of ownership by the community at large (Brownhill and Darke, 1998; Hall *et al.*, 1998). Accessing 'hard-to-reach' communities successfully can only be achieved by the use of skilled outreach workers. This approach is resource intensive in terms of time and money. However, it is clear from a number of studies that this approach is more likely than any other to have the desired effect (Hague *et al.*, 1996; Kitchin *et al.*, 1994; Lindow, 1996). On occasion this work is best undertaken by a voluntary organisation that has credibility with communities, for example Women's Aid in the case of domestic violence. Otherwise it may be undertaken by community workers who are able to develop relationships with people in the course of their daily lives, for example the guidance for 'learning cities' suggests that engaging diverse communities begins by going to the school gates as parents are most likely to spend time there waiting to collect their children (Department for Education and Employment, 1998b).

Table 9.3 *Strategies for engaging hard-to-reach groups*

Problem	Cause	Action
Targeting of high profile 'community leaders' who may not have the confidence of all of the communities	Lack of knowledge about communities. Deference to dominant political relationships	Research and outreach to identify and explore diversity of community needs
Imposition of research instruments that may not resonate with communities so leading to low-level response	Requirements of programme to work within pre-set parameters leading to specific research design and use of terms	Research instruments designed and applied with participation from respective communities
Low level of response from specific communities despite publicity/awareness raising	Lack of trust between communities and statutory bodies based on past bad experiences	Resource intensive outreach work employing skilled workers or organisations to go to where communities meet to introduce them to initiative
		Collaborations to have the scope to allow community members to get involved on their own terms
Failure of collaboration to attract diverse representation from communities	Imposition of rules of involvement with which communities do not agree leads to under-representation by some groups	Agreement with communities about rules of involvement
		Employing more than one form of involvement
	Dominance of collaboration by statutory bodies	Increasing the ratio of community to statutory members
		Develop a separate forum for community members linked to forum for statutory bodies
	Statutory bodies do not reflect wider community	Statutory bodies improving representation of minority groups among all levels of staff

(Continued)

Table 9.3 (*Continued*)

Problem	Cause	Action
Failure of community members to stay involved in collaboration	Inadequate support for community members	Resource support to individuals to enable participation, e.g. childcare, physical access, interpretation
	Use of 'jargon' and unfamiliar rules	Resource support for local groups to build capacity for participation and facilitate accountability to wider community
	Dominance of professional concerns within collaboration	Training for *all* members in developing appropriate codes of conduct and protocols for meetings etc. Development and monitoring of equal opportunities policy in collaboration Clarify roles of members in collaboration and emphasise contribution of community members as experts
	Implementation demands override changes to improve community participation in collaboration	Negotiation with relevant funder to try and create space for effective implementation
Inability to demonstrate 'what works'	Poor provision for monitoring and evaluation of experience of involvement in collaboration and impact of involvement	Development of targets for monitoring impact on specific groups Adequate resourcing of quantitative and qualitative data collection Publicising success of initiative widely

In some cases the prevailing power relationships and lack of trust between 'hard-to-reach' communities and the mainstream providers in collaboration may be such that additional support is needed for those groups in order to facilitate their participation. This can result in the creation of specialist bodies whose role is to act as a block of influence within collaborations, for example Bradford HAZ works with a body called HEAT (Health Equality Action Team) to achieve this. In other areas attempts have been made to increase the influence of 'hard-to-reach' groups by extending traditional mechanisms. In Walsall, the Local Involvement initiative has resulted in the development of neighbourhood committees who oversee and advise on the spending of regeneration money in their areas. The neighbourhoods are small (no more than 1100 people) and the committees are elected on a representative basis. Turnouts have been as high if not higher than in local elections and the resulting elected representatives have reflected the diversity of Walsall's local communities (Sullivan *et al.*, 2001).

The role played by monitoring and evaluation has become very important in recording the impact of collaborative efforts upon 'hard-to-reach' communities. The experience of SRB has led to a closer attention to the way in which targets are devised and monitored in subsequent regeneration programmes and there has been an increase in the development and application of community-based or community-led evaluation frameworks in recent years (such as Sullivan and Potter, 2001). However, there is concern that frameworks remain constrained by the use of quantitative data and are not able to complement this with the application of more qualitative findings (see Chapter 10).

The impact of citizen participation in collaboration

The importance of citizen participation in collaboration is widely accepted. However, relatively little is known about its impact. Here we draw attention to evidence that is available with specific reference to the impact of citizen involvement on individual participants, communities, the quality of the collaboration and its outcomes.

Individual participants

Individuals' experience of collaboration as 'life changing' is common. Participants will often tell of 'feeling more confident' as a result of participating, of 'knowing that they can make a difference', 'understanding better how things work' and developing the skills to function alongside professionals and others in collaborations (Sullivan and Potter, 2001). However, the positive experiences are invariably accompanied (and often overwhelmed) by negative experiences or consequences of getting involved. Experiences of feeling marginalised, excluded, used and exploited have been referred to earlier and Purdue *et al.* (2000) reveal how potentially damaging citizen participation can be in terms of stress levels and impact on family or personal life.

Communities

Early studies into the impact of citizen participation in collaboration upon communities had little to contribute largely because what was reported was the failure of the collaborations to effectively engage communities. In City Challenge, there was concern that even though community representatives might be part of the decision-making bodies their impact would be less than that of private sector stakeholders because of the emphasis of the programme on levering in significant external resources (Mabbott, 1993). More recent studies of regeneration in the UK indicate circumstances have changed, with Carley *et al.* (2000, p. 16) concluding that community capacity can grow 'steadily and sustainably through involvement in a regeneration partnership programme'.

In service-focused collaborations the outcomes for communities are similarly mixed. For example, Barnes *et al.* (1999) examined service user groups' experience of collaboration with commissioners and providers. They found that involvement in the collaboration gave the user community the opportunity 'to challenge the assumptions of welfare professionals as well as lay attitudes towards "needy" and stigmatised groups' (1999, p. 126). However, they also identified adverse impacts on the user community, including the depletion of user-group resources in trying to maintain relationships with the variety of potential collaborators, the potential for the group to become caught up in a cycle of reacting to the agenda set by others and the danger of the group becoming dominated by a consumerist philosophy.

The quality of the collaboration

The extent to which citizen participation has informed the way in which collaborations 'do business' is variable. Certainly collaborations are now more likely to draw in communities from the beginning of the process and to use a variety of means to access and support community engagement. Collaborations are also more likely to understand the complexity of community dynamics and to be more aware of the resources required to engage 'hard-to-reach' groups. However, the specific mechanisms for organising and managing collaborative processes remain the cycle of meetings, agendas and minutes. For the most part citizen participants have had to learn the 'rules' of meetings in order to participate effectively in collaborative activities.

Outcomes

Disentangling the impact of citizen participation in collaborations is difficult. However, there are indications that citizen participation can affect outcomes. Barr *et al.* (2001), for example, provide evidence of community leaders acting as catalysts for new ideas within service-focused collaborations. Other sources point to the significance of utilising local views and experience in order to both increase local ownership of programmes and to gain a better idea of 'what the problem is' and 'what works' in a particular area from the perspective of the beneficiaries (for example, Benyon and Edwards, 1996; Audit Commission, 1999).

The capacity of citizens to impact on outcomes appears to be greater in relation to local or more closely-specified collaborations. Research in York has revealed the extent to which communities have been able to influence the process and content of 'neighbourhood agreements'. These are formal statements drawn up by local partnerships of providers and citizens to outline the level of services that will be delivered to a community. While communities have no formal sanctions if services deliverers do not meet their set targets or standards, the act of having to give an account of progress or failure to a community meeting is considered by some to be sanction enough (Cole *et al.*, 2000). Citizens are most likely to influence the outcomes of activity when it is they that are in control of the collaboration. For example, Carley *et al.* (2000) cite the example of the Arts Factory in the Rhondda in Wales. This is a community development trust that employs 28 local residents and provides services to the local community funded in part by revenue it earns through commercial activity it undertakes.

This emphasis on control is revealing as it reinforces the findings of other studies, which indicate that where collaborations are reliant upon national streams of funding their capacity to develop local inclusive strategies for action will remain limited. For example, one HAZ had as its focus a concern

with children and children's services. However, central government refused
to endorse this and subsequently required all HAZs to include targets for
coronary heart disease, mental health and cancer in their programmes
(Barnes, Sullivan and Matka, 2001). Other writers are also sceptical about
the capacity of citizen participation to be influential in informing outcomes, indicating that most collaborations are simply too small to have
any major impact on outcomes for regeneration, health and community
safety which are influenced by far larger socio-economic changes (Nevin
and Shiner, 1995; Gilling, 1997).

Conclusion

Involving citizens in collaborative activity is politically complex and practically difficult. Governmental initiatives that seek citizens as partners are
frequently overlaid by visions of society that are not developed with communities but none the less form the basis of their subsequent involvement.
Citizens may be expected to engage with collaborations at different levels
and this requires different skills, roles and supporting infrastructure. The
involvement of community leaders in collaborative relationships may be
one way of efficiently engaging communities but it calls for clarity about
their role and accountability. It also necessitates some consideration of
their legitimacy within their particular community. Developing capacity
among community members to help facilitate their participation is
resource intensive in terms of time and money and also requires an examination of wider institutional and structural factors that might hinder effective capacity-building. The concept of social capital is helpful here. Power
relationships are a vitally important part of any collaboration and there is a
propensity for statutory bodies to dominate. However, citizens do bring
specific experiential and lay knowledge to collaborations and their contribution needs to be valued on this basis. This contribution may be more difficult to obtain in relation to those citizens or communities that are subject
to processes of social exclusion. Here particular attention needs to be paid
to understanding the dynamics of these groups and securing ways to
involve them. Assessing the impact of citizen participation in collaboration
is difficult and often costly. This could also be said of attempts to evaluate
collaboration more generally. Examining why the evaluation of collaboration is difficult and reviewing the available evidence about the contribution
of collaborative activity to date is the subject of the next chapter.

10 Evaluating Collaboration

Evaluation is the key tool for identifying 'what works' in terms of delivering public policy goals. It has a particular significance in an era where the pragmatic values of the Third Way place weight on policy and practice being evidence-based rather than ideologically determined (Davies *et al.*, 2000; Giddens, 2000). This agenda is of major concern in the UK, but is also apparent internationally. For example, the W. K. Kellogg Community Empowerment Programme in southern Africa and the Robert Wood Johnson Foundation Urban Health Initiative in eight US cities are both concerned with identifying 'what works' in different contexts. There is an urgency to the task of evaluation as a result of policy-makers' determination to demonstrate real improvements in the well-being of the population and to justify the 'value added' by collaboration. The 'real worldness' of evaluation (Robson, 1993, p. 170) – its concern with addressing practical problems and influencing change – is extremely valuable in the public policy context. However, this also contributes to the contention surrounding evaluation. It means that evaluators are operating in a dynamic environment and amongst a range of stakeholders who may have very different views about the purpose and design of the evaluation and the interpretation of its results. Consequently evaluation of public policy is a highly charged issue with methodological disagreements amongst academics compounded by policy-makers' concerns at the cost involved, the lack of immediate results and the political implications of findings when they are produced (Owen, 1999; Robson, 1993).

This debate about public policy evaluation offers considerable scope to devise bespoke frameworks for assessing collaborative action. Most collaborative programmes introduced by government have had an evaluation associated with them, and significant theoretical and methodological developments have taken place as a result of these. This chapter reviews the key approaches to evaluating public policy collaboration. Initially it identifies the main challenges that must be addressed by evaluators when assessing collaborative working. It then discusses approaches to impact evaluation, stakeholder evaluation and the evaluation of collaborative mechanisms. In each case we examine the strengths and limitations of available evaluation frameworks and identify ways in which approaches to evaluating collaboration can be enhanced. Public policy evaluation, especially in such a high-profile field as collaboration, is at the heart of the tension between rigorous investigation and the politics of the possible (Rein, 1976; Vickers, 1968; Wilensky, 2000). Consequently our discussion demonstrates how evaluation approaches have been subject to significant change over the last two decades, in large part reflecting the dynamic political environment. We consider the implications of this relationship in the conclusion.

The logic of evaluation

The core purpose of evaluation is to enable the effects or effectiveness of an intervention to be determined. For evaluations to have integrity in this respect it is important that they conform to what Fournier terms the 'logic of evaluation' (1995). The 'logic of evaluation' comprises a chain of activities that enable the evaluator to make valid judgements about the matter under consideration. It offers a theoretical integrity to the activity. However, its application to the field of public policy collaboration reveals some of the core challenges which evaluators must face. Fournier highlights four key elements in the chain.

Establishing criteria

Different approaches to evaluation specify different requirements for what count as the criteria for judgement, what evidence to collect and how that data is to be analysed. For example, a stakeholder-based evaluation would typically adopt a pluralistic set of criteria reflecting the different interests involved. It would gather subjective as well as objective data and analyse this evidence in terms of the values of the different stakeholders. In contrast a value-for-money evaluation would tend to have a single criterion against which data, largely of a quantitative form, could be compared. Consequently the dimensions of evaluation and who is involved in determining these are key issues that need to be addressed. Traditionally the value base of the commissioners or providers has prevailed. This is not sustainable in the evaluation of collaborative activity because its governance and delivery is increasingly the responsibility of various agencies and sectors.

Constructing standards

The determination of standards of performance in relation to each criterion will inform judgements of worth. Setting objective standards for public policy is often complicated by the lack of tangible measures of performance and the need to take account of other extraneous factors that may have hindered performance. This is because the identification of causal relationships in programmes addressing complex cross-cutting issues is extremely difficult. Collaborative activity is also relatively new in most policy fields. The absence of historic data about the efficacy of the collaborative mechanism being employed therefore makes it difficult to set objective standards for performance.

Measuring performance

Measuring the performance of collaborative mechanisms requires evaluators to establish ways of articulating the expected impact of collaboration on goal achievement and the 'value added' by the act of collaboration. This involves consideration of the counter-factual problem, that is, what would have happened without the intervention of the collaboration? It also requires consideration of the other factors that may adversely affect collaborative performance. For example, there can be tensions between organisational performance targets and collaborative goals. A 5 per cent reduction in crime may be a plausible goal for a community safety partnership, yet the community policing and crime prevention contribution to this may be detrimentally affected by requirements on the police service to target organised crime.

Synthesising and integrating evidence into a judgement of worth

The judgements made at the outcome of the investigation must be made on the basis of the evidence gathered and regardless of any inherent values or preferred findings the evaluand, evaluator or evaluation commissioners may have. However, collaborations are multi-party activities and consequently the normal processes of debate and disagreement at the end of any evaluation will be augmented. Whether these different judgements of worth can be reconciled may depend upon the extent to which the criteria and standards established at an early stage of the evaluation were agreed by all parties and are, with the benefit of hindsight, still seen as relevant and appropriate.

The application of Fournier's logic of evaluation in a context of public policy collaborations illuminates the complex political, epistemological and methodological issues involved. The questions arising from this brief discussion are now explored in greater detail throughout the remainder of the chapter.

Determining impact in collaborative endeavour

The logic of evaluation emerges from and is most closely related to the assessment of impact. Impact evaluations can focus simply on the achievement of programme or policy goals or they can examine the link between implementation and outcome through an exploration of what happened and why in the programme. They are concerned with the achievement of outcomes – defined as *the benefits for the participants of the programme*, primarily relating to changed outputs – defined as *the products of programme activity* concerned with the delivery of programme features (DETR, 2001b; Owen, 1999). The distinction between outcomes and outputs is particularly important in the context of evidence-based policy-making since much impact assessment to date has been concerned with the latter rather than the former. Value-for-money evaluations provide a case in point. However, the balance is now shifting as a result of the development of such process–outcome approaches as theories of change and realistic evaluation.

'Value-for-money' evaluation

Value-for-money evaluations give a particular emphasis to questions of economy, efficiency and – to a lesser extent – effectiveness. They were widely employed in evaluations of collaborative approaches to regeneration during the 1980s and 1990s. Central to this approach is the construction of a cost/benefit analysis enabling quantitative judgements to be made about the transformation of inputs to outputs. The most influential manifestation of value-for-money evaluation was the Treasury Model (HM Treasury, 1995) which informed the operation of regeneration programmes and consequently evaluation activity. The Treasury Model applied value-for-money criteria that had a particular emphasis on the impact of government funding on the performance of regeneration programmes (Box 10.1). The Treasury Model reflected a preference by government for quantitative approaches to evaluation. This was reinforced by the requirement on local regeneration partnerships to specify and measure on a regular basis their progress towards the achievement of key outputs. Programme delivery plans specified quantifiable outputs in relation to each goal, for example number of jobs created, number of residents attending training courses and number of houses refurbished.

Applying a value-for-money approach to evaluation has a number of important implications. The focus on quantifiable outputs enables a

---

Box 10.1   *Criteria for value-for-money evaluation of regeneration programme*

- 'Additionality' – Government funding results in outputs that would not otherwise have been achieved
- 'Deadweight' – Government funding makes no difference to outputs, and therefore is effectively wasted
- 'Displacement' – Government funding undermines existing or potential activity in the area
- 'Synergy' – The 'added value' arising from the operation of a variety of funded regeneration projects in one area
- 'Multiplier effects' – The consequences of regeneration funding beyond the immediate beneficiaries.

Source: HM Treasury (1995).

---

concern with cost to be satisfied, a particularly important feature when dealing with public money (see Chapter 8). However, questions of quality and appropriateness may be sacrificed. The knowledge that evaluation is in terms of specified quantifiable outputs will also drive the programme towards meeting these regardless of whether or not they reflect the breadth of the partnership's agenda. Specifying and measuring outputs can result in a heavy bureaucratic burden for local project managers with time spent proving the value of a project at the expense of its growth and development. Finally, the monitoring and evaluation exercise fulfils the agenda set and values held by central government. By definition this top-down perspective excludes the values and perspectives of other stakeholders involved in the collaboration, so potentially limiting the value of the evaluation.

City Challenge was the first government-sponsored regeneration partnership to formally incorporate public, private, voluntary and community sectors into its governing board. The national evaluation of this initiative was commissioned at the height of government's concern with developing and assessing value for money and reached conclusions that supported the movement towards new evaluation frameworks (Box 10.2). Among its findings were two of particular note: (1) that stakeholders appeared not to see any connection between outputs and outcomes; and (2) that there were multiple criteria of success across the stakeholder group. Similar conclusions emerged from a parallel evaluation of the regeneration partnership at Ferguslie Park in Scotland (Gaster *et al.*, 1995). This study observed that the extent to which synergy created added value in regeneration was dependent upon the definitions of and criteria for success operationalised in the programme, and especially where official criteria were disputed by other stakeholders. These were important conclusions for the time and supported the move towards stakeholder evaluation (see below).

Box 10.2   *National evaluation of City Challenge – key findings*

- Local autonomy in selecting the target area and drawing together key partners was important in determining the health of the partnership.
- Attitudes to collaboration were more important than prescribed management arrangements in enabling the partnership to operate effectively.
- City Challenge bodies were surpassing expectations in terms of outputs and spending targets. There was direct relationship between achieving private sector leverage and reaching targeted spend.
- City Challenge provided a more integrated and synergetic approach to regeneration. Without it little physical or environmental improvement work could have been resourced.
- Initiatives that were more focused on economic development/social issues were more dependent on public sector resources than those with a more physical/environmental orientation.
- Comparison with non-City Challenge areas reveals greater reliance on public sources.
- The longer lead time for partnerships to build capacity was beneficial in helping the second-round City Challenge programmes to attain targets more quickly.
- Outputs were a valuable management tool but needed to be understood in the context of wider goals and not as an end in themselves.
- Baseline and other local data reveals that 'success' means different things to different people.
- Local players were interested in the impact and outcomes of the programme rather than its outputs.

Source: Russell *et al.* (1996).

Outcome-focused evaluations of collaboration

The developing debate about evaluation between academics and policy-makers combined with a new political agenda from the late 1990s to give greater emphasis to the assessment of the outcomes of collaborative activity. For example, local crime and disorder partnerships aim to reduce the propensity for incidence and fear of crime while Sure Start partnerships work to improve the physical, intellectual and social development of children of pre-school age, especially where they come from disadvantaged families, to maximise their life chances thereafter. The concern with outcomes represents what Richards *et al.* (1999) consider to be a key element in the emergence of a new paradigm of the public policy system. This paradigm prioritises the effectiveness of resource utilisation over its efficient application and requires a closer specification of what long-term policy outcomes are sought but offers more flexibility in how those outcomes are achieved. An outcomes orientation presents major new challenges for evaluators. The evaluation of outcomes is technically difficult. There are major conceptual problems associated with formulating causal relationships between interventions and outcomes and specifying indicators towards progress present significant difficulties. Where indicators are specified they may in fact operate in tension with each other. For example, improving the quality of life may involve the demolition of high-rise flats and their replacement by low-rise accommodation at a lower density. To realise this, the blocks have to be emptied and families temporarily found alternative accommodation. This process may have adverse effects on the school attendance and performance of children, thus detrimentally affecting an outcome indicator about improving local educational attainment. Finally, many of the outcomes sought will be in relation to cross-cutting issues that require concerted action by various agencies and may only be realised in the long term.

Outcome-focused evaluation is closely associated with the notion of evidence-based policy-making which involves the identification and replication of 'what works' in relation to delivering outcomes, especially on cross-cutting issues. The use of evaluation to identify good practice has informed work in a number of policy areas, including the Home Office's formative review of Neighbourhood Warden schemes as part of the development of the National Strategy for Neighbourhood Renewal (Jacobson and Saville, 1999). However, embedding the concept of evidence-based policy-making into organisational and political routines is fraught with potential difficulty. This is accentuated when working across organisational

and professional boundaries. Davies *et al.* suggest that the institutionalisation of evidence-based approaches may be supported by a collaborative
approach to generating and collecting data. They comment that '[t]here is
much to be gained from viewing evidence-influenced practice as a partnership activity between all the key stakeholders, with no clear discontinuities
between evidence creation, validation, dissemination or use' (2000, p. 342).

Process-outcome evaluation

Outcome evaluation and the identification of 'what works' has considerable political salience. However, some authors point to the inadequacy of
evaluations that focus exclusively on outputs/outcomes (Guba and Lincoln,
1981; Strauss and Corbin, 1990; Yin, 1994). They point out that objective
measures, and particularly those relating to cause and effect, are not necessarily obtainable in applied research. They also recognise that evaluation
does not take place in a static environment. Instead changes in circumstances and the behaviour of individuals can contribute positively or negatively to the achievement of outcomes, and thus need to be accommodated
in the evaluation. Consequently they argue that an examination of the
process of implementing an initiative is vital to an understanding of
whether and how the objectives of the initiative were met. The examination of process is also helpful in elaborating the circumstances in which
particular interventions take effect, thereby aiding evidence-based practice.

The 'balanced score-card' provides one approach to evaluating partnerships from a process-outcome perspective. Originally devised by Kaplan
and Norton (1996) for use in the private sector, the approach has been
adapted by a number of public sector bodies – including the Scottish
Accounts Commission for the assessment of community safety partnerships. The scorecard has four perspectives which, in the case of community
safety, are impact, external processes (involving communities), resources,
and partnership management and improvement. Indicators of performance
are identified for each perspective and partnerships are assessed against
each to provide a 'balanced and comprehensive picture of their performance' (Accounts Commission, 2000, p. 4). The deployment of four separate perspectives is useful in requiring the definition of indicators for each.
However, it risks underplaying the way in which matters of process inform
and influence subsequent outcomes.

There are, however, several theory-based or theory-driven frameworks
that make explicit the links between process and outcome. These require a

rationale to be elaborated for the relationship between interventions and outcomes (Chen and Rossi, 1983; Funnel, 1997). One example is 'theories of change', originally developed in the US. This is an approach to evaluating complex community initiatives – activities that are community-oriented and have a focus on achieving change within individuals, families and communities. They make use of a range of instruments to address the social, economic and environmental conditions within deprived communities and seek to build communities through their interventions (Connell and Kubisch *et al.*, 1995). A 'theories of change' approach is defined as 'a systematic and cumulative study of the links between activities, outcomes and contexts of the initiative' (Connell and Kubisch, 1998, p. 16). The approach aims to clarify the overall theory of the initiative by specifying the desired long-term outcomes and the associated strategies for change. In building the theory, steps are taken to explicitly link the original problem or context in which the programme began with the activities planned to address the problem and the intended medium- and longer-term outcomes. Theory generation takes place with those involved in planning and implementing an initiative. The approach encourages stakeholders to debate how an initiative can best produce desirable outcomes by asking them to make explicit connections between the different components of a programme. In this way a theory of change approach can sharpen the planning and implementation of an initiative and facilitate the measurement and data collection elements of the evaluation. It can also reduce problems associated with causal attribution of impact as it specifies how activities will lead to immediate and long-term outcomes and identifies the contextual conditions that may affect them (Judge, 2000).

An alternative, though in many ways complementary, approach to theories of change is provided by 'realistic evaluation', a UK approach that was developed to address the difficulties of measurement and causality within complex social systems. Pawson and Tilley (1997) argue that the evaluation of social programmes takes place within dynamic environments in which the environment (its location, institutions and relationships) within which the intervention operates is as significant as the intervention itself in determining programme outcomes. The authors summarise their position through the '*CMO*' formula:

Context (C) + mechanism (M) = outcome (O)

This approach emphasises the complexity of establishing cause and effect relationships in environments where, as Judge puts it, 'cause and effect are not discrete events' (2000, p. 3). Therefore, realistic evaluation focuses its attention on increasing understanding of the programme under consideration rather than attempting to construct control or comparison sites against which to judge the programme. It does this by asking three key questions: why does a particular programme work, for whom does it work and in what circumstances?

Applying process-outcome evaluation in practice: the HAZ case

The national Health Action Zone evaluation has combined elements of these approaches to create an evaluation framework that addresses the complexities inherent in ABIs (Figure 10.1). The starting point for the evaluation is the context within which HAZs operate – the resources available in the communities and the challenges that they face. The evaluation elaborates stakeholders' rationales for intervening in relation to their objectives and describes the emergent strategies to fulfil these rationales. The evaluation then assesses the extent to which the strategies are translated into clearly defined change mechanisms, which could be either activities (such as public involvement programmes linked to primary care) or

Figure 10.1 *Evaluation framework for national Health Action Zone initiative*

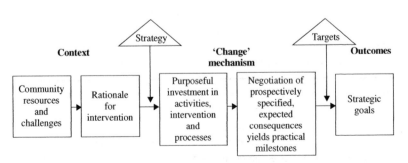

Source: Judge (2000, p. 4).

processes (for instance the development of integrated assessment protocols). The framework requires the HAZs to specify targets. Ideally, these should be articulated *in advance* of the expected consequences of actions and they should be accompanied by milestones that indicate progress towards the agreed strategic goals. The targets should reflect the cross-cutting nature of the issues being addressed and hence the collaborative nature of the projects undertaken.

There are several ways in which this framework is appropriate to the prevailing policy environment. First, it focuses on the achievement of outcomes. These are defined locally but set within the context of (frequently stringent) national policy expectations. They also reflect the joined-up policy agendas that are necessary to deliver cross-cutting results. Second, it intends to identify 'what works' through an examination of the development of bespoke strategies pertinent to the local context, and thus to generate explanations of relevance to evidence-based policy-making. Third, it considers the utilisation of all of the resources relevant to the achievement of desired outcomes rather than simply those provided through partnership-specific funding streams. Finally, its emphasis upon the involvement of a whole range of interested stakeholders fits well with the notion of pluralistic evaluation (see below).

However, the UK-wide evaluation of Health Action Zones identified a number of limitations to this approach (Sullivan, Barnes and Matka, forthcoming). The requirement to involve all stakeholders in theory generation assumes that consensus can be reached between them. In practice though, competing theories will emerge and it is those associated with the most powerful groups that will hold sway. In addition, theories of change is a resource intensive exercise for evaluators which assumes their engagement in the programme from the beginning. In practice, evaluations of HAZ (and, indeed, many other collaborations) were not commissioned until the programme started, thereby creating a disjunction between HAZ and evaluation timetables. Finally, theories of change is a long-term process which may sit uncomfortably in a political environment where learning is expected to emerge in the short term. An additional complication has arisen for some evaluators. The wide variety of public policy collaborations has resulted in particular localities being in receipt of up to 10 area-based initiatives (ABIs) at any one time. This raises questions about the causal interconnections between collaborations and their consequent impact on the achievement or dilution of specified outcomes (DETR, 2000).

The HAZ case reflects the general concern that the evaluation of collaborative activity should include the examination of the contribution of partners across all sectors. These partners may have different views about the nature and value of the evaluation and about the process and outcomes of the collaboration. The capacity of different partners to influence how the evaluation is undertaken will vary, a feature which pertains even in the employment of frameworks that attempt to be more inclusive such as theories of change (Sullivan, Barnes and Matka, forthcoming; Jacobs, 2000). Therefore some evaluators have suggested that a key part of the evaluation process is the examination and exploration of the respective roles and relationships of key stakeholders in the process. It is this issue that we now consider.

Stakeholder evaluation of collaboration

A number of writers (Coulson, 1988; Hambleton and Thomas, 1995) express concern about attempts to perform 'value free' evaluation. They suggest that valid evaluation requires the consideration of a range of stakeholders' views, since different stakeholders will have differential access to and influence over the evaluation process. Therefore to comply with Fournier's logic of evaluation it is important to be aware of whose values underpin and prevail in evaluation. As Loftman and Nevin (1998, p. 3) comment, 'evaluation studies cannot be separated from the political context within which they are set, and the motives behind their establishment'. Thomas and Palfrey (1996) identify three groups of stakeholders: those who pay, such as the government on behalf of the taxpayer, beneficiaries and other customers; those who benefit, for example clients; and those who provide, including professionals, managers and politicians. Conventionally those stakeholders who exercise most influence over how evaluations are conducted and what is evaluated are those with some responsibility for both payment and provision. Those with the least amount of influence over the evaluation process are those who are intended beneficiaries or individual 'customers'. For Thomas and Palfrey power relationships are hugely important in determining the shape, criteria and use of evaluations involving many stakeholders and the greatest influence will invariably rest with the stakeholder groups that can 'call the shots' at any given moment. Consequently they argue that the contestability of the evaluative terrain means that:

one needs to be sceptical and explicit about how evaluations are being conducted and accept that evaluations are invariably subjective, controversial and political. The choice of criteria, the relative weightings given to them, decisions about who undertakes the evaluation work and the subsequent action taken (or not taken) as a result of evaluations all depend crucially on which stakeholders have the decisive power at the time in question ... Greater acceptance of the need to use explicit criteria is needed to inform the political process. (1996, p. 140)

Some forms of evaluation allow for the incorporation of the views of a range of stakeholders. Owen (1999) describes this as 'interactive' evaluation and characterises it as valuing local experience and expertise in delivering change and improvement, seeing evaluation as an empowering activity for those involved in the programme and attempting to address problems not addressed before or employing approaches that are new to the organisation. The value of interactive evaluation lies in the fact that it aims to encourage a learning culture and is appropriate for use in innovative programmes. The logic of evaluation is applied in a very different manner in interactive evaluation. Practitioners themselves interpret the logic of evaluation based upon their own practice knowledge and experience and contribute this to the development of the evaluation framework. The role of the evaluator is to help practitioners reach new understandings and so encourage improved practice. This is partly achieved via regular communication between the formal evaluator and the practitioners throughout the evaluation.

Interactive evaluation is appropriate for use in relation to collaborations. This is because its focus on regular interaction with key stakeholders to develop and refine the evaluation and to encourage a 'learning culture' emphasises the significance of learning to the success of the initiative. By taking account of the different value bases of stakeholders and reflecting the power differentials inherent in relationships between them, interactive evaluation reveals the tensions that exist across governance levels and between governance agents and enables a focus on activity and its implications, allowing close examination of obstacles and opportunities to change.

Recent research has re-emphasised the significance of stakeholder involvement (at all levels) in the design and delivery of evaluation programmes (Barnes, Sullivan and Matka, 2001). However, it also reveals that the political and performance imperatives that public providers work within remain significant obstacles to the effective and sustainable involvement of stakeholders in evaluation, for example in relation to best value reviews (Foley and Martin, 2000). Other writers have focused their attention on developing alternative approaches with particular reference to the role of community stakeholders. This is because communities appear to be least influential in informing the process of evaluation while at the same time are cited as vitally important stakeholders in collaborative activity. The approaches adopted can be categorised in two ways: approaches to evaluating the role and effectiveness of communities in collaborative activity and approaches to developing community-led evaluation capacities and programmes. Each is considered below.

Evaluating communities in collaborations

There are several evaluation frameworks that focus in different ways on the experience of communities in collaboration, for example Burns and Taylor (2000), COGS (2000), Skelcher *et al.* (1996), Smith and Beazley (2000). Comparing these frameworks reveals some important differences between them in relation to their use in evaluating community involvement in collaboration (Table 10.1). Burns and Taylor's 'Audit Tools' are the most flexible as they facilitate assessment at all stages of collaboration and can be applied to a variety of arrangements. Skelcher *et al.*'s framework is the simplest and least costly evaluative tool, having been designed for self-evaluation. While Burns and Taylor identify key indicators in relation to different components of collaboration, Skelcher *et al.* focus on the different influences on communities' participation at different stages of the collaborative cycle and specify a range of influences that help or hinder its effective working (see Chapter 7). However, the authors point out that the focus on individual behaviours precludes an examination of the impact of other structural factors. This issue is accommodated in Smith and Beazley's 'Wheel of Involvement' which employs power, partnership and participation as key evaluative criteria. A further advantage of this tool is that it can be applied at different stages of the collaborative cycle thereby illuminating changes over time. The COGS framework can also be applied over time but is more closely focused on utilising forms of assessment that are integral to the performance-monitoring processes associated with regeneration, for instance benchmarking. Their framework aims to enable partnerships to focus on continuous improvement in relation to community involvement through the use of the designated benchmarks. In addition to the differences between the frameworks there are also some important commonalties. Central among these is coverage of issues of power and

Table 10.1 Assessing the role of communities in collaborations

	Burns and Taylor's Audit (2000)	Skelcher et al. framework for self-evaluation (1996)	Smith and Beazley's 'Wheel of involvement' (2000)	COGS' Benchmarks (2000)
Focus	Community participation	Community network	Partnership	Partnership
Elements	*Context of participation* – range, communities present, barriers	*Factors helping/hindering network development* – goals, purpose and benefits, resources and time	*Power* – extent of power sharing, access to resources for participation, devolution of decision-making	*Influence* – community equal partner, meaningful representation, access to resources, access to all community members, community agenda incorporated
	Quality of participation strategies – rule setting, power relationships, community influence, resourcing participation, leadership	*Factors helping/hindering network membership* – consistency, accessibility, confidentiality, role clarity	*Partnership* – shared goals sought, valuing difference and openness to learning	*Inclusivity* – equal opportunities implemented, volunteers valued, diversity reflected
	Capacity of partners to support community participation – where decisions are taken, permeability to community influence	*Factors helping/hindering network operation* – structures, processes, rules of engagement, focus, permeability, culture, trust, communication, success	*Participation* – accountability of arrangements, legitimacy of members, open processes	*Communication* – two-way communication, clear and accessible implementation processes

(Continued)

Table 10.1 (Continued)

	Burns and Taylor's Audit (2000)	Skelcher et al. framework for self-evaluation (1996)	Smith and Beazley's 'Wheel of involvement' (2000)	COGS' Benchmarks (2000)
	Capacity of communities to participate – accessibility, inclusivity and accountability of community processes *Impact assessment* – effectiveness of community participation, outcomes and beneficiaries			*Capacity* – communities resourced, partners have requisite capacities
Who evaluates?	Peer group with external support	Individuals/whole network	External evaluator	Partnership officers
Criteria	Indicators	Helping/hindering factors	Points on a scale	Benchmarks
Stage of collaboration	Pre-collaboration to impact assessment	Initiation to implementation	Implementation	Implementation

influence, leadership and capacity building, and accountability and inclusivity in influencing the effective involvement of communities.

Community-led evaluations

Finding ways of assessing community participation is only a part of the evaluation role. Communities also need to be able to undertake evaluation themselves in order to assess the impact of policy programmes designed to support them. Community-led evaluations take two forms. The first focuses on the development of tools for evaluation that can be used by communities to evaluate different aspects of the collaboration. These evaluation frameworks work on the premise that community capacity-building is central to the achievement of sustainability. Here the work of the Scottish Community Development Council (1996, 1999) has been influential in setting out tools for measuring and assessing community development based around 10 key 'building blocks' relating to community empowerment and quality of community life. Latterly, a consortium of bodies has produced *Prove It!* (Walker *et al.*, 2000), a 'method of measuring the effect of community projects on local people, on the relationships between them and on their quality of life'. *Prove It!* aims to provide communities with the necessary tools and information to undertake their own impact assessments of projects and programmes designed for their benefit.

One important aspect of these frameworks is the emphasis that is placed on community members taking control of the evaluation and applying it for their own purposes (Nyden *et al.*, 1997). Community researchers are no longer unusual in policy initiatives designed to benefit communities and examples of community members undertaking service audits and community needs analysis are now relatively common. They have also been supported by the development of programmes such as Community Profiling in Leeds (Hawtin *et al.*, 1994). However, community members are often involved in conducting evaluations in relation to specific community projects rather than the partnership as a whole.

One type of community-led evaluation that seeks to provide a comprehensive approach to programme assessment is the Monitoring and Evaluation Pyramid (Sullivan and Potter, forthcoming) (Figure 10.2). The pyramid has two important features. First, it suggests that all of the elements in the evaluation are interlocking and part of a continuous process. Second, it emphasises the importance of 'a bottom-up' rather than 'top-down' approach to evaluation by focusing attention on the potential role

Figure 10.2   *Monitoring and evaluation pyramid*

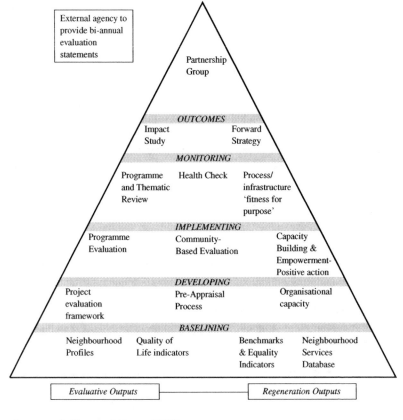

Source: Sullivan and Potter (2001).

of the baseline information and the need to involve stakeholders from the beginning in programme design and evaluation. The right side of the pyramid highlights the regeneration outputs arising from the key stages of the process, while the left side describes the evaluation outputs. Both sets of outputs derive from the same activities described through the middle of the pyramid. At the centre of the pyramid is 'community-based evaluation of implementation'. This is the pivotal part of the programme as it is here that community members develop their role as evaluators of activity. The Neighbourhood Initiatives Foundation has developed a training programme – 'Evaluation for Real' – which provides community members with the skills and capacities to evaluate and to manage evaluators (Neighbourhood Initiatives Foundation, 1999). There are a number of important implications that arise from the adoption of this model. This type of evaluation will be resource intensive, requiring the active involvement of a number of stakeholders complemented by external input to facilitate skills acquisition and the setting up of the relevant systems. In addition external involvement will be important in two other areas – the development and collection of key baseline data, where specific technical skills are required, and the undertaking of a particular role in relation to the monitoring and impact evaluation stages of the process where an independent view on progress is desirable. Proactive steps would need to be taken to ensure that representation from all relevant sections of the community is facilitated within the evaluation. Key outcomes should be established early on and baseline data collected to help determine programme priorities which should be spelled out for no more than two or three years at a time. Annual reviews of the programme with key stakeholders, possibly through community conferences, will enable scrutiny of performance to date and the introduction of new priorities. This approach builds flexibility into the programme. It enables changing circumstances and new opportunities to be taken advantage of in keeping with working towards the desired outcomes. It is also in keeping with more recent approaches to evaluating complex community initiatives.

Evaluating collaborative mechanisms

In addition to evaluating the outcomes of collaboration it is important to devote some attention to the assessment of the means of collaboration, namely the partnerships themselves. Recently a number of frameworks for evaluating the performance of partnerships have been developed, ranging from those that consider partnerships in general (Cropper, 1996; Audit Commission, 1998; Huxham and Vangen, 2000) to those that focus on a particular policy area such as regeneration (Wilson and Charlton, 1997) or health and social care (Hardy *et al.*, 2000; WHO, 2000). A number of the partnership evaluation frameworks are outlined in Table 10.2. One approach adopted by the frameworks for partnership development is to take participants through the different stages of collaborative action from inception to review. Others highlight partnership development in relation to a set of principles or elements.

Table 10.2 *Stages of partnership development – evaluation frameworks*

Key Aspects	Wilson and Charlton (1997)	Audit Commission (1998)	Hardy et al. (2000)	WHO (2000)
Imperatives	Develop relationships following recognition of need to collaborate Agree mission and goals	Deciding to go into partnership – is rationale clear?	Recognise and accept need for partnership Develop purpose	Leadership – vision, commitment, relationships People – membership, development, skills Resources Policy and Strategy – development
The form taken		Getting started – is partnership appropriate?		
Building capacity	Identify partner capacity and potential training needs	Operating efficiently and effectively – issues of trust, authority and skills	Ensure ownership – leadership, skills, rewards and commitment Secure trust in partnership – partner equality, fairness in operating, involving the right people	
Implementing: good governance issues	Establish partnership structures and processes – governance, management and consultative aspects Implement programme	Operating efficiently and effectively – developing appropriate governance and management arrangements	Create sound working arrangements – resources, responsibilities and accountabilities	Processes – managing, governing and involving communities Programmes – delivery
Evaluation	Plan exit strategy	Reviewing success – measuring achievements, costs and benefits and securing acceptability	Monitor and learn – criteria, institutionalize review and celebrate success	Policy and strategy – review and evaluation

The Wilson and Charlton and Audit Commission frameworks are self-assessment tools which combine key questions and learning points to draw out perceptions of partnership performance. The WHO framework is rather more complex containing a number of benchmarks of partnership performance with respect to each of six elements. Participants are expected to complete a questionnaire in relation to these elements but the process of assessment is a joint one requiring external facilitation. Hardy *et al.*'s framework (2000) combines elements of each, with a self-assessment tool for 'rapid appraisal' and a more in-depth assessment process for partnerships that find themselves to be underperforming. Regardless of the different emphases and approaches of the frameworks, certain common issues emerge in relation to the assessment of partnership performance. They pertain to: an examination of the imperatives for collaboration; attention to the development of overarching goals and purposes; an exploration of partners' capacity for collaboration (leadership, commitment and skills) along with the partnership capacity for collaboration (trust, resources, and ownership); examination of key issues to effect implementation (governance and management structures and processes); and a review of mechanisms to evaluate activity and improve performance.

Cropper's (1996) approach is rather different. He sees evaluation as a tool to assess the sustainability of collaborative relationships. He understands sustainability as being directly related to the capacity of the collaborative arrangement to create value. The creation of value in turn engenders commitment to the relationship and this secures its long-term existence. Value is created in two ways: through 'consequential value' that arises from the operation of collaborative arrangements, and from 'constitutive value' that is related to the individual character of the collaborative relationship (and which in turn is influenced by the conduct of the various partners). The elements that comprise the two values are similar to those incorporated into the frameworks developed by others, for example context, shared purpose, trust. However, Cropper's identification of two value bases, one of which is actively influenced by the partners themselves, emphasises the significance of relationships to the sustainability of partnerships and the need to appreciate that partnerships operate in a dynamic environment (see Chapter 7).

Conclusion

Collaborative activity is becoming more plentiful and more embedded as a means of delivering public policy. Consequently the need for evaluators to build adequate frameworks to monitor, understand and assess this activity will intensify. Collaboration can take a number of forms, some of which will present little difficulty to evaluators seeking to assess its performance. However, evaluators will need to be able to devise frameworks that can accommodate the logic of evaluation in different ways if the current concern with the application of cross-sector collaborative mechanisms to achieve key public policy outcomes persists. Our analysis of evaluation in collaborations leads us to conclude that there are four main ways in which such approaches need to develop.

In the first place, evaluations of collaboration will need to *distinguish between implementation, outputs and outcomes*, be able to establish indicators of the attainment of outputs and outcomes, and trace a pathway between these and the activities that contributed to them. Theories of change and realistic evaluation have a great deal to offer in this regard, particularly where there are a variety of inter-related factors that contribute to the desired outcome. While not without their critics, for example Hollister and Hill (1999), theory-based approaches do make an important contribution to thinking about how to determine and assess the attainment of particular outcomes in the real world. Secondly, evaluation frameworks will need to *facilitate an examination of the implementation process*. Poor implementation will compromise the capacity of collaborations to achieve their objectives. But equally there may be evidence of successful approaches which demonstrate how cross-cutting – and even cross-collaboration – implementation can be achieved. Focusing attention on the functionality of the collaborative instrument will be important in explaining what happened and why. Merely establishing a cross-sector collaboration will not secure the equitable participation of all stakeholders. Our third point, therefore, is that evaluations of such collaborations need to be able to secure the *involvement of a range of stakeholders and to address issues of power relationships between them*. The degree of involvement of different stakeholders will vary depending on the collaboration but at the very least the evaluator should be aware of the different perspectives that exist in relation to a collaborative endeavour. In some circumstances it may be appropriate to adopt a more stakeholder-focused perspective in the evaluation. Finally, the experience of collaboration can provide partners with valuable insights into the processes, relationships and ways of working that facilitate and diminish collaborative capacity and the achievement of collaborative outcomes. Therefore an important feature of evaluative activity is some assessment of *partners' capacity to learn*. Learning organisations are understood to be increasingly important in the development and delivery or public policy (for example, Department for Education and Employment, 1998b). However, evidence suggests that partners remain equivocal about the contribution of evaluation in this regard (Newchurch, 1999a). Emerging findings from the national evaluation of Health Action Zones suggests that this equivocation persists particularly in relation to increasing understanding of how best to work in partnership. As a result relatively few HAZ partnerships have regularised reviews of their partnership capacity, preferring instead to rely on informal means of learning (Barnes, Sullivan and Matka, 2001). The necessity for organisations to improve their capacity to act as learning organisations in relation to collaboration will in part depend on the role of collaboration in future public policy initiatives. The next chapter considers this issue, examining the emergent policy agendas in the UK and considering what they imply for the future of collaborative activity.

11 Collaboration and Modernisation

The collaborative agenda has emerged as a major theme in contemporary public sector activity in the UK and internationally. It is stimulated – indeed even directed – by national and supra-national government initiatives and funding regimes, but also arises spontaneously as local public bodies look for ways to deliver their policy objectives and meet the needs of their communities and users. It is a consequence of the renewal of public services in the post-market era and a reaffirmation of their primary role in serving communities. Inter-agency working has now penetrated into the *modus operandi* of public service professionals and managers. Networking, building alliances and putting together co-operative projects are expected behaviours of the modernised public manager. The promise of collaborative endeavour is also recognised by those outside the public sector – the private companies, voluntary organisations and community groups that have an interest in shaping or benefiting from public policy.

This development, however, exists in parallel with other significant policy streams. In the UK these include the performance agenda with its array of targets, inspectorates and sanctions, the impetus on democratic renewal which stresses accountability and responsiveness to citizens, and the emphasis on proper procedures for transparent and high standards of decision-making in the public interest. There are tensions between these agendas, as Painter and Clarence point out:

> Local collaborative networks and partnerships to promote more robust approaches to cross-cutting public policy problems and more integrated service delivery rest uneasily alongside 'top-down' leveraging of change. There are underlying tensions between experimental multi-agency working and the more directive performance management regime that had earlier become associated with the New Public Management. (2000, p. 484)

The analysis of collaboration needs to be undertaken with an acute awareness of this wider context. Yet this is often absent in the literature. Academic analysis frequently omits to locate collaboration and partnership in the context of other forces acting on public services. Much advisory and good practice material directed at practitioners also fails to do this, instead presenting partnership working as something that can be delivered through the adoption of a toolkit of techniques rather than the negotiation of powerful and sometimes contradictory forces.

In this chapter we consider these broader questions about the collaborative agenda in public services. Initially we review those other elements of the modernisation agenda and reflect on the compatibilities and inconsistencies with the development of partnerships. We then move on to discuss some fundamental dilemmas in the way partnerships can be understood through their practice. Finally, we revisit the four questions laid out in Chapter 1 and draw on our analysis to develop a framework for understanding public policy collaboration.

The modernisation agenda

Governments since 1997 have set about the task of radical institutional redesign. The collaborative agenda is a central theme within this programme for modernising public services. It intersects with five other strands of change, namely modernising state institutions, redefining public policy problems, delivering outcomes, developing state employees and renewing democracy (Figure 11.1). The modernisation of state institutions involves a package of measures. There has been a fundamental redistribution of legislative and governmental power and authority from the Westminster Parliament to the Scottish Parliament and Executive and, to a more limited extent, to the National Assembly of Wales. More modest changes have been introduced in the regions of England, with an elected strategic authority for London, and elsewhere strengthened regional administration through the RDAs, regional chambers and regional offices of government. This introduces a new dynamic into the processes of multi-level governance, as we discussed in Chapter 5. There has also been a number of initiatives designed to join up government at the centre. These include the creation of special teams such as the Social Exclusion Unit to integrate and drive policy and a stronger central policy and performance delivery resource within the Prime Minister's office (Kavanagh and Richards, 2001). These changes to the structure of state institutions establish new organisational boundaries and centres of power which will need to be negotiated to enable joined-up public action, but also give some of

Figure 11.1   *The collaborative agenda in the context of modernisation*

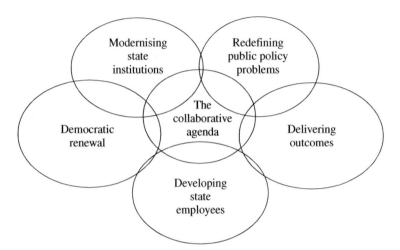

these bodies the responsibility for ensuring co-ordinated policy-making and delivery, for example the Regional Co-ordination Unit which monitors the development of new ABIs (Regional Co-ordination Unit, 2000).

The redesign of state institutions is connected in part to a further element of the modernisation programme – the redefinition of public policy problems. The emphasis has moved from a functional definition of policy problems to an outcome definition (see Chapter 1). This functional orientation has dominated for many years. It focuses on the provision of education, housing, transport and the other activities of government that are deeply embedded in departmental structures and areas of professional expertise (Richards *et al.*, 1999). The prevailing public policy agenda of reducing social exclusion, ensuring sustainable development and enabling life-long learning reflects a shift in concern towards the achievement of outcomes. Such formulations transect jurisdictional, organisational and professional boundaries and therefore require collaborative activity if they are to be successful addressed. However, merely to redefine public policy problems is insufficient to drive change. The modernisation programme places great weight on the delivery of these outcomes. This is apparent in the promotion of evidence-based policy, management and practice which seeks to identify what works most effectively and to disseminate this throughout relevant bodies (see Chapter 10). Ensuring that the findings are implemented will require the collaborative engagement of a host of service-providing agencies, professions, occupational bodies and staff. There is, however, a further dimension to the outcome delivery agenda. This is the growth of the performance regime with its array of indicators, targets and inspectorates. Indicators and targets have themselves traditionally been defined in functional terms. Latterly there has been interest in establishing cross-cutting measures. For example, the targets set for the Connexions service, which promotes educational attainment for 13- to 19-year-olds, require the contribution of a number of partners to secure their achievement. Yet at the same time agencies such as the police and schools are subject to functionally-defined indicators and targets, backed-up with regular external inspections, which may or may not be consistent with the cross-cutting agenda (Davies *et al.*, 2000; Rogers, 1996).

There is a key link between delivering outcomes and the development of state employees, and especially their capacity to manage the process of policy development and service delivery across various organisational and occupational boundaries. Joining-up services to ensure performance requires individuals who are able to exercise leadership outside the bureaucratic conventions of authority and status (Chapters 6 and 7). Interestingly, collaboration generates a powerful motivation for public service employees in the aftermath of the new public management:

> the language and practice of partnership working ... opened up the possibility of new sources of meaning and identity for those delivering public services ... Boundary spanning workers developed new skills and cultural orientations, and alternative routes for career development. (Newman, 2001, p. 167)

However, professional and occupational competencies remain clearly delimited within the public sector. For example, collaboration between health and social services requires the resolution of the debate between the medical and social models of care in which the condition of an individual is perceived respectively as a function of their physiology or their environment. Differences in training, values and notions of good practice between professional groups reinforce these world views and limit collaborative activity.

The final modernisation theme with which the collaborative agenda intersects is democratic renewal. Fundamental to this is the notion of active citizenship derived from the Third Way (Giddens, 2000). Active citizenship embraces two main ideas. The first is the normative position that citizens should actively exercise their right to engage in the governance of their society and to forgo the passive dependence arising from welfare state provision. The second is that citizens also have responsibilities as members of that society, including the responsibility to care for their fellow citizens (see Chapter 9). The collaborative agenda provides new mechanisms through which citizens can fulfil both roles. Their involvement in partnership boards and consultative groups offers an active contribution to governance, but also enables them to develop a wider understanding of the community in which they live or work. This is where the participative democracy encouraged through community- or user group-based collaborations intersects with new ideas about deliberative democracy. The basic proposition informing deliberative democracy is that an informed dialogue between different interests can lead the individuals involved to transform their understandings and value sets and on this basis reach a collectively agreeable conclusion (Fishkin, 1991; Habermas, 1994; Young, 2000). Collaborative settings provide a more amenable location for this process. Greer's analysis of the district partnerships for peace and reconciliation in Northern Ireland illustrates this process. He observes the feelings of intimidation and undervaluing which voluntary and community sector members of a partnership felt during its meetings in the local council's chamber. Eventually the location was moved. A participant in the process commented:

> The shift from the Council Chamber to a neutral venue has created neutral space ... At the neutral venue a strong sense of people getting together has been created with the District Partnership members relating to one another as individuals, not as individuals within their own attached boxes. (Greer, 2001, p. 86)

Collaborative activity, therefore, can provide an important opportunity for deliberative forms of democracy to develop.

Collaboration and modernisation at the local level

The modernisation programme is evident across all levels of government, but finds a particular focus at the local level. It is here, where residents live, businesses operate and many public services are delivered, that policy interventions to transform governance arrangements have been particularly marked (Figure 11.2). The drive to redefine the policy problems of localities in relation to outcomes rather than functions has been central to this development, with particular attention being placed on the promotion of

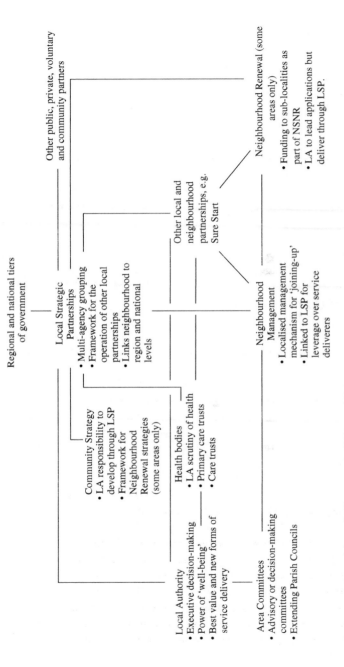

Figure 11.2 *Collaboration and modernisation in the local governance system*

Regional and national tiers of government

Other public, private, voluntary and community partners

Local Strategic Partnerships
• Multi-agency grouping
• Framework for the operation of other local partnerships
• Links neighbourhood to region and national levels

Community Strategy
• LA responsibility to develop through LSP
• Framework for Neighbourhood Renewal strategies (some areas only)

Health bodies
• LA scrutiny of health
• Primary care trusts
• Care trusts

Other local and neighbourhood partnerships, e.g. Sure Start

Neighbourhood Renewal (some areas only)
• Funding to sub-localities as part of NSNR
• LA to lead applications but deliver through LSP.

Neighbourhood Management
• Localised management mechanism for 'joining-up'
• Linked to LSP for leverage over service deliverers

Local Authority
• Executive decision-making
• Power of 'well-being'
• Best value and new forms of service delivery

Area Committees
• Advisory or decision-making committees
• Extending Parish Councils

Source: Adapted from Sullivan *et al.* (2001, p. 11).

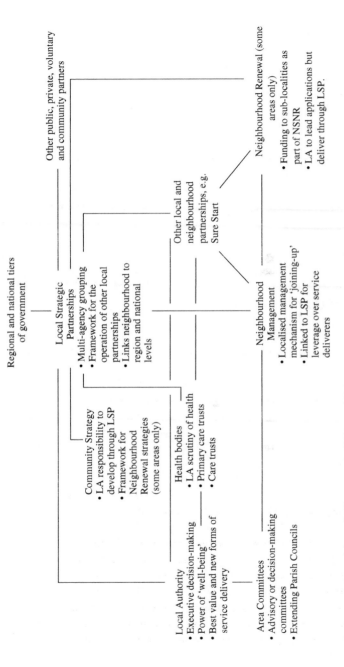

213

'well-being' and the reduction of social exclusion. The cross-cutting nature of these outcomes has generated new collaborative arrangements through which strategies and delivery programmes can be developed in concert by the relevant stakeholders and informed by past experiences of using collaborative mechanisms to tackle cross-cutting issues (Chapter 4). Local Strategic Partnerships are the principal vehicles to achieve this since they bring together key players in the locality and provide an umbrella body for existing public policy partnerships (Chapter 2). The planning mechanism through which LSPs operate is the community strategy, the preparation of which is a duty on the local authority working in co-operation with partners. The community strategy has an interactive relationship with other planning systems, and especially the Health Improvement and Modernisation Programme (HIMP) developed at a local level and led by NHS bodies. Those local authorities who rank highly on deprivation indices will also be part of the National Strategy for Neighbourhood Renewal (NSNR), which promotes economic and social regeneration through a combination of targeted funding to improve neighbourhood quality of life and improved co-ordination of mainstream service delivery (Social Exclusion Unit, 2000). Authorities coming within the NSNR must agree their local strategies through the LSP.

These developments have implications for the way in which local public service agencies are organised and governed. Executive decision-making by a small cabinet of councillors, and in some cases a directly-elected mayor, has replaced the traditional committee system in most English and Welsh local authorities. This executive is expected to exercise community leadership, especially through the new duty on local councils to prepare a community strategy in the context of the LSP. Local authorities also have an important new general power to do anything that enables them to promote or improve the economic, social or environmental well-being of their area. This includes the authority to establish new collaborative arrangements. The health–social care interface is also being remodelled. Local councils have the power to scrutinise the activities of health bodies in the locality and to call before them senior local NHS figures. Partnership flexibilities under the Health Act 1999 are being used more widely and primary care trusts (PCTs) include local authority representatives. This collaboration is being extended by the introduction of care trusts. These are statutory partnerships between health trusts and local authorities which will integrate particular areas of activity that cross the boundary between the two partners, for example provision of mental health services or commissioning for individual client groups. More generally, the best value process for reviewing council services and the debate about alternative forms of service delivery, including strategic partnering (Chapter 5), offer the prospect of new collaborative arrangements being established.

The modernisation agenda is associated with a renewed interest in neighbourhood management of public services. The NSNR has a strong emphasis on the very local level:

> The Strategy requires action at many levels of governance. Action at the neighbourhood level is crucial. It is at this level that local intelligence is best gathered, that community motivation is best harnessed and renewal momentum achieved. (Social Exclusion Unit, 2000, p. 7)

This focus follows similar developments in cities in the USA where, since the 1960s, neighbourhoods have been the locus for community-led revitalisation programmes. This in turn has generated much debate about their potential contribution to urban governance systems (Box, 1998; Keating *et al.*, 1996; Peterman, 2000). Joined-up activity at the local level has been a feature of UK public policy since the 1970s, with a series of experiments in neighbourhood management, budgeting and policy-making (Gaster, 1994; Hambleton, Hoggett and Razzaque, 1996; Taylor, 2000; Webster, 1982). The National Strategy for Neighbourhood Renewal promotes the role of neighbourhood management as the tool for 'joining-up' at a sub-local level, and advocates five principles:

1. a responsible individual at neighbourhood level;
2. community involvement and leadership;
3. applying the right tools, for example agreements with service providers, purchasing capacity, use of special resources;
4. planned approach to local problems;
5. effective delivery mechanisms.

The NSNR introduces delivery of these principles through a designated manager who will bring together all local stakeholders to plan and deliver neighbourhood renewal. The manager would be responsible for overseeing the programme but would need the co-operation of local service deliverers to make this happen. In addition, a neighbourhood management board is proposed with representation from the local community and key agencies. Community representation on the board is considered essential in securing the legitimacy of the renewal programme and giving voice to emergent community leaders. This reflects the place of active citizenship in the modernisation agenda and the priority attached to facilitating deliberation between stakeholders in relation to local problems and issues. There is a relationship here with ward or similar local committees created by councils. These bodies may be advisory or have the authority to make certain decisions, for example on the allocation of Neighbourhood Renewal Fund, grants to voluntary bodies or service initiatives to tackle local problems. Increasingly these are multi-agency meetings to which the police, health and other bodies send representatives in addition to the presence of councillors and their officials (Sullivan *et al.*, 2001).

The impact of the modernisation programme at the local level clearly demonstrates how strategic, sectoral and neighbourhood partnerships have a key role in formalising collaborative activity and thus are integral to the notion of the congested state (Chapter 2). The hierarchical nature of the local governance system is evidenced in the overarching role of the local strategic partnership. This collaborative body becomes the prime voice for the locality, undermining the position held by the elected local council, and the shaper and arbiter of public, private, voluntary and community activity in respect of public policy goals. Hierarchical linkages from locality to regional and national level are also apparent in the relationship between local neighbourhood renewal programmes and the National Strategy, which in England is owned by the Neighbourhood Renewal Unit inside Whitehall. This reflects our analysis of Sure Start and the other recent policy initiatives which use partnerships as the local implementation mechanisms (Chapter 8). The effective operation of this system of collaborative and multi-level governance requires that a number of issues are addressed. Here we concentrate on three: leadership, centre–local relations and the role of the citizen.

Leadership is of prime concern to a collaborative system of local governance. Many local councils will be operating with executive decision-making, thus giving a greater visibility to the leader or elected mayor. The expectation behind the new arrangements is that they will use their position to construct and advance a community agenda. However, leadership may also emerge at other points in the system, for example the chair of the LSP or local residents with key roles on the boards of sectoral or neighbourhood partnerships. There have, of course, always been many leaders in a locality. However, the new system is different in two respects. First, there are more opportunities for individuals to claim with some legitimacy that they speak on behalf of a significant constituency. Secondly, the insights of regime theory suggest that old models of leadership based on systemic and command power must be replaced by new models related to collaborative and social production power. Stone (1993) comments that the power struggle is to gain and fuse a capacity to act; it is about power *to* not power *over*. This poses a challenge for British political culture which has deeply embedded assumptions about politics as an adversarial process and the state as the prime mover. New models of community governance, however, provide a way forward (Sullivan, 2001b).

The second issue concerns the relationships between tiers in the multi-level system of governance. Collaborations required or sponsored by national and European levels of government introduce a new dimension into the relationships between semi-autonomous actors. The academic study of central–local relationships in the UK has been largely ignored since the mid-1980s and new conceptualisations are needed to accommodate the changes that have occurred since then and which we map in this book. The traditional debate examined the autonomy of local authorities in the context of a principal–agent model, considering such issues as their legal powers and political and professional linkages with central government, although insights from the resource-dependency literature were subsequently introduced into the field (Goldsmith, 1986; Jones, 1980; Rhodes, 1999). The pattern of the local state revealed by our analysis suggests that a wider understanding of centre–local relations is required. It is no longer sufficient to focus solely on local authorities; rather analysis must take in the local system of governance. Theorising the centre–local relationship must accommodate both the old functional silos as well as the new hierarchical relationships structured around cross-cutting issues.

Finally, an analysis of collaboration in the context of multi-level governance must incorporate the citizen, an actor notably absent from earlier formulations. Active citizenship and community involvement are central to the local system of governance in a way that has transformed the local political landscape. As indicated above there are leadership opportunities for citizens at a variety of levels in this new governance framework: at neighbourhood level through programmes such as Sure Start and HAZ, and at strategic level through participation in the LSP. These opportunities for leadership are accompanied by a new commitment to making citizen and community participation more meaningful through the adoption of deliberative approaches to planning and decision-making. Despite this commitment, powerful forces remain which may dilute or marginalise such initiatives. These are centred upon the extent to which key institutions such as central and local government, the police and health service bodies are both prepared and able to relinquish control and develop new ways of working that are inclusive of community stakeholders.

Collaborative dilemmas

Our analysis of the collaborative agenda and its relationship to contemporary processes of governance leads us to conclude that there are an underlying set of dilemmas in these institutions of public policy (Box 11.1). These are dilemmas to be managed, rather than to be resolved in favour of one element rather than another. This is because the dilemmas are inherent in any form of collaboration that concerns matters of public policy.

The first tension is between collaboration as a delivery mechanism and as a governance process. Formal collaborative arrangements have become a key means for government to deliver its policy promises. They give a new focus to the work of agencies with interrelated missions and domains. In this sense they are powerful interventions by a third party into the underlying political economy of the inter-organisational network (see Chapter 3). These interventions affect, or at least strongly influence, the prevailing distribution of authority and resources and as a result structure new forms of relationship between organisations at the surface level. The resulting partnerships often have a strong connection with higher tiers of government through the requirement to deliver outcome targets. Consequently they become local agents for a central principal. This places weight on what March and Olsen (1989a) term the logic of consequentiality, where action is driven by a calculation of outcomes. Although these outcomes are mandated to a large extent by government at the centre and are related to funding streams and upward accountability for achievement, they sit in contrast to the values of governance in the public domain. Here are important matters of transparency, due process, standards of conduct and public debate. Questions of local autonomy and self-determination also come into focus when partnerships are viewed in terms of theories of local democracy and community governance (Sharpe, 1974; Stoker, 1996; Sullivan, 2001a).

Box 11.1 *Collaborative dilemmas*

Collaborations as ...
- delivery mechanisms and governance arrangements?
- political fora and managerial devices?
- capacity releasing and control exerting?
- structural entities and dynamic processes?

This perspective emphasises the logic of appropriateness, in other words that action is driven by the obligation of role. The roles of decision-makers in a system of elected local government, for example, are representative and decisional. Councillors represent their constituents, their party (if they have one) and the community at large. They make decisions following rules and procedures that are intended to ensure personal impartiality and reasonableness of judgement (Skelcher and Snape, 2001). Our analysis of partnership governance demonstrates a general weakness in relation to the regulation of decision-making and the conduct of board members (Chapter 8). This can be rationalised by the desire to maximise flexibility in order to deliver outcomes, but this sits oddly with an agenda in local government and quangos which is about strengthening corporate governance. The tension between procedural conformance and outcome performance is resolved in favour of the latter. The pragmatism of 'what works' to deliver outcomes sits uncomfortably alongside the virtue placed on high standards of conduct and democratic renewal.

A second tension exists between collaboration as a political process and as a managerial technique. Many collaborations, and especially those constituted as partnerships, have a strong emphasis on consultation with and involvement of the public (see Chapter 9). They open up a new political opportunity space in the locality (Maloney *et al.*, 2000). The clear geographical or issue focus of partnerships and the absence of electoral and party politics may give them a particular appeal for citizens in comparison with local government, and especially where councils have not created accessible ward or sub-locality opportunities for debate and decision-making. Connexions partnerships are required to involve young people on their boards and regeneration partnerships typically include elected or nominated resident representatives. There is, therefore, a dynamic political process around and within partnerships. However, new public management and the constitutional changes to local government have altered the balance between politicians and officials. Officials have greater delegated authority while conversely politicians are being encouraged to have an arm's-length relationship to detailed decision-making. This move is predicated in the notion of elected politicians as the strategic decision-makers, within whose policies officials then manage the meso- and micro-levels of activity. Whether such a detached role for politicians is either achievable or desirable is a matter for debate. Nevertheless it is part of the agenda and its impact can be seen in the predominance of managers as members of partnership boards (see Chapter 2). This suggests partnerships are a managerial device for inter-agency service delivery. The duality between political process and management technique is inherent to all public sector institutions. However, it is more pronounced in partnerships because their complex governance arrangements do not distinguish clearly between political and managerial roles.

The third tension is that between collaboration as a means to release capacity and to exert control. Collaborations provide vehicles to exercise the power of social production, that is the potential collective benefit arising from the pooling of resources by a number of agencies. The willingness to engage offers the possibility for creativity and synergy and to develop in ways which were not previously understood. Regime theory provides one intellectual justification for this view and local strategic partnerships offer a practical manifestation. This is a positive perspective on the development of the collaborative governance system, but one which presupposes a commonality of interest and a degree of equality in the power available to key actors in the locality. Such a view reflects a political desire by New Labour to move beyond the uncomfortable distributional questions of 'who wins, who loses?' and towards a vision of society as consensual and inclusive (Newman, 2001). The notion that it is possible to define an overall public interest should be challenged, and particularly in metropolitan areas with a diversity of economic, social, ethnic and cultural populations. Creating an LSP composed of representatives of peak groups, even where this relates to a broader consultative conference, does not ensure an adequate reflection of such diversity. The selection of participants and the process by which preferences are aggregated will both filter in and filter out certain interests. What it does do, however, is to structure a powerful alliance of key actors behind a particular vision for the locality in a way that has not previously been possible. Here is a powerful instrument for controlling the activities of a host of public, private, voluntary and community players around a common purpose, and one which has as its symbol the common good of the community. Regime theory reflects the neo-pluralist perspective that power is not evenly distributed, but argues that the blending of the resources of major actors can create a capacity to address collective action problems. The problem is that only some may be involved in the blending, and that the result may not be to everyone's benefit. Analysis of collaboration therefore requires an awareness of both its narrow, close-ended control dimension and its fluid, open-ended potentiality.

The final tension is between collaboration as a structural entity and as a dynamic process. Collaborations are easily identified with reference to formal partnerships structures – the board, the budget, the form of constitution.

These are important manifestations of agencies' commitment to work together in their mutual interest and for the benefit of the community. As with any formal structure, the partnership will take on a life of its own. There will be routines of board and consultative group meetings to hold, agendas and monitoring reports to prepare, and human resource management issues to deal with where the partnership directly employs staff or funds them to work in other agencies. Logos may be developed – indeed Connexions partnerships are expected to develop a distinctive branding – and public relations strategies developed. Partnerships begin to take on the trappings of mainstream public organisations, and to develop a presence in the system of local governance. Those associated with the partnership will develop a sense of loyalty to its mission and to the continuation of the organisation. The social processes identified by Ring and van de Ven (1994) will have a particular resonance in terms of the individuals who pioneer a partnership's emergence from a looser collaborative arrangement, and who take the risk of boundary-spanning activity to achieve this. Yet collaborations are fundamentally about dynamic processes through which actors – both individual and organisational – negotiate their relationships around mutual interests. Their interests will change over time, responding to internal political imperatives, the policy context in which they operate and the nature of their communities. The partnership itself, especially if it is time-limited, will also change as activities develop and funding patterns evolve (see Chapter 7). This tension raises important questions about organisational flexibility and personal loyalties in the new collaborative environment (see Chapter 6).

Theorising public policy collaboration

Working in collaboration has become institutionalised both as a form of practice and a value set within the normative regime extant in the public sector, yet also exhibits features which are in contradiction to the traditional values of good public governance (Brereton and Temple, 1999). The centrality of collaboration within contemporary governance and the tensions that it generates poses questions for the way in which this new environment can be theorised. How, in other words, can we explain the nature of collaboration in the current period? One way forward is to return to the four questions that we posed in the first chapter. These questions are:

- why does collaboration happen?
- what forms does collaboration take?

- how can collaborative performance be explained?
- how can collaborative activity be evaluated?

Reflecting on these in the light of the evidence presented in this volume enables us to develop a theoretically informed pathway through this issue (Table 11.1).

The starting point is to consider imperatives for collaboration. Our analysis isolates three key factors. The changing pattern of public governance is clearly a major force. Developments internationally are reconstituting the roles of public agencies and their relationships with each other and with other sectors. The complexity of the outcome-oriented tasks with which they engage motivates collaborative activity across organisational boundaries (Chapters 2, 4 and 5). This process should be seen in the context of two factors. The first is resource control and distribution, and particularly the active intervention by central government into the inter-organisational political economy. This has a significant impact on collaborative form and capacity, since it determines who the key players are and what their agenda is. The second is to do with a vision driven by values of social justice and public service and the desire to join-up agencies to deliver improved outcomes. This impacts upon the nature of collaborative capacity, including leadership and inter-agency and inter-professional histories (Chapter 3).

Successful motivation generates the question of collaborative forms. Our discussion of the dynamics of collaboration illustrates the importance of pre-existing networks to the emergence and shape of subsequent more formalised structures (Chapter 7). Equally, notions of collaborative betterment and collaborative empowerment (Chapter 3) and agency exclusive–community inclusive board composition are central to the corporate governance of the collaboration (Chapter 2). The forms chosen are explained both by agency concerns with resource dependencies, for example the degree to which there is a willingness to create a corporate body and integrate activities, staff and budgets, as much as by direction from superior tiers of government (Chapter 8). Communities do not appear to be significant in determining the questions (compared with local government in England and Wales where the adoption of new constitutions has required consultation and occasionally referenda). However, the wide extent of public consultation around partnerships (if not directly through membership of their boards) can be explained with reference to the democratic deficit of partnerships and the need to legitimise such significant public interventions (Chapter 9). This is particularly the case given the role of partnerships in managing power relationships between and within sectors (Chapters 4 and 5).

Table 11.1 *A framework for understanding public policy collaboration*

Imperatives for collaboration	Collaborative forms	Collaborative capacity	Evaluation of collaboration
• Context: multi-level, political imperatives, complexity and scope of task	• Constitution: prior relationships, network/partnership, corporate/non-corporate, accountability	• Individual and organisational factors: strategy, leadership, relationship skills, risk, trust	• Outcomes: targets, policies, well-being
• Resources: acquiring, exchanging, controlling	• Membership: defined/flexible, inclusive/exclusive	• Balance: external pressures and internal routines, demands on staff and communities	• Stakeholders: communities, users, agencies
• Vision: supporting, resisting	• Management of power: within and across sectors, citizens and communities	• Building capacity: institutional opportunities and constraints	• Collaborative governance: efficient, accountable, democratic

The dynamic of collaboration and the effective operation of its governance leads to questions of collaborative capacity (Chapter 6). There is a series of individual and organisational factors that are important in explaining the propensity of collaborations to emerge beyond the initial good idea, and to function effectively over time. These include leadership, risk and trust. Beyond these, there are questions of balance between the demands of the collaboration and of the partner organisations. At a micro-level, there can be particular pressures on community members who are actively involved in partnerships (Chapter 9). The nature of institutional capacity and constraint, especially as it is shaped by the prevailing local context (histories, traditions and conditions), pre-existing cultures and routines of partner organisations, are also significant explanatory variables (Chapter 6).

The final question we posed in the introductory chapter is of a different order to the other three. It concerns the ways in which collaborations can be evaluated, rather than explanations of the development and operation of these phenomena. Because of this our comments here are more normative. The evaluation of substantive outcomes is particularly important given their place in motivating collaboration. However, these should be seen not just as specific policies or targets achieved, but in terms of their contribution to the well-being of the overall community and to its diverse constituencies. This can be reflected in part through an understanding of stakeholder views and through the active engagement of stakeholders in and throughout the evaluative process. Evaluation should also be concerned with collaborative governance and assess its efficiency, accountability and democratic contribution. In the drive for outcomes, it is important to remember that collaboration is for public purpose and therefore should engage with public debate, scrutiny and choice (Chapters 10 and 11).

Conclusion

The powerful momentum for collaboration is unlikely to be diminished, despite the problems of accountability, the complexities of the organisational relationships which emerge and the time and energy necessary to maintain these relationships at an organisational and individual level. The state is joining-up with a vengeance and in the process is constructing a configuration that is significantly different from that found prior to the mid-1990s. The emergence of partnerships as tertiary structures – in contrast to primary elected bodies and secondary arm's-length unitary quangos – poses new problems of legitimacy and accountability for public action. They accentuate the problems arising from hollowing-out which themselves 'erode accountability ... [and] obscures who is accountable for what' (Rhodes, 1996, p. 662). In an era of collaboration and performance orientation, authority is based more on nodality in networks and the ability to deliver on objectives; accountability to organisational partners and funders is strong, but that to citizens is weak.

Collaborations establish new jurisdictions – functional and geographical domains – for public action. Yet there is little debate about their rationale, nor the implications for existing jurisdictions such as local councils and health bodies, nor the impact on local political systems. This suggests that governance is perceived as an essentially negotiative process in which first movers can gain advantage by creating or mandating collaborations and others must then accommodate to them. But there must be more to public governance than this. Questions of order, rationality and purpose should surely be debated. These major developments in the system of governance deserve attention. They deserve particular attention in a nation such as the UK which, especially in England, has a highly centralised governmental system and lacks a written constitution. Membership of the European Union, which itself is undergoing major change, accentuates the issue. However, it is beyond the centre – in neighbourhoods, cities, towns and counties – that the greatest impact of the congested state is felt. Here we find a plethora of overlapping jurisdictions constructed in the name of public benefit while also confusing the nature of accountability. Our discussion provides some clarity to and explanation of this rapid, confusing and significant change. There is an important research agenda here to be exploited.

Appendix 1 Note on Sources and Research Method

This book draws on original research by the authors undertaken since the mid-1990s, some of which has been published previously. This research has investigated questions of accountability, governance, collaboration and citizenship. It has adopted an interdisciplinary approach, although the main theoretical content draws from public management, political science and organisational sociology. Studies have generally employed plural methodologies within a largely ethnographic tradition. Methods adopted have included quantitative surveys, case study and critical incidents, diary-keeping by respondents, semi-structured interviews and observation. Action-research has been employed in several cases. The empirical focus of the research includes City Challenge, SRB, HAT, HAZ, Sure Start, NDC, community safety, public involvement programmes and neighbourhood management.

Research studies of particular relevance are:

1. The national evaluation of Health Action Zones – **'Building Capacity for Collaboration component'** (1999–2002). Helen Sullivan is leading on the evaluation of partnership working as part of this study and findings from the early experiences of HAZ partnerships contribute particularly to Chapter 6. Outputs include Sullivan, Barnes and Matka (forthcoming), Barnes and Sullivan (forthcoming) and Barnes, Sullivan and Matka (2001).

2. **Effective Partnership and Good Governance: Conformance or Performance?** Early contributions from this ESRC research award, for which Chris Skelcher is the principal investigator, are reflected in the discussion of dilemmas in the concluding chapter of the book. The study also involves Mike Smith at the University of Birmingham.

3. **Power, Participation and Political Renewal (2000–2002).** A study funded as part of the ESRC Democracy and Participation Programme. This study is concerned with exploring new ways of involving citizens and communities in decision-making with particular reference to deliberative approaches. A variety of initiatives in two major cities are being explored, including partnerships involving the community sector. Initial outputs from the study have contributed to Chapter 9. Helen Sullivan is a named researcher on this project, which is led by Marian Barnes who is also at the University of Birmingham.

4. **Community networks in urban regeneration.** This project, funded by the Joseph Rowntree Foundation, was undertaken by a team led by Vivien Lowndes

and including Chris Skelcher, Angus McCabe and Philip Nanton. It employed an action-research methodology to identify and examine informal and formal collaborative arrangements for urban regeneration in three localities. The project developed an understanding of partnership dynamics which contributed to Chapter 7. Outputs include: Lowndes and Skelcher (1998); McCabe *et al.* (1997); Skelcher *et al.* (1996).

5. **Democratic Participation and Social Inclusion**. This project was supported by the Local Government Information Unit and Joseph Rowntree Foundation and was undertaken as a collaboration between INLOGOV and the Local Government Centre at Warwick. It was led by Helen Sullivan. The project examined the opportunities available to local authorities and others to 'join up' the modernisation and social inclusion agendas for the maximum benefit to local communities. The work contributed particularly to Chapters 3, 6 and 11. The report of the research was published in 2001 (Sullivan *et al.*, 2001)

6. **Advance of the Quango State**. A study of quangos under new Labour undertaken jointly by Chris Skelcher and Lynne Wilson from the Institute of Local Government Studies at the University of Birmingham and Stuart Weir from Democratic Audit, the University of Essex, for the Local Government Information Unit. The study drew on secondary sources, including internet searches. It has informed Chapters 2 and 8, and the initial mapping of partnerships it contained has been developed in Appendix 2. Outputs include Skelcher *et al.*, 2000.

7. **Governing Bodies in the Public and Non-profit Sectors**. An early version of Chapter 2 was presented to, and benefited from discussion at, an ESRC research seminar series convened jointly by Chris Skelcher from the University of Birmingham and Margaret Harris from Aston Business School.

8. **Cross-cutting Issues in Public Policy and Public Service**. This research project, funded by DETR in 1998, examined the challenge to central government of 'joining-up' policy-making and implementation. Led by Sue Richards at the University of Birmingham, the team included Helen Sullivan. The study explored a number of cross-cutting issues including social exclusion, environmental sustainability, disaffected young people and community safety. It has contributed to Chapters 3 and 6. The research report was published in 1999 (Richards *et al.*, 1999).

Appendix 2   Number and Value of Multi-Agency Partnerships, 2001/02[*]

Partnership	Purpose	Start date	Number	Public sector contribution	Identifiable funding through the partnership 2001/2
Action Team for Jobs	Assist those disadvantaged in labour market get and keep jobs	2000	70[5]	£45 m 2000/01; £135 m for 3 years from 2001/2[5]	£40 m[12] (p)
Active Community Programme	Pilot new ways of increasing public involvement in the Community	1999	5[5]	£4.5 m over 3 years[5]	£1.5 m (e)
Black and Minority Ethnic Twinning Voluntary Partnerships	Assist black and ethnic minority voluntary sector twinning activities	1999	N/a	£0.8 m over 3 years	£0.3 m (e)
Childcare Partnerships in Scotland	To support pre-school education and affordable childcare	1998	32	£14 m p.a 2001/2 to 2003/4[10]	£14 m (p)

Childrens's Fund	Help tackle child poverty and social exclusion	2001	40 initially; final number depends on bids[5]	£450 m over 3 years[5]	£150 m (e)
Children and Youth Partnerships in Wales	Tackle causes and effects of social exclusion among children and young people	1999	Up to 22[9]	£10 m p.a. for 4 years 2000/1–2003/4[9]	£10 m (p)[9]
Coalfields Programme	Regeneration of coalfield areas	1998	–	£350 m over 10 years; plus £399 m over 4 years from 1998[5]	£135 m (e)
Community Chests	Support community involvement in deprived areas	2001	88, managed through local strategic partnerships[5]	£10 m 2001/2; £15 m 2002/3; £25 m 2003/4[5]	£10 m (p)[5]
Community Consortia for Education and Training in Wales	Prepare plans to meet education and training needs of individuals, communities and employers	2001	Currently being decided	£1.4 m 2000/1; £5 m 2001/2[9]	£5 m (p)[9]
Community Rural Transport Partnerships in Northern Ireland	To improve mobility in rural areas	1998	17 at Nov. 2001[15]	£1.3 m	N/a
Community Safety Partnerships in Northern Ireland	Address issues of community safety and fear of crime	1996	7 at Nov. 2001	Resourced by partners	N/a
Community Safety Partnerships in Scotland	Address issues of community safety and fear of crime	1999	32	Resourced by partners plus bids to other programmes	N/a

(Continued)

Partnership	Purpose	Start date	Number	Public sector contribution	Identifiable funding through the partnership 2001/2
Community Legal Service Partnerships in England and Wales	Improve access to good quality legal advice	2000	182[5], more to be established	To be determined; £15 m innovation fund over 3 years[5]	£5 m + (e)
Connexions	Support young people in the transition to adulthood and work	2001	47[1]	Central grant of additional £177 m in 2002/3; also resourced by partners plus bids to other funds[11]	N/a
Creative Partnerships	Provision of creative experiences for school-children in deprived areas	2002	12[1]	£15 m 2002/3; £25 m 2003/4 with possible extension[5]	Commences 2002/3
Crime and Disorder Partnerships in England and Wales	Address issues of community safety and fear of crime	1998	376[1]	Bid for resources from other programmes, including the Crime Reduction Programme in England and Wales: £40 m 1999/00; £100 m 2000/1; £110 m 2001/2; plus £153 m for CCTV initiative[5]	£160 m (e) from Crime Reduction Programme

Drug Action Teams	Local implementation of national drugs strategy	1999	Approx. 100	Resourced by partners plus Drugs Prevention Advisory Service.	N/a
Early Excellence Centres	Develop, demonstrate and disseminate integrated services to meet needs of children and families	2000	Up to 100 by 2004[5]	£45 m over 4 years[5]	£11 m (e)
Early Years Development and Childcare Partnerships in England and Wales	Develop nursery provision and affordable childcare	1998	150[7]	£145 m childcare funding and £290 m early education funding in 2001/02[7] plus £14 m in Wales over 4 years 1999/00 –2002/3[9]	£435 m (p)[7] plus £3.5 (e)
Education Action Zones	Raise educational standards of groups of schools	1998	73 large zones plus 100 small zones by 2002[5]	£274 m over 5 years[4]	£72 m (e)
Employment Zones	Assist long-term unemployed people into work	2000	15[5]	£112 m over 2 years 2001/02–2002/3; £81 m 2002/3[5]	£56 m (e)
Excellence in Cities	Drive up standards in schools in major cities	1999	58[5]	£300 m over 4 years[5]	£75 m (e)
Further Education Partnerships in Wales	Facilitate collaboration between schools and colleges	1998	N/a	N/a	N/a

(Continued)

Partnership	Purpose	Start date	Number	Public sector contribution	Identifiable funding through the partnership 2001/2
Health Act 1999 Partnerships	Facilitate joined-up working between NHS bodies and social services at a local level	1999	64 at Nov 2001	Partnership grant of £887 m 1999/00–2001/2 plus partners' resources[16]	637 m (e)[16]
Health Action Zones	Targeting localities where health can be improved by better integrating care and treatment	1998	26[1]	Resourced by partners plus £499 m over 1998/9–2001/2[13]	£160 m[13]
Healthy Living Centres	To promote health in its broadest sense	1999	Being developed at Nov. 2001	£300 m over 5 years[5]	£60 m (e)
Healthy Schools Programme (Education and Health Partnerships)	Create health ethos within schools	1998	149	£1 m 1998/99; £2 m 1999/00; plus £15 m via Standards Fund in 2001/2[5]	£15 m (p)[5]
Joint Committees	Created by local authorities for various purposes	Since late C19th	N/a	N/a	N/a
Joint Boards	For certain function in metropolitan counties	1986	15	Data not available for all services	£377 m (p) for fire joint boards[14]

Lifelong Learning Partnerships	Local delivery of national learning targets for participation in post-16 education	1999	100[1]	Bids for resources from DfES Standards Fund plus access to £10m p.a. partnership fund[9]	£10m+ (e)
Local Agenda 21 throughout UK	Sustainable development at the local level	1991	285[1]	Resourced by partners or bids for funding	N/a
Local Enterprise Forums in Scotland	Advise on local economic development	2001	12[9]	Resourced by partners	N/a
Local Health Alliances in Wales	Contribute to health improvement	1998	22	Resourced by partners	N/a
Local Partnership Agreements in Scotland	Comprehensive and intensive support and care scheme for all client groups	2000	32[9]	Resourced by partners	N/a
Local Strategic Partnerships	Develop and oversee implementation of long-term vision for the locality	2001	Approx. 400	Resourced by partners	N/a
Neighbourhood Management	Improve local outcomes by increasing integration and responsiveness of local services	2001	20 pathfinders plus 10 further projects[8]	£45 m over 3 years[8]	£15 m (e)
Neighbourhood Renewal Fund	Improve services in 88 most deprived districts	2001	88 managed by local strategic partnerships[8]	£200 m 2001/2; £300 m 2002/3; £400 m 2003/4[8]	£200 m (p)[8]

(Continued)

234

Partnership	Purpose	Start date	Number	Public sector contribution	Identifiable funding through the partnership 2001/2
Neighbourhood Support Fund	Re-engage into education and training the most disaffected 13–19-year-olds living on poorest estates	2000	Over 600 projects managed in a variety of ways[5]	£60 m over 3 years[5]	£20 m (e)
Neighbourhood Wardens	Using wardens to tackle problems of poorest neighbourhoods	2000	Depends on number of applications	£13 m over 3 years[5]	£4 m (e)
New Commitment to Regeneration	Develop comprehensive and integrated regeneration strategies	1998	22[1]	Resourced by Partners	N/a
New Deal for Communities	Tackle multiple deprivation in the most deprived neighbourhoods in the country	1998	39[5]	£1.12 bn over 10 years[5]	£112 m(e)
New Deal Partnerships throughout UK	Plan and co-ordinate New Deal for Unemployed	1998	140[17]	£3.5 bn over 4 years, some of which may be delivered by partnerships[9]	N/a
On Track	Identify ways of stopping development of anti-social and offending behaviour in children	1999	24[9], but encouraged to use an existing partnership forum	£30 m over first two years, but initiative will run for 7 years in total[9]	£15 m (e)

Partnership Action for Continuing Employment in Scotland	Address effect on communities when major employers close	2000	Dependent on local choice[9]	Resourced by partners	N/a
Partnership Projects	Partnerships between state and independent schools to raise educational standards	1996	120	£1.75 m over 1998–2001, plus £0.45 m from educational charity[18]	£350 m
People in Communities Partnerships in Wales	Build sustainable communities (will phase into Communities First partnerships)	1999	Up to 22[9]	£2.5 m 2000/1[9]	0
Regional Cultural Consortia	Development of cultural strategy in each English region	2000	8[1]	Resourced by partners	N/a
Regional Transport Partnerships	Integrate transport strategies across council boundaries	2000	4[9] to date	May bid for Scottish Executive funding[9]	N/a
Rural Transport Partnerships	Social inclusion of people living in rural areas	2001	Dependent on local choice[9]	£4 m. p.a.[9]	£4 m (p)[9]
Single Regeneration Budget	Economic, social and cultural regeneration of deprived areas	1994	900+[5]	900+ schemes will receive over £5.6 m over their 7 year lifetime[5]	£700 m (e)
Social Inclusion Partnerships	Tackle social exclusion	1999	48[9]	£150 m for 3 years 2000/1–2002/3[9]	£50 m (e)
Sport Action Zones	Bring benefits of sport to deprived communities	1999	30 by 2002[6]	£750 m over 10 years[6]	£75 m (e)

(Continued)

Partnership	Purpose	Start date	Number	Public sector contribution	Identifiable funding through the partnership 2001/2
Supporting People Partnerships	Commissioning and purchasing social care support services	2001	150 approx.	To be determined at time of writing	N/a
Sure Start	Promote development of children of disadvantaged families	1999	500 Sure Start by 2004[2]	£580 m over 5 years[3]	£284 m (p)[3]
Sure Start Plus	Reduce social exclusion and poverty arising from teenage pregnancy	2001	20[2]	Within Sure Start budget[3]	–
Sure Start Scotland	Promote development of children of disadvantaged families	1999	Integrate within social inclusion partnerships[9]	£42 m over 3 years 1999/00–2001/2[9]	£14 m (e)
Sure Start Wales	Promote development of children of disadvantaged families	1999	22[9]	£11 m p.a.[9]	£11 m (p)[9]
Vehicle Crime Reduction Action Team	Develop and implement a strategy to reduce vehicle crime	1998	1	Funded through Crime Reduction Programme	N/a
Youth Offending Teams	Formulate and implement youth justice plans	1999	149	Resourced by partners	N/a

Notes: *All initiatives are for England unless otherwise specified. The final column gives identifiable public funding through the partnership. In general the figures provided are special funds rather than mainstream spending directed through or influenced by the partnership. Figures for the latter are not available.

(e) contribution for the year estimated from global figures.

(p) is a published figure for that year.

Sources:

1. House of Commons (2001)
2. DfES (2001a)
3. HM Treasury (2000)
4. National Audit Office (2001a)
5. www.rcu.gov.uk/
6. www.sportengland.org
7. DfEE (2001)
8. Social Exclusion Unit (2001)
9. CIPFA (2001)
10. Scottish Executive (2001)
11. DfES (2001b)
12. HM Treasury (2001)
13. www.ohn.gov.uk
14. CIPFA (2000). The figure given is 2000/01; 2001/02 data not available at time of writing.
15. www.nics.gov.uk
16. www.doh.gov.uk/jointunit
17. www.newdeal.gov.uk
18. www.dfes.gov.uk

References

Accounts Commission (2000) *How Are We Doing? Measuring the Performance of Community Safety Partnerships* (Edinburgh: Audit Scotland).

Alter, C. and Hage, J. (1993) *Organisations Working Together* (London: Sage).

Anastacio, J., Gidley, B., Hart, L., Keith, M., Mayo, M. and Kowarzik, U. (2000) *Reflecting Realities: Participants' Perspectives on Integrated Communities and Sustainable Development* (Bristol: Policy Press).

Ariño, A. (1997) 'Veracity and Commitment: Co-operative Behaviour in First-time Ventures' in Beamish, P. W. and Killing, J. P. (1997) *Co-operative Strategy: European Perspectives* (San Francisco: The New Lexington Press).

Audit Commission (1986) *Making a Reality of Community Care* (London: HMSO).

Audit Commission (1989) *Urban Regeneration and Economic Development: The Local Government Dimension* (London: HMSO).

Audit Commission (1996) *Misspent Youth: Young People*, 2nd edn (London: Audit Commission).

Audit Commission (1998) *A Fruitful Partnership* (London: Audit Commission).

Audit Commission (1999) *Safety in Numbers* (London: Audit Commission).

Ayres, S. and Davis, P. (2000) ' "Welcome to the Party"? Inclusion, Mutuality and Difference in the West Midlands Regional Development Agency Network in the UK', paper to the *Fourth International Research Symposium on Public Management*, Erasmus University, April.

Bailey, N. with Barker, A. and MacDonald, K. (1995) *Partnership Agencies in British Urban Policy* (London: UCL Press).

Balloch, S. and Taylor, M. (eds). (2001) *Partnership Working* (Bristol: Policy Press).

Barnekov, T., Boyle, R. and Rich, D. (1990) *Privatism and Urban Policy in Britain and the USA* (Oxford: Oxford University Press).

Barnes, M. and Bowl, R. (2001) *Taking over the Asylum: Empowerment and Mental Health* (Basingstoke: Palgrave Macmillan).

Barnes, M., Harrison, S., Mort, M., Shardlow, P. and Wistow, G. (1999) 'The New Management of Community Care: User Groups, Citizenship and Co-Production' in Stoker, G. (ed.) (1999), *The New Management of Local Governance* (Basingstoke: Palgrave Macmillan).

Barnes, M. and Prior, D. (2000) *Private Lives as Public Policy* (Birmingham: Venture Press).

Barnes, M. (1999) 'Social Exclusion' in Richards, S., Barnes, M., Coulson, A., Gaster, L., Leach, B. and Sullivan, H. (1999) *Cross-Cutting Issues in Public Policy and Public Services* (London: DETR).

Barnes, M., Newman, J., Knops, A. and Sullivan, H. (2001) 'Constituting "the Public" in Public Participation', Paper presented at an ESRC Democracy and Participation Programme conference, January.

Barnes, M., Sullivan, H. and Matka, E. (2001) *Context, Strategy and Capacity. Initial Findings from the Strategic Level Analysis. Building Capacity for Collaboration: The National Evaluation of Health Action Zones*, A Report to the Department of Health, (Birmingham: University of Birmingham).

Barnes, M. and Sullivan, H. (forthcoming) 'Building Capacity for Collaboration in English HAZs' in Powell, M., Glendinning, C. and Rummery, K. (eds) (forthcoming), *Partnerships, the Third Way and the Governance of Welfare* (Bristol Policy Press).

Barr, A., Stenhouse, C. and Henderson, P. (2001) *Caring Communities: A Challenge for Social Inclusion* (York: York Publishing Service).

Barton, A. and Quinn, C. (2001) 'The Supremacy of Joined-up Working: A Pandora's Box for Organisational Identity?', *Public Policy and Administration*, vol. 16, no. 2, pp. 49–62.

Benington, J. and Harvey, J. (1998) 'Transnational Local Authority Networking Within the European Union: Passing Fashion or New Paradigm?' in Marsh, D. (ed.) (1998), *Comparing Policy Networks* (Buckingham: Open University Press).

Benson, J. K. (1975) 'The Interorganisational Network as a Political Economy', *Administrative Science Quarterly*, vol. 20, pp. 229–49.

Benyon, J. and Edwards, A. (1996) 'Local Strategies for Crime Prevention', paper presented at an ESRC Local Governance Programme seminar, University of Strathclyde.

Benyon, J. and Edwards, A. (1999) 'Community Governance of Crime Control' in Stoker, G. (ed.) (1999), *The New Management of British Local Governance* (London: Palgrave Macmillan).

Birmingham City Council (1999) *Birmingham – Setting the Agenda: Dynamic Liaisons: Partnerships in Birmingham* (Birmingham: Birmingham City Council).

Blau, P. M. (1964) *Exchange and Power in Social Life* (London: John Wiley).

Börzel, T. A. (1998) 'Organizing Babylon – On the Different Conceptions of Policy Networks', *Public Administration*, vol. 76, no. 2, pp. 253–74.

Box, R. C. (1998) *Citizen Governance* (London: Sage).

Boyle, R. (1993) 'Changing Partners: The Experience of Urban Economic Policy in West Central Scotland, 1980–90', *Urban Studies*, vol. 30, no. 2, pp. 309–24.

Boyne, G., Gould-Williams, J., Law, J. and Walker, R. (1999) 'Best Value in Welsh Local Government: Progress and Prospects', *Local Government Studies*, vol. 25, no. 2, pp. 68–86.

Bradford, H. A. Z. (1998) *Breaking Barriers: Improving Health – Practical Steps to Better Health* (Bradford: Bradford Health Authority).

Bradford, M. and Robson, B. (1995) 'An Evaluation of Urban Policy' in Hambleton, R. and Thomas, H. (eds) (1995), *Urban Policy Evaluation: Challenge and Change* (London: Paul Chapman).

Brereton, M. and Temple, M. (1999) 'The New Public Service Ethos: An Ethical Environment for Governance', *Public Administration*, vol. 77, no. 3, pp. 455–74.

Bright, J. (1997) *Turning the Tide: Crime, Community and Prevention* (London: DEMOS).

Brownhill, S. and Darke, J. (1998) *'Rich Mix': Inclusive Strategies for Urban Regeneration* (Bristol: Policy Press).

Burns, D. and Taylor, M. (2000) *Auditing Community Participation* (Bristol: Policy Press).

Byatt, I. (2001) *Delivering Better Services for Citizens: A Review of Local Government Procurement in England* (London: DTLR).

Carley, M., Chapman, M., Hastings, A., Kirk, K. and Young, R. (2000) *Urban Regeneration Through Partnership: A Study in Nine Urban Regions in England, Scotland and Wales* (Bristol: Policy Press).

Cavanagh, M. (1998) 'Offshore Health and Safety Policy in the North Sea: Policy Networks and Policy Outcomes in Britain and Norway' in Marsh, D. (ed.) (1998), *Comparing Policy Networks* (Buckingham: Open University Press).

Challis, L., Fuller, S., Henwood, M., Klein, R., Plowden, W., Webb, A., Whittingham, P. and Wistow, G. (1988) *Joint Approaches to Social Policy* (Cambridge: Cambridge University Press).

Chanan, G. (1991) *Taken for Granted: Community Activity and the Crisis of the Voluntary Sector* (London: Community Development Foundation).

Chapman, M. (1995) 'Urban Policy and Urban Evaluation: The Impact of the European Union' in Hambleton, R. and Thomas, H. (eds) (1995), *Urban Policy Evaluation: Challenge and Change* (London: Paul Chapman).

Chau, R. C. M. and Yu, S. W. K. (2001) 'Social Exclusion of Chinese People in Britain', *Critical Social Policy*, vol. 21, no. 1, pp. 103–25.

Chelliah, R. (2001) *Local Authorities and Companies: Partnership Working* (London: Local Government Information Unit).

Chen, H. T. and Rossi, P. H. (1983) 'Evaluating with Sense: The Theory Driven Approach', *Evaluation Review*, vol. 7, pp. 283–302.

Chen, H. T. (1990) *Theory-Driven Evaluations* (London: Sage).

Chumrow, J. (1995) 'Housing Action Trusts: A Possible Role Model?', *Parliamentary Affairs*, vol. 48, no. 2, pp. 254–70.

CIPFA (2000) *Estimates of Expenditure 2000/01* (London: CIPFA).

CIPFA (2001) *The CJC Guide to Partnerships and Partnering* (London: CIPFA).

Clarence, E. and Painter, C. (1998) 'Public Services under New Labour: Collaborative Discourses and Local Networking', *Public Policy and Administration*, vol. 13, no. 3, pp. 8–22.

Clarke, G. (2000) 'The Decline of Leviathan: State, Market and Civil Society in South East Asia 1986–1998' in Osborne, S. P. (ed.) (2000), *Public–Private Partnerships: Theory and Practice in International Perspective* (London: Routledge).

Clarke, M. and Stewart, J. (1988) *The Enabling Council* (Luton: Local Government Management Board).

Clarke, M. and Stewart, J. (1997) *Handling the Wicked Issues: A Challenge for Government* (Birmingham: INLOGOV, University of Birmingham).

Clegg, S. (1990) *Modern Organizations: Organization Studies in the Post-modern World* (London: Sage).

COGS (2000) *Active Partners: Benchmarking Community Participation in Regeneration* (Leeds: COGS/Yorkshire Forward).

Cole, I., McCoulough, E. and Southworth, J. (2000) *Neighbourhood Agreements in Action* (York: York Publishing Service).

Commission on Public Private Partnerships (2001) *Building Better Partnerships: The Final Report of the Commission on Public Private Partnerships* (London: Institute for Public Policy Research).

Connell, J. P., Kubisch, A. C., Schorr, L. B. and Weiss, C. H. (eds) (1995), *New Approaches to Evaluating Community Initiatives: Concepts, Methods and Contexts*, (Washington, DC: Aspen Institute).

Connell, J. P. and Kubisch, A. C. (1998) 'Applying a Theory of Change Approach to the Evaluation of Comprehensive Community Initiatives: Progress, Prospects and Problems', in Fulbright-Anderson, K., Kubisch, A. C. and Connell, J. P. (eds) (1998), *New Approaches to Evaluating Community Initiatives,* vol. 2: *Theory, Measurement and Analysis* (Washington, DC: Aspen Institute).

Corby, S. (1999) 'The National Health Service' in Farnham, S. and Horton, D. (eds) (1999), *Public Management in Britain* (Basingstoke: Palgrave Macmillan).

Corrigan, P., Steele, J. and Parston, G. (2001) *The Case for the Public Interest Company: A New Form of Enterprise for Public Service Delivery* (London: Public Management Foundation).

Coulson, A. (1988) 'The Evaluator: Inquisitor, Comrade or Spy?', *Local Economy*, vol. 2, no. 4, pp. 229–36.

Coulson, A. (1998) 'Trust and Contract in Public Sector Management' in Coulson, A. (ed.) (1998), *Trust and Contracts: Relationships in Local Government, Health and Public Services* (Bristol Policy Press).

Craig, G., Taylor, M., Szanto, C. and Wilkinson, M. (1999) *Developing Local Compacts: Relationships Between Local Public Sector Bodies* (York: York Publishing Service).

Crawford, C., Sauvain, S., Coulson, A. and Clarke, M. (2000) *Law Relating to Local Government: A Research Report* (London: DETR).

Cropper, S. (1996) 'Collaborative Working and the Issue of Sustainability' in Huxham, C. (1996) (ed.), *Creating Collaborative Advantage* (London: Sage).

Daemen, H. and Schaap, L. (eds) (2000), *Citizen and City: Developments in Fifteen Local Democracies in Europe* (Delft: Eburon).

Daugbjerg, C. (1998) 'Linking Policy Networks and Environmental Policies: Nitrate Policy Making in Denmark and Sweden 1970–1995', *Public Administration*, vol. 76, no. 2, pp. 275–94.

Daugbjerg, C. and Marsh, D. (1998) 'Explaining Policy Outcomes: Integrating the Policy Network Approach with Macro-level and Micro-level Analysis' in Marsh, D. (ed.) (1998), *Comparing Policy Networks* (Buckingham: Open University Press).

Davies, H. T. O., Nutley, S. M. and Smith, P. C. (2000) *What Works? Evidence-based Policy and Practice in Public Services* (Bristol: Policy Press).

Davies, M., Croall, H. and Tyrer, J. (1995) *Criminal Justice: An Introduction to the Criminal Justice System in England and Wales* (London: Longman).

Davis-Smith, J. (1995) 'The Voluntary Tradition: Philanthropy and Self-help in Britain 1500–1945' in Davis-Smith, J., Rochester, C. and Hedley, R. (1995) *An Introduction to the Voluntary Sector* (London: Routledge).

Davoudi, S. and Healey, P. (1995) 'City Challenge: A Sustainable Mechanism or Temporary Gesture' in Hambleton, R. and Thomas, H. (eds) (1995), *Urban Policy Evaluation: Challenge and Change* (London: Paul Chapman).

Deakin, N. (1995) 'The Perils of Partnership: The Voluntary Sector and the State 1945–1992' in Davis-Smith, J., Rochester, C. and Hedley, R., *An Introduction to the Voluntary Sector* (London: Routledge).

Deakin, N. (2001) 'Putting Narrow-mindedness out of Countenance: The UK Voluntary Sector in the New Millennium' in Anheier, H. K. and Kendall, J. (eds) (2001), *Third Sector Policy at the Crossroads* (London: Routledge).

Department for Education and Employment (1998a) *The EAZ Handbook* (London: DFEE).

Department for Education and Employment (1998b) *Practice, Progress and Value – Learning Communities: Assessing the Value they Add* (London: DFEE).

Department for Education and Employment (2001) *Early Years Childcare and Development Partnerships Planning Guidance 2001–2002* (London: DFEE).

Department for Education and Skills (2001a) *SureStart: A Guide to Fifth Round Programmes* (London: DFES).

Department for Education and Skills (2001b) *Connexions Service Business Planning Guidance 2001/2001* (London: DFES).

Department for Environment, Food and Rural Affairs (2001) *Our Countryside: The Future – A Fair Deal for England* (London: The Stationery Office).

Department of Health (DoH) (1989) *Caring for people: community care in the next decade and beyond* Cm. 849 (London: HMSO).

Department of Health (1997) 'Health Action Zones – Invitation to Bid', *Executive Letter*, No. 65 (London: DoH).

Department of Health (DoH) (1998a) *Partnership in Action* (London: The Stationery Office).

Department of Health (DoH) (1998b) *Saving Lives: Our Healthier Nation* (London: The Stationery Office).

Department of Health (1999) *Summary of Responses to the Government's Discussion Document 'Partnership in Action'* (London: DoH).

Department of Health (2000) *The NHS Plan: A Plan for Investment: A Plan for Reform* (London: DoH).

Department of Health (2001) *Involving Patients and the Public in Healthcare: A Discussion Document* (London: DoH).

Department of Health and Social Security (DHSS) (1971) *Better Services for the Mentally Handicapped*, Cmnd 4683 (London: HMSO).

Department of Health and Social Security (DHSS) (1978) *Collaboration in Community Care* (London: HMSO).

Department of Health and Social Security (DHSS) (1981) *Priorities for Health and Personal Social Services: The Way Forward* (London: HMSO).

Department of the Environment (DoE) (1977) *Policy for the Inner Cities*, Cm 6845 (London: HMSO).

Department of the Environment, Transport and the Regions (1998) *Local Evaluation: Draft Good Practice Guide* (London: DETR).

Department of the Environment, Transport and the Regions (2000) *Collaboration and Co-ordination in Area-based Regeneration Initiatives*, Regeneration Research Summary No. 35 (London: DETR).

Department of the Environment, Transport and the Regions (2001a) *Working with Others to Achieve Best Value* (London: DETR).

Department of the Environment, Transport and the Regions (2001b) *New Deal for Communities: Outcomes and Milestones* (London: DETR).

Devas, N. and Horváth T. (1997) 'Client–Contractor Splits: Applying a Model of Public Management Reform to Local Community Services in Hungary', *Local Government Studies*, vol. 23, no. 4, pp. 100–9.

DiGaetano, A. (1997) 'Urban Governing Alignments and Realignments in Comparative Perspective: Developments Politics in Boston, Massachusetts and Bristol, England 1980–1996', *Urban Affairs Quarterly*, vol. 32, no. 6, pp. 844–70.

DiGaetano, A. and Klemanski, J. S. (1993) 'Urban Regime Capacity: A Comparison of Birmingham, England and Detroit, Michigan', *Journal of Urban Affairs*, vol. 15, no. 4, pp. 367–84.

DiMaggio, P. and Powell, W. (1991) 'Introduction' in Powell, W. and DiMaggio, P. (eds) (1991), *The New Institutionalism in Organisational Analysis* (Chicago: University of Chicago Press).

Dobash, R. E. and Dobash, R. P. (1996a) *Research Evaluation of Programmes for Violent Men* (Edinburgh: Central Research Unit, Scottish Office).

Dobash, R. E. and Dobash, R. P. (1996b) *Re-education Programmes for Violent Men – An Evaluation*, Research Findings No. 46 (London: Research and Statistics Directorate, Home Office).

Doig, A. (1995) 'Mixed Signals? Public Sector Change and the Proper Conduct of Public Business', *Public Administration*, vol. 73, pp. 191–212.

Dowding, K. (1995) 'Model or Metaphor? A Critical Review of the Policy Network Approach', *Political Studies*, vol. 43, no. 2, pp. 136–58.

Dowding, K. (2001) 'There Must Be End to Confusion: Policy Networks, Intellectual Fatigue, and the Need for Political Science Methods Courses in British Universities', *Political Studies*, vol. 49, no. 1, pp. 89–105.

Dungey, J. (ed.) (2000) *The Democratic Region* (London: Local Government Information Unit).

Dunleavy, P. (1991) *Democracy, Bureaucracy and Public Choice* (London: Harvester Wheatsheaf).

Edwards, B., Goodwin, M., Pemberton, S. and Woods, M. (1999) *Partnership Working in Rural Regeneration*, Findings 039 (York: Joseph Rowntree Foundation).

Elster, J. (ed.) (1998) *Deliberative Democracy* (Cambridge: Cambridge University Press).

Emerson, R. M. (1962) 'Power Dependence Relations', *American Sociological Review*, vol. 27, no. 1, pp. 31–40.

Etzioni, A. (1995) *The Spirit of Community: Rights, Responsibility and the Communitarian Age* (London: Fontana).

Etzioni, A. (2000) *The Third Way to a Good Society* (London: DEMOS).

Evans, M. (2001) 'Understanding Dialectics in Policy Network Analysis', *Political Studies*, vol. 49, pp. 542–50.

Falconer, P. K. and McLoughlin, K. (2000) 'Public–Private Partnerships and the "New Labour" Government in Britain' in Osborne, S. P. (ed.) (2000), *Public–Private Partnerships: Theory and Practice in International Perspective* (London: Routledge).

Faulkner, D. O. and de Rond, M. (2000) 'Perspectives on Co-operative Strategy' in Faulkner, D. O. and de Rond, M. (eds) (2000), *Co-operative Strategy: Economic, Business and Organisational Issues* (Oxford: Oxford University Press).

Feyerherm, A. E. (1994) 'Leadership in Collaboration: A Longitudinal Study of Two Interorganizational Rule Making Groups', *Leadership Quarterly*, vol. 5, no. 3–4, pp. 253–70.

Filkin, G., Allen, E. and Williams, J. (2001) *Strategic Partnering for Local Service Delivery* (London: New Local Government Network).

Fishkin, J. (1991) *Democracy and Deliberation: New Directions for Democratic Reform* (London: Yale University Press).

Flynn, N. (1997) *Public Sector Management*, 3rd edn (London: Prentice Hall-Harvester Wheatsheaf).

Flynn, N. and Leach, S. (1984) *Joint Boards and Joint Committees: An Evaluation* (Birmingham: Institute of Local Government Studies, University of Birmingham).

Foley, P. and Martin, S. (2000) 'A New Deal for the Community? Public Participation in Regeneration and Local Service Delivery', *Policy and Politics*, vol. 28, no. 4, pp. 479–91.

Fortmann, L., Roes, E. and Van Eeten, M. (2001) 'At the Threshold Between Governance and Management: Community Based Natural Resource Management in Southern Africa', *Public Administration and Development*, vol. 21, no. 2, pp. 171–85.

Foster, J. (2001) 'Thoroughly Modern Middlesborough', *Public Finance*, 20–26 July.

Fournier, D. (1995) 'Establishing Evaluative Conclusions: A Distinction Between General and Working Logic', *New Directions for Program Evaluation*, vol. 68, pp. 15–32.

Friend, J., Power, J. and Yewlett, C. (1974) *Public Planning: The Inter-corporate Dimension* (London: Tavistock).

Fukuyama, F. (1995) *Trust: Social Relations and the Creation of Prosperity* (London: Hamish Hamlyn).

Funnel, S. (1997) 'Program Logic: An Adaptable Tool for Designing and Evaluating Programs', *Evaluation News and Comment*, July, pp. 5–17.

Gaster, L. (1994) *Area Co-ordination – Developing Our Approach: An Evaluation of the Wood End/Bell Green Area Management Initiative* (Bristol: School for Advanced Urban Studies).

Gaster, L., Stewart, M. and associates (1995) *Interim Evaluation of the Ferguslie Park Partnership* (Edinburgh: HMSO).

Gaster, L. (1995) *Management Skills in Decentralised Environments* (Luton: Local Government Management Board).

Gaster, L. (1999) 'Disaffected Young People' in Richards, S., Barnes, M., Coulson, A., Gaster, L., Leach, B. and Sullivan, H. (1999) *Cross-Cutting Issues in Public Policy and Public Services* (London: DETR).

Geddes, M. (2000) 'Tackling Social Exclusion in the European Union? The Limits to the New Orthodoxy of Local Partnership', *International Journal of Urban and Regional Research*, vol. 24, no 4, pp. 782–800.

Giddens, A. (1991) *Modernity and Self Identity* (Cambridge: Polity Press).

Giddens, A. (2000) *The Third Way and its Critics* (Cambridge: Polity Press).

Gilliat, S., Fenwick, J. and Alford, D. (2000) 'Public Services and the Consumer – Empowerment or Control?', *Social Policy and Administration*, vol. 34, no. 3, pp. 333–49.

Gilling, D. (1997) *Crime Prevention* (London: UCL Press).

Glass, N. (1999) 'Sure Start: The Development of an Early Intervention Programme for Young Children in the UK', *Children and Society*, vol. 13, no. 4, pp. 257–64.

Goldsmith, M. (1986) *New Research in Central–Local Relations* (Aldershot: Gower).

Grant, G. (1995) *Assessment and Care Management: A Service Sector View* (Bangor) Centre for Social Policy and Research, University of Wales Newsletter, Summer, 5–12.

Gray, B. (1996) 'Cross-sectoral Partners: Collaborative Alliances Among Business, Government and Communities' in Huxham, C. (ed.) (1996), *Creating Collaborative Advantage* (London: Sage).

Greer, J. (2001) *Partnership Governance in Northern Ireland* (Aldershot: Ashgate).

Griffiths, R. (1988) *Community Care: Agenda for Action* (London: HMSO) ('The Griffiths Report').

Guba, E. G. and Lincoln, Y. S. (1981) *Effective Evaluation* (London: Jossey-Bass).

Gutch, R., Kunz, C. and Spencer, K. (1990) *Partners or Agents? Local Government and the Voluntary Sector – Changing Relationships in the 1990s* (London: NCVO).

Habermas, J. (1984) *The Theory of Communicative Action* (Cambridge: Polity Press).

Hadley, R. and Clough, R. (1996) *Care in Chaos* (London: Cassell).

Hague, G. and Malos, E. (1996) *Tackling Domestic Violence* (Bristol: Policy Press).

Hague, G., Malos, E. and Dear, W. (1996) *Multi-Agency Work and Domestic Violence: A National Study of Inter-agency Initiatives* (Bristol: Policy Press).

Hague, G. and Malos, E. (1998) 'Inter-Agency Approaches to Domestic Violence and the Role of Social Services', *British Journal of Social Work*, vol. 28, pp. 369–86.

Hall, R., Heafey, M. and King, D. (2000) 'Managing the PFI Process for a New High School', *Public Management*, vol. 2, no. 2, pp. 159–79.

Hall, S., Beazley, M. and associates (1996) *The Single Regeneration Budget: A Review of Challenge Fund Round II* (Birmingham: Centre for Urban and Regional Studies, University of Birmingham).

Hall, S., Nevin, B. and associates (1998) *Competition, Partnership and Regeneration: Lessons from Three Rounds of the Single Regeneration Budget Fund* (Birmingham: Centre for Urban and Regional Studies, University of Birmingham).

Hambleton, R., Hoggett, P. and Razzaque, R. (1996) *Freedom within Boundaries, Developing Effective Approaches to Decentralisation* (Luton: Local Government Management Board).

Hambleton, R. and Thomas, H. (1995) 'Urban Policy Evaluation – the contours of the debate', in Hambleton, R. and Thomas, H. (eds) *Urban Policy Evaluation* (London: Paul Chapman).

Harding, A. (1994) 'Urban Regimes and Growth Machines: Towards a Cross-national Research Agenda', *Urban Affairs Quarterly*, vol. 29. no. 3, pp. 356–82.

Hardy, B., Hudson, B. and Waddington, E. (2000) *What Makes a Good Partnership?* (Leeds: Institute for Health/NHS Executive Trent).

Hastings, A. and McArthur, A. (1995) 'A Comparative Assessment of Government Approaches to Partnership with the Local Community' in Hambleton, R. and Thomas, H. (eds) (1995), *Urban Policy Evaluation: Challenge and Change* (London: Paul Chapman).

Hastings, A., McArthur, A. and McGregor, A. (1996) *Less Than Equal? Community Organisations and Estate Regeneration Partnerships* (Bristol: Policy Press).

Haughton, G. (1996) 'Local Leadership and Economic Regeneration in Leeds' in Haughton, G. and Williams, C. C. (eds) (1996), *Corporate City? Partnership, Participation and Partition in Urban Development in Leeds* (Aldershot: Avebury).

Hawtin, M., Hughes, G., Percy-Smith, J. with Foreman, A. (1994) *Community Profiling: Auditing Social Needs* (Buckingham: Open University Press).

Hay, C. (1998) 'The Tangled Webs we Weave: The Discourse, Strategy and Practice of Networking' in Marsh, D. (ed.) (1998), *Comparing Policy Networks* (Buckingham: Open University Press).

Heclo, H. and Wildavsky, A. (1981) *The Private Government of Public Money: Community and Policy Inside British Government*, 2nd edn (London: Palgrave Macmillan).

Himmelman, A. T. (1996) 'On the Theory and Practice of Transformational Collaboration: From Social Service to Social Justice' in Huxham, C. (ed.) (1996), *Creating Collaborative Advantage* (London: Sage).

Hirst, P. and Thompson, G. (1999) *Globalisation in Question: The Myths of the International Economy and the Possibilities of Governance*, 2nd edn (Cambridge: Polity Press).

HM Inspectorate of Constabulary (1998) *Beating Crime: Thematic Inspection Report* (London: HM Inspectorate of Constabulary).

HM Treasury (1995) *A Framework for the Evaluation of Regeneration Projects and Programmes* (London: HM Treasury).

HM Treasury (2000) *Prudent for a Purpose: Building Opportunity and Security for All – Spending Review 2000: New Public Spending Plans for 2001–2004*, Cm 4807 (London: The Stationery Office).

HM Treasury (2001) *Budget Report 2001 – Investing for the Long Term: Building Prosperity and Opportunity for All*, HC 279 (London: The Stationery Office).

Hodges, R., Wright, M. and Keasey, K. (1996) 'Corporate Governance in the Public Services: Issues and Concepts', *Public Money and Management*, vol. 16, no. 2, pp. 7–13.

Hoggett, P. (ed.) (1997) *Contested Communities* (Bristol: Policy Press).

Hollister, R. G. and Hill, J. (1999) 'Problems in the Evaluation of Community-wide Initiatives' in Connell, J. P., Kubisch, A. C., Schorr, L. B. and Weiss, C. H. (eds) (1995), *New Approaches to Evaluating Community Initiatives: Concepts, Methods and Contexts* (Washington, DC: Aspen Institute).

Home Office (1991a) *Safer Communities: The Local Delivery of Crime Prevention Through the Partnership Approach* (London: Home Office) ('The Morgan Report').

Home Office (1991b) *The Response to Racial Attacks: Sustaining the Momentum*. The Second Report of the Inter-departmental Racial Attacks Group (London: Home Office).

Home Office (1997) *Getting to Grips with Crime: A New Framework for Local Action* (London: HMSO).

Home Office (1998) *Getting it Right Together: Compact on Relations Between Government and the Voluntary and Community Sector in England*, Cm 4100 (London: The Stationery Office).

Hood, C. (1991) 'A Public Management for All Seasons?', *Public Administration*, vol. 69, no. 1, pp. 3–19.

House of Commons (2001) *Report of the Select Committee on Public Adminis-tration: Mapping the Quango State*, HC 367, Session 2000–01 (London: The Stationery Office).

Hudson, B. (1986) 'In Pursuit of Co-ordination – Housing and the Personal Social Services', *Local Government Studies*, vol. 12, no. 2, pp. 53–66.

Hudson, B. (1987) 'Collaboration in Social Welfare: A Framework for Analysis', *Policy and Politics*, vol. 15, no. 3, pp. 175–82.

Hudson, B., Hardy, B., Henwood, M. and Wistow, G. (1999) 'In Pursuit of Inter-agency Collaboration in the Public Sector', *Public Management*, vol. 1, no. 2, pp. 235–60.

Hughes, J., Knox, C., Murray, M. and Greer, J. (1998) *Partnership Governance in Northern Ireland: The Path to Peace* (Dublin: Oak Tree Press).

Huxham, C. (ed.) (1996) *Creating Collaborative Advantage* (London: Sage).

Huxham, C. and Vangen, S. (2000a) 'Leadership in the Shaping and Imple-mentation of Collaborative Agendas: How Things Happen in a (Not Quite) Joined Up World', *Academy of Management Journal*, vol. 43, no. 6, pp. 1159–75.

Huxham, C. and Vangen, S. (2000b) 'What Makes Partnerships Work?' in Osborne, S. P. (ed.) (2000), *Public–Private Partnerships: Theory and Practice in Inter-national Perspective* (London: Routledge).

Huxham, C. and Vangen, S. (2000c) 'Ambiguity, Complexity and Dynamics in the Membership of Collaboration', *Human Relations*, vol. 53, no. 6, pp. 771–806.

Jacobs, B. (1999) *Strategy and Partnership in Cities and Regions: Economic Development and Urban Regeneration in Pittsburgh, Birmingham and Rotterdam* (Basingstoke: Palgrave Macmillan).

Jacobs, B. (2000) 'Partnerships in Pittsburgh: The Evaluation of Complex Local Initiatives', in Osborne, S. P. (ed.) (2000), *Public–Private Partnerships: Theory and Practice in International Perspective* (London: Routledge).

Jacobson, J. and Saville, E. (1999) *Neighbourhood Warden Scheme: An Overview*, Policing and Crime Reducing Unit, Crime Reduction Research Series Paper 2 (London: Home Office).

James, R. (ed.) (2001) *Power and Partnership? Experiences of NGO Capacity Building* (Oxford: INTRAC).

John, P. and Cole, A. (1999) 'Political Leadership in the New Urban Governance: Britain and France Compared', *Local Government Studies*, vol. 25, no. 4, pp. 98–115.

Johnston, R. and Lawrence, P. R. (1991) 'Beyond Vertical Integration – The Rise of the Value-adding Partnership' in Thompson, G., Frances, J., Levacic, R. and Mitchell, J. (eds) (1991), *Markets, Hierarchies and Networks: The Co-ordination of Social Life* (London: Sage).

Jones, G. (1980) *New Approaches to the Study of Centre–Local Relationships* (London: Social Science Research Council).

Jones, G. R. and George, G. M. (1998) 'The Experience and Evolution of Trust: Implications for Co-operation and Teamwork', *Academy of Management Review*, vol. 23, no. 3, pp. 531–46.

Jones, K. (1989) 'Community Care: Old Problems and New Answers' in Carter, P., Jeffs, T. and Smith, M. (eds) (1989), *Social Work and Social Welfare Yearbook 1* (Milton Keynes: Open University Press).

Jones, R. W. and Trystan, D. (2001) 'Wales', *Parliamentary Affairs*, vol. 54, pp. 712–24.

Jones, T., Newburn, T. and Smith, D. (1994) *Democracy and Policing* (London: Policy Studies Institute).

Jordan, A. G. and Schubert K. (1992) 'A Preliminary Ordering of Policy Network Labels', *European Journal of Political Research*, vol. 21, no. 1–2, pp. 7–27.

Judge, K., Barnes, M. and associates (1999) *Health Action Zones – Learning to Make a Difference* (London: Department of Health).

Judge, K. (2000) 'Testing Evaluation to the Limits: The Case of English Health Action Zones', *Journal of Health Services Research and Policy*, vol. 5, no. 1, pp. 1–3.

Kaplan, R. S. and Norton, D. P. (1996) *The Balanced Scorecard* (Harvard: Harvard Business School Press).

Kavanagh, D. and Richards, D. (2001) 'Departmentalism and Joined-up Government: Back to the Future?', *Parliamentary Affairs*, vol. 54, no. 1, pp. 1–18.

Keating, D., Krumholtz, N. and Star, P. (1996) *Revitalizing Urban Neighbourhoods* (Kansas: University Press of Kansas).

Kendall, J. and Knapp, M. (1996) *The Voluntary Sector in the UK* (Manchester: Manchester University Press).

Kerestes, R. and Lenniham, M. (2001) 'Project Impact: Building Public and Private Sector Partnerships in Disaster Prevention Programmes', *Paper to the Fifth International Research Symposium on Public Sector Management*, Barcelona, April.

Keywood, K., Fovargue, A. and Flynn, M. (1999) *Best Practice? Health Care Decision-making by, with and for Adults with Learning Disabilities* (Manchester: National Development Team).

Kickert, W., Klijn, E.-H. and Koppenjan, J. (eds) (1997), *Managing Complex Networks: Strategies for the Public Sector* (London: Sage).

King, A. (1975) 'Overload: Problems of Governing in the 1970s', *Political Studies*, vol. 23, nos. 2–3, pp. 162–74.

Kitchin, H., Chelliah, R. and Evans, J. (1994) *Women and Urban Regeneration* (London: Local Government Information Unit).

Klein, N. (2000) *No Logo* (London: Flamingo).

Klijn, E.-H. (1996) 'Analysing and Managing Policy Processes in Complex Networks: A Theoretical Examination of the Concept Policy Network and its Problems', *Administration and Society*, vol. 28, no. 1, pp. 90–119.

Klijn, E.-H. and Teisman, G. R. (2000) 'Governing Public–Private Partnerships: Analysing and Managing the Process and Institutional Characteristics of Public–Private Partnerships' in Osborne, S. P. (ed.) (2000), *Public–Private Partnerships: Theory and Practice in International Perspective* (London: Routledge).

Kooiman, J. and van Vliet, M. (1993) 'Governance and Public Management' in Eliassen, K. A. and Kooiman, J. (eds) (1993), *Managing Public Organisations: Lessons from Contemporary European Experience* (London: Sage).

Lane, C. and Bachmann, R. (1998) *Trust Within and Between Organisations* (Oxford: Oxford University Press).

Lane, J.-E. (ed.) (1987), *Bureaucracy and Public Choice* (London: Sage).

Lansley, S., Goss, S. and Wolmar, C. (1989) *Councils in Conflict: The Rise and Fall of the Municipal Left* (Basingstoke: Palgrave Macmillan).

Lawless, P. (1981) *Britain's Inner Cities: Problems and Policies* (London: Harper and Row).

Lawless, P. (1991) *Public–Private Sector Partnerships in the United Kingdom*, Working Paper 16, Centre for Regional, Economic and Social Research (Sheffield: Sheffield City Polytechnic).

Leach, S., Davis, H. and associates (1996) *Enabling or Disabling Local Government* (Buckingham: Open University Press).

Leach, S. and Wilson, D. (1998) 'Voluntary Groups and Local Authorities: Rethinking the Relationship', *Local Government Studies*, vol. 24, no. 2, pp. 1–18.

Leach, S. and Wingfield, M. (1999) 'Public Participation and the Democratic Renewal Agenda: Prioritisation or Marginalisation?' in Pratchett, L. (ed.) (1999), *Renewing Local Democracy?: The Modernisation Agenda in British Local Government* (London: Frank Cass).

Leach, S., Davis, H., Game, C. and Skelcher, C. (1992) *After Abolition: The Operation of the Post-1986 Metropolitan Government System in England* (Birmingham: INLOGOV, the University of Birmingham).

Levine, S. and White, P. E. (1962) 'Exchange as a Conceptual Framework for the Study of Interorganisational Relationships', *Administrative Science Quarterly*, vol. 5, pp. 583–601.

Lewis, J., Bernstock, P. and Bovell, V. (1995) 'The Community Care Changes: Unresolved Tensions and Policy Issues in Implementation', *Journal of Social Policy*, vol. 24, no. 1, pp. 73–94.

Liddle, M. and Gelsthorpe, L. (1994) *Inter-Agency Crime Prevention: Further Issues*, Police Research Group Supplementary Paper to Crime Prevention Unit Series Nos 52 and 53 (London: Home Office).

Lindow, V. (1996) *User Involvement: Community Service Users as Consultants and Trainers* (London: Department of Health).

Local Government Association (2000) *Partnerships with Health: A Survey of Local Authorities* (London: Local Government Association).

Local Government Association (2001) *Examples of Local Strategic Partnerships in Development* (London: Local Government Association).

Local Government Management Board (1996) *Survey of Community Safety Activities in Local Government in England and Wales* (London: Local Government Management Board).

Loftman, P. and Beazley, M. (1998) *Race and Regeneration* (London: Local Government Information Unit).

Loftman, P. and Nevin, B. (1998) *'Evaluation for Whom?' – The Politics of Evaluation Research*, School of Public Policy Occasional Paper 15 (Birmingham: University of Birmingham).

Loney, M. (1983) *Community Against Government – The British Community Development Project 1968–78* (London: Heinemann).

Lorenz, E. H. (1991) 'Neither Friends Nor Strangers: Informal Networks of Subcontracting in French Industry' in Thompson, G., Frances, J., Levacic, R. and Mitchell, J. (eds) (1991), *Markets, Hierarchies and Networks: The Co-ordination of Social Life* (London: Sage).

Lowndes, V. (1995) 'Citizenship and Urban Politics' in Judge, D., Stoker, G. and Wolman, H. (1995) *Theories of Urban Politics* (London: Sage).

Lowndes, V. (1996) 'Varieties of New Institutionalism: A Critical Appraisal', *Public Administration*, vol. 74, no. 2, pp. 181–97.

Lowndes, V. (1997) 'Change in Public Service Management: New Institutions and New Managerial Regimes', *Local Government Studies*, vol. 23, no. 2, pp. 42–66.

Lowndes, V., Stoker, G. and associates (1998) *Enhancing Public Participation in Local Government*, Research Report (London: DETR).

Lowndes, V. and Skelcher, C. (1998) 'The Dynamics of Multi-organisational Partnerships: An Analysis of Changing Modes of Governance', *Public Administration*, vol. 76, no. 2, pp. 313–34.

Lowndes, V. (2000) 'Women and Social Capital: A Comment on Hall's "Social Capital in Britain"', *British Journal of Political Science*, vol. 30, pp. 533–40.

Lowndes, V. and Wilson, D. (2001) 'Social Capital and Local Governance: Exploring the Institutional Design Variable', *Political Studies*, vol. 49, pp. 629–47.

Luhman, C. (1979) *Trust and Power* (Chichester: Wiley).

Luke, J. S. (1997) *Catalytic Leadership: Strategies for an Interconnected World* (New York: Jossey-Bass).

Mabbott, J. (1993) 'The Role of Community Involvement', *Policy Studies*, vol. 14, no. 2, pp. 27–35.

McCauley, M., Emanuel, E., Dan, A. and Ford, Z. (1997) 'Putting a Face to Lesbian Health Risk: A Collaborative Research Project' in Nyden, P., Figert, A., Shibley, M. and Burrows, D. (eds) (1997), *Building Community: Social Science in Action* (California: Pine Forge Press).

McGann, J. and Gray, B. (1986) 'Power and Collaboration in Human Service Domains', *International Journal of Sociology and Social Policy*, vol. 8, pp. 56–67.

McKeganey, N. and Hunter, D. (1986) 'Only Connect … : Tightrope Walking and Joint Working in the Care of the Elderly', *Policy and Politics*, vol. 14, no. 3, pp. 335–60.

Mackintosh, M. (1992) 'Partnerships: Issues of Policy and Negotiation', *Local Economy*, vol. 7, no. 3, pp. 210–24.

Macpherson of Cluny, Sir William (1999) *Report of the Stephen Lawrence Inquiry* (London: The Stationery Office).

Mainwaring, R. (1998) *The Walsall Experience* (London: HMSO).

Maloney, W., Smith, G. and Stoker, G. (2000) 'Social Capital and Urban Governance: Adding a More Contextualized 'Top-Down' Perspective', *Political Studies*, vol. 48, pp. 802–20.

March, J. and Olsen, J. (1989a) 'The New Institutionalism: Organizational Factors in Political Life', *American Political Science Review*, vol. 78, pp. 734–49.

March, J. and Olsen, J. (1989b) *Rediscovering Institutions* (New York: Free Press).

Marsh, D. (1998) 'The Utility and Future of Policy Network Analysis' in Marsh, D. (ed.) (1998), *Comparing Policy Networks* (Buckingham: Open University Press).

Marsh, D. and Rhodes, R. A. W. (eds) (1992), *Policy Networks in British Government* (Oxford: Clarendon).

Marsh, D. and Smith, M. J. (2000) 'Understanding Policy Networks: Towards a Dialectual Approach', *Political Studies*, vol. 48, pp. 4–21.

Marsh, D. and Smith, M. J. (2001) 'There is More Than One Way To Do Political Science: On Different Ways to Study Policy Networks', *Political Studies*, vol. 49, pp. 528–41.

Martin, S. and Pearce, G. (1999) 'Differentiated Multi-level Governance? The Response of British Sub-national Governments to European Integration', *Regional and Federal Studies*, vol. 9, no. 2, pp. 32–52.

Mawson, J. and Spencer, K. (1997) 'The Government Offices of the English Regions: Towards Regional Government?', *Policy and Politics*, vol. 25, no. 1, pp. 71–84.

Mawson, J., Hall, S. and associates (1995) *The Single Regeneration Budget: The Stocktake* (Birmingham: Centre for Urban and Regional Studies, University of Birmingham).

May, M. and Brunsdon, E. (1999) 'Social Services and Community Care' in Farnham, S. and Horton, D. (eds) (1999), *Public Management in Britain* (Basingstoke: Palgrave Macmillan).

Mayer, R. C., Davis, J. H. and Schoorman, F. D. (1995) 'An Integrative Model of Organizational Trust', *Academy of Management Review*, vol. 20, no. 3, 709–34.

Mayo, M. and Taylor, M. (2001) 'Partnerships and Power in Community Regeneration' in Balloch, S. and Taylor, M. (eds) (2001), *Partnership Working* (Bristol: Policy Press).

Meyer, J. and Rowan, B. (1991) 'Institutionalized Organizations: Formal Structure as Myth and Ceremony' in Powell, W. and DiMaggio, P. (eds) (1991), *The New Institutionalism in Organizational Analysis* (Chicago: The University of Chicago Press).

Middlesbrough Council (2000) *Decision Day for Public/Private Partnership*, http://www.middlesbrough.gov.uk.

Midwinter, A. and McGarvey, N. (2001) 'In Search of the Regulatory State: Evidence from Scotland', *Parliamentary Affairs*, vol. 79, no. 4, pp. 825–49.

Millan, G. S. and Acosta, A. G. (2000) 'Versalles: Healthy Municipality for Peace', Paper to the Fifth Global Conference for Health Promotion, Geneva, June.

Milward, H. B. and Provan, K. G. (1998) 'Measuring Network Structure', *Public Administration*, vol. 76, no. 2, pp. 387–407.

Monbiot, G. (2000) *Captive State* (London: Palgrave Macmillan).

Montanheiro, L., Haigh, B., Morris, D. and Linehan, M. (eds) (1999), *Public and Private Sector Partnerships: Furthering Development* (Sheffield: Sheffield Hallam University Press).

National Audit Office (1997) *The PFI Contracts for Bridgend and Fazakerly Prisons*, HC 253, Session 1997/98 (London: The Stationery Office).

National Audit Office (1999) *The Private Finance Initiative: The Contract to Complete and Operate the A74(M)/M74 in Scotland*, HC 356, Session 1998/99 (London: The Stationery Office).

National Audit Office (2001a) *Education Action Zones: Meeting the Challenge – The Lessons from Auditing the First 25 Zones*, HC 130, session 2000–2001 (London: The Stationery Office).

National Audit Office (2001b) *The Channel Tunnel Rail Link*, HC 302, Session 2000–2001 (London: The Stationery Office).

National Council of Voluntary Organisations (1994) 'The Single Regeneration Budget', *Urban Issues*, October, 7.

National Council of Voluntary Organisations (1996) *Meeting the Challenge of Change: Report of the Commission on the Future of the Voluntary Sector* (London: NCVO).

Neighbourhood Initiatives Foundation (1999) *Evaluation for Real* (Telford: Neighbourhood Initiatives Foundation).

Nelson, S. (2001) 'The Nature of Partnership in Urban Renewal in Paris and London', *European Planning Studies*, vol. 9, no. 4, pp. 483–502.

Nevin, B., and Shiner, P. (1995) 'Community Regeneration and Empowerment: A New Approach to Partnership', *Local Economy*, vol. 9, no. 4, pp. 308–22.

Newchurch (1999a) *Local Authority Partnerships: A Review of the Literature*, Newchurch/DETR Partnership Series Paper 2 (London: DETR).

Newchurch (1999b) *Service Delivery Partnerships in English Local Authorities: Survey Findings*, Newchurch/DETR Partnership Series Paper 5 (London: DETR).

Newman, J. (1994) 'Beyond the Vision: Cultural Change in the Public Sector', *Public Money and Management*, vol. 14, no. 2, pp. 59–64.

Newman, J. (1996) *Shaping Organisational Cultures in Local Government* (London: Pitman).

Newman, J., Richards, S. and Smith, P. (1998) 'Market Testing and Institutional Change in the UK Civil Service: Compliance, Non Compliance and Engagement', *Public Policy and Administration*, vol. 13, no. 4, pp. 96–110.

Newman, J., Raine, J. and Skelcher, C. (2000) *Innovation and Best Practice in Local Government: A Research Report* (London: DETR).

Newman, J. (2001) *Modernising Governance: New Labour, Policy and Society* (London: Sage).

Niskanen, W. A. (1994) *Bureaucracy and Public Economics* (Aldershot: Edward Elgar).

North, D. (1990) *Institutions, Institutional Change and Economic Performance* (Cambridge: Cambridge University Press).

Northumberland HAZ (1999) *Implementation Plan 1998–2002: A Vision of Health – An Ideal for Life* (Morpeth: Northumberland Health Authority).

Nottingham CVS (2001) *Directory of Initiatives* (www.nottinghamcvs.co.uk/ regeneration).

Nyden, P., Figert, A., Shibley, M. and Burrows, D. (eds) (1997), *Building Community: Social Science in Action* (California: Pine Forge Press).

Osborne, S. P. (ed.) (2000), *Public–Private Partnerships: Theory and Practice in International Perspective* (London: Routledge).

Ostrom, E. (1986) 'An Agenda for the Study of Institutions', *Public Choice*, vol. 48, pp. 3–25.

Ostrom, E. (2000) 'Crowding Out Citizenship', *Scandinavian Political Studies*, vol. 23, no. 1, pp. 3–16.

Ouchi, W. (1991) 'Markets, Bureaucracies and Clans' in Thompson, G., Frances, J., Levačić, R. and Mitchell, J. (eds) (1991), *Markets, Hierarchies and Networks: The Co-ordination of Social Life* (London: Sage).

Owen, J. M. with Rogers, P. J. (1999) *Program Evaluation: Forms and Approaches* (Australia: Sage).

Painter, C., Isaac-Henry, K. and Rouse, J. (1997) 'Local Authorities and Non-elected Agencies: Strategic Responses and Organisational Networks', *Public Administration*, vol. 75, no. 2, pp. 225–46.

Painter, C. and Clarence, M. (2000) 'New Labour and Inter-governmental Management: Flexible Networks or Performance Control?', *Public Management*, vol. 2, no. 4, pp. 477–98.

Parsons, D. W. (1995) *Public Policy: An Introduction to the Theory and Practice of Policy Analysis* (Aldershot: Edward Elgar).

Patton, M. Q. (1996) 'A World Larger than Formative and Summative Evaluation', *Evaluation Practice*, vol. 17, no. 2, pp. 131–44.

Pawson, R. and Tilley, N. (1997) *Realistic Evaluation* (London: Sage).

Pennings, J. (1980) *Interlocking Directorates* (London: Jossey-Bass).

Performance and Innovation Unit (2000) *Reaching Out: The Role of Central Government at Regional and Local Level* (London: Cabinet Office).

Peterman, W. (2000) *Neighbourhood Planning and Community-Based Development* (London: Sage).

Peters, B. G. (1993) 'Managing the Hollow State' in Eliassen, K. and Kooiman, J. (eds) (1993), *Managing Public Organisations: Lessons from Contemporary European Experience* (London: Sage).

Peters, B. G. (1997) 'Shouldn't Row, Can't Steer: What's a Government to Do?', *Public Policy and Administration*, vol. 12, no. 2, pp. 51–61.

Peters, B. G. and Pierre, J. (2001) 'Developments in Intergovernmental Relations: Towards Multi-level Governance', *Policy and Politics*, vol. 29, no. 2, pp. 131–36.

Pettigrew, A. and McNaulty, G. (1995) 'Power and Influence In and Around the Boardroom', *Human Relations*, vol. 48, pp. 845–73.

Pfeffer, J. and Salancik, G. (1978) *The External Control of Organisations* (New York: Harper).

Phillips, A. (1993) *Democracy and Difference* (Cambridge: Polity Press).

Pierre, J. and Peters, B. G. (2000) *Governance, Politics and the State* (London: Palgrave Macmillan).

Pollitt, C. (1993) *Managerialism and the Public Services*, 2nd edn (Oxford: Blackwell).

Powell, M., Glendinning, C. and Rummery, K. (eds) (forthcoming) *Partnerships, the Third Way and the Governance of Welfare* (Bristol: Policy Press).

Powell, W. (1991) 'Neither Market Nor Hierarchy: Network Forms of Organisation' in Thompson, G., Frances, J., Levacic, R. and Mitchell, J. (eds) (1991), *Markets, Hierarchies and Networks: The Co-ordination of Social Life* (London: Sage).

Powell, W. and DiMaggio, P. (eds) (1991), *The New Institutionalism in Organizational Analysis* (Chicago: The University of Chicago Press).

Prior, D. (1996) ' "Working the Network": Local Authority Strategies in the Reticulated Local State', *Local Government Studies*, vol. 22, no. 2, pp. 92–104.

Purdue, D., Razzaque, K., Hambleton, R., Stewart, M., Huxham, C. and Vangen, S. (2000) *Community Leadership in Area Regeneration* (Bristol: Policy Press).

Putnam, R. D. (1993) *Making Democracy Work* (Chichester: Princeton University Press).

Qaiyoom, R. (1993) *Empty Vessels, Hollow Sounds* (London: Sia).

Raab, C. D. (2001) 'Understanding Policy Networks: A Comment on Marsh and Smith', *Political Studies*, vol. 49, pp. 551–56.

Raelin, J. A. (1980) 'The Mandated Basis of Interorganisational Relations: The Legal-political Network', *Human Relations*, vol. 33, no. 1, pp. 57–68.

Ranson, S. and Stewart, J. (1994) *Management for the Public Domain: Enabling a Learning Society* (Basingstoke: Palgrave Macmillan).

Razzaque, K. (2001) 'Men in Suits Make Me Fall Silent' in Taillieu, T. (ed.) (2001), *Collaborative Strategies and Multi-organizational Partnerships* (Levveu/ Apeldoorn: Garant).

Regional Co-ordination Unit (2000) *Collaboration and Co-ordination in Area-based Initiatives*, Second research working paper (London: DETR).

Registrar of Friendly Societies (2000) *Report of the Chief Registrar 1999–2000* (London: The Stationery Office).

Rein, M. (1976) *Social Science and Public Policy* (Harmondsworth: Penguin).

Rhodes, R. (1994) 'The Hollowing Out of the State: The Changing Nature of the Public Service in Britain', *Political Quarterly*, vol. 65, pp. 138–51.

Rhodes, R. (1996) 'The New Governance: Governing Without Government', *Political Studies*, vol. 44, pp. 652–667.

Rhodes, R. (1997) *Understanding Governance: Policy Networks, Governance, Reflexivity and Accountability* (Buckingham: Open University Press).

Rhodes, R. A. W. (1999) *Control and Power in Central–Local Governmental Relations*, 2nd edn (Aldershot: Ashgate).

Richards, S., Barnes, M., Coulson, A., Gaster, L., Leach, B. and Sullivan, H. (1999) *Cross-Cutting Issues in Public Policy and Public Services* (London: DETR).

Richards, S. and Jervis, P. (1997) 'Public Management: Raising the Game', *Public Money and Management*, vol. 17, no. 1, pp. 1–8.

Ring, P. and Van de Ven, A. (1994) 'Developmental Processes of Co-operative Interorganisational Relationships', *Academy of Management Review*, vol. 19, no. 1, pp. 90–118.

Riseborough, M. and White, J. (1994) *Women and Community Safety in Birmingham: A Report to Birmingham City Council* (Birmingham: School of Public Policy, University of Birmingham).

Roberts, V. and associates (1995) *Public/Private/Voluntary Partnerships in Local Authorities* (Luton: Local Government Management Board).

Robinson, F., Shaw, K. and associates (2000) *Who Runs the North-East Now? A Review and Assessment of Governance in North East England* (Durham: Dept of Sociology and Social Policy, Durham University).

Robson, B., Parkinson, M. and Robinson, F. and associates (1994) *Assessing the Impact of Urban Policy* (London: HMSO).

Robson, C. (1993) *Real World Research* (Oxford: Blackwell).

Rogers, S. (1998) *Community Planning and Engagement* (Birmingham: INLO-GOV, University of Birmingham).

Rogers, S. (1996) *Performance Management in Local Government*, 2nd edn (London: Pitman).

Ross, K. and Osborne, S. P. (1999) 'Making a Reality of Community Governance: Structuring Government–Voluntary Sector Relationships at the Local Level', *Public Policy and Administration*, vol. 14, no. 2, pp. 49–61.

Rousseau, D. M., Sitkin, S. B., Burt, R. S. and Camerer, C. (1998) 'Not So Different After All: A Cross-discipline View of Trust', *Academy of Management Review*, vol. 23, no. 3, pp. 339–404.

Russell, H., Dawson, J., Garside, P. and Parkinson, M. (1996) *City Challenge: Interim National Evaluation* (London: HMSO).

Sartori, G. (1997) *Comparative Constitutional Engineering* (Basingstoke: Palgrave Macmillan).

Saulsbury, W. and Bowling, B. (1991) *The Multi-Agency Approach in Practice: The North Plaistow Racial Harassment Project*, Research and Planning Unit Paper 64, (London: Home Office).

Savas, E. S. (2000) *Privatization and Public–Private Partnerships* (New York: Seven Bridges Press).

Schmitter, P. (1996) 'Imagining the Future of the Euro-polity With the Help of New Concepts' in Marks, G., Scharpf, F., Schmitter, P. and Streek, W. (eds) (1996), *Governance in the European Union* (London: Sage).

Scott, W. (1991) 'Unpacking Institutional Arguments' in Powell, W. and DiMaggio, P. (eds) (1991), *The New Institutionalism in Organizational Analysis* (Chicago: The University of Chicago Press).

Scottish Community Development Centre (1996) *Measuring Community Development in Northern Ireland* (Belfast: Voluntary Activity Unit).

Scottish Community Development Centre (1999) *Measuring Community Development* (Glasgow: Scottish Community Development Centre).

Scottish Council of Voluntary Organisations (1997) *Head and Heart: Report of the Commission on the Future of the Voluntary Sector in Scotland* (Edinburgh: SCVO).

Scottish Executive (2001) *Early Education and Childcare Plan 2001–4: Guidance to Partnerships* (Edinburgh: Scottish Executive).

Scottish Office (1988) *New Life for Urban Scotland* (Edinburgh, Scottish Office).

Sharman, Lord (2001) *Holding to Account: The Review of Audit and Accountability for Central Government* (London: HM Treasury).

Sharpe, L. J. (1974) 'Theories and Values of Local Government', *Political Studies*, vol. 18, no. 2, pp. 153–74.

Siedentop, L. (2000) *Democracy in Europe* (London: Allen Lane).

Sink, D. (1996) 'Five Obstacles to Community-based Collaboration and Some Thoughts on Overcoming Them' in Huxham, C. (ed.) (1996), *Creating Collaborative Advantage* (London: Sage).

Skelcher, C. and Davis, H. (1995) *Opening the Boardroom Door: The Membership of Local Appointed Bodies* (York: Joseph Rowntree Foundation).

Skelcher, C., McCabe, A. and Lowndes, V. with Nanton, P. (1996) *Community Networks in Urban Regeneration* (Bristol: Policy Press).

Skelcher, C. (1998) *The Appointed State: Quasi-governmental Organisations and Democracy* (Buckingham: Open University Press).

Skelcher, C. (2000) 'Changing Images of the State: Overloaded, Hollowed Out, Congested', *Public Policy and Administration*, vol. 15, no. 3, pp. 3–19.

Skelcher, C., Weir, S. and Wilson, L. (2000) *Advance of the Quango State* (London: Local Government Information Unit).

Skelcher, C. and S. Snape (2001) 'Ethics and Local Councillors: Modernising Standards of Conduct', *Parliamentary Affairs*, vol. 54, no. 1, pp. 72–87.

Slater, R. (2001) 'Local Government Partnerships in Urban Management: The Case of South Asia', *Local Government Studies*, vol. 27, no. 3, pp. 79–96.

Smith, M. and Beazley, M. (2000) 'Progressive Regimes, Partnerships and the Involvement of Local Communities: A Framework for Evaluation', *Public Administration*, vol. 78, pp. 855–78.

Smith, M. M. (2001) 'Community Regimes: An Analysis of Power, Participation and Partnership in an English Locality', unpublished PhD thesis (Birmingham: University of Birmingham).

Social Exclusion Unit (2000) *National Strategy for Neighbourhood Renewal – a Framework for Consultation* (London: The Stationery Office).

Social Exclusion Unit (2001) *A New Commitment to Neighbourhood Renewal, National Strategy Action Plan* (London: The Stationery Office).

Stewart, J. (1995) 'A Future for Local Authorities as Community Government', in Stewart, J. and Stoker, G. (eds) (1995), *Local Government in the 1990s* (Basingstoke: Palgrave Macmillan).

Stewart, J. (2000) *The Nature of British Local Government* (Basingstoke: Palgrave Macmillan).

Stewart, J. and Davis, H. (1994) 'A New Agenda for Local Governance', *Public Money and Management*, vol. 14, no. 4, pp. 29–36.

Stewart, J. and Walsh, K. (1994) 'Performance Measurement When Performance Can Never be Finally Defined', *Public Money and Management*, vol. 14, no. 2, pp. 45–9.

Stewart, M. (1994) 'Between Whitehall and Town Hall: The Realignment of Urban Regeneration Policy in England', *Policy and Politics*, vol. 22, no. 2, pp. 133–45.

Stoker, G. (1995) 'Regime Theory and Urban Politics' in Judge, D., Stoker, G. and Wolman, H. (1995) *Theories of Urban Politics* (London: Sage).

Stoker, G. (1996) 'Redefining Local Democracy' in Pratchett, L. and Wilson D. (eds) (1996), *Local Democracy and Local Government* (Basingstoke: Palgrave Macmillan).

Stone, C. N., Orr, M. and Imbroscio, D. (1991) 'The Reshaping of Urban Leadership in US Cities: A Regime Analysis' in Gottdiener, M. and Pickvance, C. (eds) (1991), *Urban Life in Transition* (London: Sage).

Stone, C. N. (1993) 'Urban Regimes and the Capacity to Govern: A Political Economy Approach', *Journal of Urban Affairs*, vol. 15, no. 1, pp. 1–28.

Strauss, A. and Corbin, J. (1990) *Basics of Qualitative Research* (Newbury Park: Sage).

Sullivan, H. and Lowndes, V. (1996) *City Challenge Succession Strategies: Governance Through Partnership – A Report to Aston-Newtown City Challenge* (Birmingham: INLOGOV, University of Birmingham).

Sullivan, H. and Beazley, M. (1998) 'Evaluation of SSTARI Community Capacity Building Initiative, 1997/8', unpublished consultancy report (Birmingham: School of Public Policy: University of Birmingham.

Sullivan, H., Barnes, M. and Matka, E. (forthcoming) 'Building Collaborative Capacity Through "Theories of Change": Early Lessons from the Evaluation of Health Action Zones in England' *Evaluation*.

Sullivan, H., Barnes, M., and Matka, E. (2000) 'Building Capacity for Collaboration: early lessons from English HAZs' *Paper presented to the Evaluation Society Conference*, December.

Sullivan, H., Gaster, L. and Griffiths, P. (2000) 'Evaluating Local Involvement, Local Action in Birmingham', unpublished consultancy report (Birmingham: INLOGOV, University of Birmingham).

Sullivan, H. and Potter, T. (2001) 'Doing "Joined-up" Evaluation in Community Based Regeneration', *Local Governance*, vol. 27, no. 1, pp. 19–31.

Sullivan, H., Root, A., Moran, D. and Smith, M. (2001) *Area Committees and Neighbourhood Management* (London: Local Government Information Unit).

Sullivan, H. (2001a) 'Maximising the Contributions of Neighbourhoods – The Role of Community Governance', *Public Policy and Administration*, vol. 16, no. 2, pp. 29–48.

Sullivan, H. (2001b) 'Modernisation, Democratisation and Community Governance', *Local Government Studies*, vol. 27, no. 3, pp. 1–24.

Sure Start Unit (*c*.2000) *Guide to Fourth Wave Programme* (London: DfES).

Taillieu, T. (ed.) (2001), *Collaborative Strategies and Multi-organizational Partnerships* (Levveu/Apeldoorn: Garant).

Taylor, M. (2000) *Top-down Meets Bottom-up: Neighbourhood Management* (York: York Publishing Service).

Teisman, G. R. and Klijn, E.-H. (2000) 'Public–Private Partnerships in the European Union' in Osborne, S. P. (ed.) (2000), *Public–Private Partnerships: Theory and Practice in International Perspective* (London: Routledge).

The Community Work Group (1973) *Current Issues in Community Work: A Study by the Community Work Group* (London: Routledge and Kegan Paul).

Thomas, P. and Palfrey, C. (1996) 'Evaluation: Stakeholder-focused Criteria', *Social Policy and Administration*, vol. 30, no.2, pp. 125–42.

Thompson, G., Frances, J., Levacic, R. and Mitchell, J. (eds) (1991), *Markets, Hierarchies and Networks: The Co-ordination of Social Life* (London: Sage).

Tilley, N. (1993) 'Crime Prevention and the Safer Cities Story', *The Howard Journal*, vol. 32, no. 1, pp. 40–52.

Tyne and Wear HAZ (1997) *Health Action Zone Implementation Plan* (Newcastle: Health Authority).

Van de Ven, A. (1992) 'Suggestions for Studying Strategy Process: A Research Note', *Strategic Management Journal*, vol. 13, no. 2, pp. 169–88.

Vickers, G. (1968) *Value Systems and Social Progress* (London: Tavistock).

Walker, B. and Davis, H. (1999) 'Perspectives on Contractual Relationships and the Move to Best Value in Local Authorities', *Local Government Studies*, vol. 25, no. 2, pp. 16–37.

Walker, P., Lewis, J., Lingayah, S. and Sommer, F. (2000) *Prove It!. Measuring the Effect of Neighbourhood Renewal on Local People* (London: The New Economics Foundation and Barclays Plc).

Walsh, K. (1995) *Public Services and Market Mechanisms: Competition, Con-tracting and the New Public Management* (Basingstoke: Palgrave Macmillan).

Webb, A. (1991) 'Co-ordination: A Problem in Public Sector Management', *Policy and Politics*, vol. 19, no. 4, pp. 229–41.

Webster, B. A. (1982) 'Area Management and Responsive Policy Making' in Leach, S. and Stewart, J. D. (eds) (1982), *Approaches in Public Policy* (London: George Allen and Unwin).

Weir, S. and Hall, W. (1994) *EGO-Trip: Extra-governmental Organisations in the United Kingdom and their Accountability* (London: Charter 88).

Wilensky, J. (2000) *If Only we Knew: Increasing the Public Value of Social Science Research* (London: Routledge).

Williamson, O. E. (1985) *The Economic Institutions of Capitalism* (New York: Free Press).

Williamson, V. (2001) 'The Potential of Project Status to Support Partnerships' in Balloch, S. and Taylor, M. (eds) (2001), *Partnership Working* (Bristol: Policy Press).

Wilson, A. and Charlton, K. (1997) *Making Partnerships Work* (York: York Publishing Service).

Wilson, D. and Game, C. (1998) *Local Government in the United Kingdom* (Basingstoke: Palgrave Macmillan).

Wistow, G., Knapp, M., Hardy, B. and Allen, C. (1994) *Social Care in a Mixed Economy* (Buckingham: Open University Press).

World Bank (1997) *The State in a Changing World: World Development Report 1997* (Oxford: Oxford University Press).

WHO (2000) *The Verona Benchmark: A Guide to the Assessment of Good Practice within Partnership Working* (Geneva: World Health Organization).

Wragge and Co. (n.d.) *A Guidance Code for Councillors and Officers on Outside Bodies*, mimeo (Birmingham: Wragge and Co.).

Yin, R. (1994) *Case Study Research Design and Methods*, 2nd edn (Thousand Oaks: Sage).

Young, I. M. (2000) *Inclusion and Democracy* (Oxford: Oxford University Press).

Young, S. (1999) 'Slowing Down on LA21, or Pausing Before Accelerating?' in Lafferty, W. M. (ed.) (1999), *Implementing LA21 in Europe* (Oslo: ProSus).

Yuchtman, E. and Seashore, S. E. (1967) 'A System Resource Approach to Organisational Effectiveness', *American Sociological Review*, vol. 32, pp. 891–903.

Index